Advocate

Advocate

On History's Front Lines
from Watergate to the
Keating Five, Clinton
Impeachment, and Benghazi

James Hamilton

With a Foreword by David Ignatius

 University Press of Kansas

© 2022 by James Hamilton

Published by the University Press of Kansas (Lawrence, Kansas
66045), which was organized by the Kansas Board of Regents
and is operated and funded by Emporia State University,
Fort Hays State University, Kansas State University, Pittsburg
State University, the University of Kansas, and Wichita State
University.

Library of Congress Cataloging-in-Publication Data

Names: Hamilton, James, 1938- author.
Title: Advocate : on history's front lines from Watergate to the
Keating Five, Clinton Impeachment, and Benghazi / James
Hamilton.
Description: Lawrence : University Press of Kansas, 2022. |
Includes index.
Identifiers: LCCN 2021060200
  ISBN 9780700633517 (cloth)
  ISBN 9780700633524 (ebook)
Subjects: LCSH: Hamilton, James, 1938- | Lawyers—
Washington (D.C.)—Biography. | Law—Political aspects—United
States. | United States—Politics and government—1989- |
United States—Politics and Government—1945-1989.
Classification: LCC KF373.H278 A3 2022 | DDC 340.092 [B]—
dc23/eng/20220519
LC record available at https://lccn.loc.gov/2021060200.

British Library Cataloguing-in-Publication Data is available.

Printed in the United States of America

10 9 8 7 6 5 4 3 2 1

The paper used in this publication is acid free and meets the
minimum requirements of the American National Standard for
Permanence of Paper for Printed Library Materials Z39.48-1992.

For Kristina and our children, William, Erik, and Kathryn, who were along for the ride and made it all worthwhile.

And for Erik's wife, Kara Stiles, and granddaughter, Juniper, who brings new joy to the family.

Contents

Foreword

A good Washington, DC, lawyer sees every side of life. He represents heroic public servants and dishonest scoundrels. He sees the noble purposes of government and the sometimes misshapen results. If he's lucky, he has a window on the drama of US democracy—watching, listening, and sometimes counseling the principals as the story unfolds.

Jim Hamilton had one of those precious ringside seats for more than fifty years. He was the go-to lawyer for a generation of Democrats, vetting every Democratic vice presidential nominee for sixteen years. When prominent politicians needed good advice, they often went to Jim; when they got in trouble, they also went to Jim. The reason is that people trusted his judgment. Even in a crazy partisan town like Washington, trust is still the coin of the realm.

There's an illustrious tradition of Washington lawyers. In modern times, that list has included James H. Rowe, Abe Fortas, Edward Bennett Williams, Clark Clifford, Lloyd Cutler, and Vernon Jordan. But many of these prominent figures became power brokers in their own right—more political fixers than independent counselors.

Jim Hamilton avoided that treacherous terrain, as this book explains. He never put himself ahead of the interests of his clients. He never tried to look good in the press at the expense of the people who had hired him. He didn't leak secrets to reporters. I know that because I'm a journalist and for many years a good friend of Jim, and he didn't tell me a damn thing.

Part of Jim's success in Washington was that he began as an outsider. He was born in a small town in South Carolina. His family had been prominent in the state's politics since before the Civil War. One ancestor, a governor in the early eighteenth century, is said to have fought fourteen duels. (Those, like me, who have been regular tennis partners of Jim's, will find that detail believable.) His boyhood was the perfect small-town résumé: Eagle Scout, leader of the Presbyterian youth group, basketball and tennis letterman, high school class salutatorian.

Jim continued his outsider status a little longer by attending Davidson College, a small school in North Carolina. But he decisively joined the establishment when he enrolled at Yale Law School, usually reckoned the top in the country. (He had also been accepted at Harvard and Duke.) He served in the US Army, mostly in Germany, then spent a year at the London School of Economics. And then to Washington and the premier law firm in town, Covington & Burling.

Jim had the talent and good luck to join what would prove to be the launching pad for many in his generation of Washington lawyers—the Watergate investigation. As assistant chief counsel for the Senate Watergate Committee he helped to oversee the investigation of President Richard Nixon as well as step-by-step proof of the crimes that would lead Nixon to resign the presidency. Jim recounts that history superbly, bringing to life the colorful personalities of people like Senator Sam Ervin (D-NC), the chair of the committee. And he emphasizes what, in retrospect, is the most striking fact about the Watergate investigation: although the country was sharply divided at the time, the committee was studiously bipartisan. It approved its subpoena of Nixon's tapes and its final report by unanimous votes.

Hamilton explained what he had learned from the Watergate process in a 1976 book, *The Power to Probe: A Study of Congressional Investigations.* It's still one of the best guides on how Congress can exercise its too-little-used authority to hold the executive branch accountable.

After this Watergate baptism Jim fashioned a career as a private lawyer dealing with government ethics issues. Sometimes his clients were unfairly accused; other times he probably cut them a break. But as these pages illustrate, a lawyer's job isn't to judge his clients but to advocate their cases.

Jim had a remarkable record of success over several decades. Among those he represented were Sen. Herman Talmadge who was caught (by his wife, inadvertently) having allegedly stuffed $100 bills in his overcoat, who avoided "censure" with Hamilton's help; Sen. Dave Durenberger, who was accused of various ethical misdeeds but likewise avoided censure; Sen. Dennis DeConcini, who was accused of impropriety in the Savings and Loan scandal but escaped with only a mild rebuke from the Senate Ethics Committee; and Rep. Otto Passman, who was caught in the Koreagate scandal but acquitted by a jury in his home state of Louisiana after Jim and cocounsel managed to transfer the case there.

An especially powerful case involved Vincent Foster, who as deputy

White House counsel under President Bill Clinton was rumored to have played a role in a flap known as "Travelgate" and who was a close adviser to his former Arkansas law partner, Hillary Clinton. Foster visited Jim seeking legal advice; nine days later he died by suicide. Jim had marked his notes "privileged" and successfully protected their confidentiality in a case that went all the way to the Supreme Court. Interestingly, his opposing counsel was Brett Kavanaugh, then a member of the special prosecutor's team investigating Clinton and now a Supreme Court justice. It was Kavanaugh's only argument before the court, and he lost.

Hamilton counseled journalists (columnist Bob Novak in the Valerie Plame case), baseball players (including one falsely accused of taking steroids), and a chair of the Joint Chiefs of Staff (Mike Mullen, who was unfairly attacked by a House committee investigating the Benghazi tragedy). And for every Democratic presidential candidate from 2000 to 2016—a line that stretches from Al Gore to Hillary Clinton—he was in charge of vetting the vice-presidential candidates.

Calvin Coolidge is often quoted as observing that "the business of America is business." Maybe so, but the business of Washington is law—and as these pages demonstrate, few people have practiced it as well as Jim Hamilton.

David Ignatius
August 2021

Acknowledgments

A book of this sort, even though it is substantially based on personal recollections, is not just an individual effort but requires considerable help. Fortunately, I was able to call on others for the help I needed, and they have my lasting gratitude.

From the beginning I was aided by my able assistant, Crystal Moses. Being perhaps from a different era, I compose in longhand. Crystal is one of the few who can decipher my handwriting, which she diligently did while typing the entire manuscript.

My first reader was my astute law firm colleague and trusted friend, Raechel Kummer. Always willing to devote time to improving this book, Raechel made numerous useful suggestions to both substance and style.

Other wise friends read the entire book and offered salient advice: Michael Helfer (former general counsel and vice chair of Citi Group); Charles Buffon (former chair of the DC Bar's Ethics Committee); Harrison Wellford (a Davidson College colleague and former law partner); and John Kuhnle (my brother-in-law and a former English professor who is a stickler for correct usage). Respected authors Norm Ornstein and David McKean commented on several chapters.

Librarian Andrew Zimmerman was invaluable in retrieving hard-to-find documents and photographs. Expert paralegal Adam Wingard made sure that citations and quotes were accurate and in proper form.

As the book neared completion, family members—my wife, Kristina, and children William and Kathryn—pitched in. They each made helpful suggestions. Kathryn incorporated final edits into the text.

I also am indebted to my editor at the University Press of Kanas, David Congdon. David was patient in steering me through the intricacies of the publishing process. He also arranged for peer reviewers Philip Bobbitt and Lori Cox Han to read the book in draft form and to provide useful comments.

Finally, and sincerely, I want to thank esteemed *Washington Post* columnist

David Ignatius for writing the foreword to this book. David is a longtime friend and tennis companion. For his efforts I owe him some good line calls.

While I have had considerable assistance in writing this book, the observations and opinions expressed in it are solely my own. They should not be attributed to any lawyers, law firms, or others with whom I have been associated.

Jim Hamilton
November 2021

1

The Path to Washington

I have spent much of my professional career on history's front lines. I say that because, by a combination of serendipity and effort, I have been able to participate, as a lawyer or otherwise, in many of the major legal and political events of the last fifty years. Watergate, the investigation of John F. Kennedy's assassination, President Bill Clinton's impeachment, and heading the vetting of vice-presidential candidates for four Democratic nominees for president are prime examples but far from the only ones. Along the way I have interacted with a number of persons who have shaped history, including Sam Ervin, Howard Baker, John Dean, Bill and Hillary Clinton, Barack Obama, Joe Biden, Marina Oswald, Admiral Mike Mullen, Prince Phillip, Bob Novak, Ken Starr, Brett Kavanaugh, Ruth Bader Ginsburg, James Baker, Bill Casey, and the Keating Five among many others.

This book has been written in part to fill in various interstices of history, bringing my recollections to events that are incompletely known. I will, of course, honor my obligations to preserve attorney-client confidences and my commitment not to reveal nonpublic substantive information from the numerous political vettings I have done for presidents and presidential candidates. Nonetheless I have much to recount. I hope my revelations and stories prove interesting, revealing, at times humorous, and perhaps instructive. I have done some things right, but I also have made mistakes and come up short. I will tell you about some of those missteps as cautionary tales.

But this book does more than just present stories. It also lays out lessons from the history I have observed. For example:

- The chapter on the Senate Watergate Committee demonstrates that a highly charged investigation can be conducted fairly and in a non-partisan manner by persons of honest purpose. In contrast, the chapter on the Benghazi hearing involving Admiral Mike Mullen shows the flaws in a proceeding marred by partisanship and incivility.
- The chapter on vetting sets forth procedures I have developed and followed to ensure that suitable candidates are chosen for vice president, the president's cabinet, and the Supreme Court.
- The Keating Five chapter discusses the dangers existing when elected officials do significant favors for major campaign contributors.
- The chapters on Senators Talmadge and Durenberger underscore the perils facing those in Congress in a costly city where expenses are not covered by their salaries.
- The two chapters on the Supreme Court cases resulting from Vince Foster's suicide demonstrate the importance of the Court's holdings that the attorney-client privilege survives the death of the client and that survivors have a right of privacy under the Freedom of Information Act.
- The chapter on the Clinton impeachment presents the "proper test," which I described in testimony to the House Judiciary Committee, to determine whether a president has committed a high crime or misdemeanor that requires removal from office.
- The chapter about Bob Novak reveals the religious fervor with which journalists seek to protect their sources.
- The chapter on DNC chair Don Fowler discusses the personal sacrifices a lawyer may be called on to make to provide loyal, zealous representation to a client.
- The Debategate chapter emphasizes the need to remove dirty tricks from election politics.
- The chapter on the Lawyers' Committee for Civil Rights highlights the continuing need to provide legal representation to victims of racial injustice.
- The book also provides insights into the prominent roles lawyers play in the affairs of Washington, DC, where the practice of law involves unique, at times bizarre, issues not found elsewhere. It also presents my views on the societal obligations lawyers bear.

*   *   *

Let me start with some brief words about how I became an attorney involved at the intersection of law and politics in Washington, DC, and the values motivating this journey.

I was born in December 1938 in Chester, South Carolina. Chester was then—and was when I departed for college in 1956—a town of around seven thousand. It was a very southern town—segregated and infused with the southern mores of the time.

In the mid-1980s CBS aired a miniseries called *Chiefs* about three police chiefs in a small southern town. The story, which starred Charlton Heston among others, began in 1924, ended in 1962, and was filmed in the early 1980s. The producers thus needed a southern town that essentially had not changed in appearance in sixty years. They searched all over the South and chose Chester.

The family of my father (Herman Hamilton) was old South Carolina. One ancestor had been a hero in the American Revolution and was given the honor of receiving the British flag surrendered by General Cornwallis at Yorktown, Virginia. (Lafayette supposedly had called Major James Hamilton "the handsomest man" in General George Washington's army.[1]) Two of my ancestors had signed the Declaration of Independence. Two had been governors of the state, including James Hamilton Jr., who signed the Nullification Proclamation in 1832. Hamilton went on to be a diplomat for the Republic of Texas.

Governor Hamilton has not been treated kindly by history. He had serious faults and committed serious wrongs. As the intendant (major) of Charleston, he harshly put down a suspected slave rebellion in 1822. He fought fourteen duels. The later part of his life was marred by debt and financial indiscretions. But at the end, an admirable feature emerged.

Because of his connections to Texas, he lent the republic much of his wealth. Texas, however, would not repay the debt. (There is a county in the state named after him.) In 1857 Hamilton traveled to Texas to obtain repayment. He was sailing from New Orleans to Galveston, Texas, when his ship collided with another vessel and sank. Hamilton, who was injured in the wreck, gave up his life preserver to a woman and her small child and stood on the deck of the doomed ship with his pistol drawn to ensure that women and children were the first to enter the lifeboats. A wave swept him from the ship and he drowned in the Gulf. At the moment of his death, according to family legend, his wife, Elizabeth, awoke in her bed in Charleston in the dead of night with a premonition that Hamilton had drowned.

Hamilton's seventh child, Samuel Prioleau Hamilton (my great-grand-father) lost part of his right arm in a hunting accident. Nonetheless, he volunteered for the Confederate Army when the Civil War began. The musket he fired with his left hand, which had the flint on the left rather than the right side of the barrel was in the family's possession until it was stolen.

There is a family story about Colonel Samuel Hamilton that may be apocryphal but which I relate anyway since it cannot at this late stage be disproven. At the end of the war, matters were not going well for General Lee, who needed all the manpower he could muster. A private who had lost the fingers of one hand in battle came to General Lee and asked if he could go home because of his injury.

General Lee, family lore has it, asked the private whether he had ever heard of Colonel Hamilton "who entered the Confederate Army with only one arm?" "No sir," said the private. "Well," Lee said, "what do you think of that?" To which the private purportedly answered, "I think he's the biggest damn fool in the Confederate Army!"

The parents of my mother (Edith Gilchrist Hamilton) were English. Her father immigrated to the States in 1898. He and his three brothers were on their way to Australia, but her father and one brother decided to stay in the States after receiving offers of employment.

My father was a talented musician and accomplished speaker who was known for both talents throughout South Carolina. He sold municipal bonds, built houses, and for a while was mayor of Chester. My mother was a homemaker and the conscience of the family; I still govern my actions by what I think she would have me do. I never heard her speak an unkind word about anyone. I'm certain no one ever said an unkind word about her.

There are advantages and disadvantages in growing up in a small town. One advantage is you can try many things; you learn quickly what you do well and where you are deficient. You learn who you are.

In high school I played on the tennis and basketball teams, wrote for the school paper (I was the sports editor), sang in the chorus, and was salutatorian of my class. (The valedictorian had better conduct grades.) I was an Eagle Scout at age twelve and was the youth leader of my Presbytery (a district of the Presbyterian Church).

I discovered that I could write a good sentence. I found that I had a proficient backhand and jump shot, which brought me some success on high school teams. I also developed a capacity to find humor in diverse circumstances.

However, I was a lousy saxophonist and often out-of-step when the band was marching. In a chorus, I could carry the bass part, but barely. (My sister, Edith Kuhnle, inherited my father's musical talents.[2]) One of my mother's most nervous moments came one Sunday when half the choir was ill and I was the only bass. Perhaps the Lord helped me through the anthem.

I had an advantage that others growing up in Chester did not. In 1908 my mother's father built a summer home in Montreat, North Carolina, about twenty miles from Asheville in the Blue Ridge Mountains. My family acquired the house in the mid-to-late-1940s. At the time, Montreat was the main conference ground for the Southern Presbyterian Church. In the 1950s conference leaders invited liberal preachers and educators from the North and major educational institutions to preach and lecture. Many of them advocated the social gospel and promoted the civil rights movement. These speakers caused me to contemplate matters not given much thought in Chester. My social, ethical, and political views were altered. (My interest in civil rights continued into my legal career, as chapter 6 demonstrates.) I also realized that a small town was limiting.

I came to recognize that, wherever I lived, I did not want a mundane life. In that goal, at least, I have been successful.

The only college I considered was Davidson College in North Carolina. There were family connections and many of my Montreat friends were enrolled.

Davidson, then as now, was a rigorous place with no grade inflation. It provided me with an excellent education and a safe place to gain needed maturity. At Davidson I played on the tennis team and wrote for the school paper as the sports editor and associate editor. I majored in English and philosophy but was not a high-achieving student. This frustrated my principal mentor, philosophy professor George Abernethy. George, who remained a good friend until he passed away, never gave me an A because he didn't think I worked hard enough. He would say, "Mr. Hamilton, you're like the quarterback who knows all the plays but forgets to block." George didn't know much about football and didn't know that quarterbacks rarely block, but I got his point.

Somehow, undoubtedly with George's help and good LSAT scores, I was accepted at Yale Law School and at Harvard and Duke, which offered me its best scholarship. I didn't think I could turn Yale down, so I convinced my dad, who was far from wealthy, to help fund my education there. Attending Yale Law was life-changing and one of my best decisions.

I didn't know for sure I wanted a career in law when I went to Yale but thought I'd give law school a try. I had contemplated being a journalist but decided I'd rather do things than write about other people doing things. I also considered being a preacher but became increasingly theologically challenged. It's not clear that the law benefited from my choice, but the church certainly did!

I ended up being a respectable student at Yale, but I really made my name on campus by cracking an impromptu joke. My first semester I took Civil Procedure from J. William Moore, a renowned, diminutive scholar famous for terrorizing students, especially women. Moore concentrated mainly on the Federal Rules of Civil Procedure, about which he had written a massive treatise, and did not turn to the antiquated common-law pleading forms—trover, assumpsit, and the like—until the remaining few days of the semester after the winter holidays.

But once he did, he wanted quickly to move through these topics. However, his students, who like me had spent the vacation on more pleasurable matters, were not assisting.

After one student failed to answer a question about these old pleading forms, Moore banged on his desk and exclaimed, "We need to move quickly through this topic. I am General Sherman and I want to get to the sea!"

The next student asked was also ill prepared and unable to answer. Moore banged again on his desk, repeating his desire quickly to dispose of these subjects. He said again, "I am General Sherman and I want to get to the sea!"

Then he called on me. I had not a clue what the answer was and was desperate to avoid embarrassment. So I said in my best southern accent: "Well, frankly Mr. Moore, I'm not very interested in getting to the sea."

The class (which had few southerners) gave me a standing ovation!

At Davidson, I participated in the ROTC program and was commissioned as a lieutenant in the US Army. I thus had a military commitment after law school. I decided to remain in the artillery rather than apply to the Judge Advocate General's Corps, which had a longer service requirement. I also concluded I would prefer to spend the bulk of my military service in Germany. How I achieved that result was unusual; I did not leave matters to fate.

On my way home to South Carolina from Yale in May 1963, I stopped by the Pentagon. In those days, one could just stroll into the Pentagon and by judicious questioning find the office sought. (In our age of terror and caution, this of course is no longer possible.) So I walked into the building looking for the officer who made assignments for young artillery officers. I hiked around the building for three hours, probably covering five miles. Finally I found Colonel Smith, who was likely on his last posting and also likely had never been visited in his remote office by a young officer seeking assignment to a specific location. Colonel Smith was delighted to see me. "Sure son," he said, "I'll send you to Germany."

I told two of my Davidson friends about my successful endeavor. They also contacted Colonel Smith. One of them was stationed about one hundred miles from me in Nuremberg. The other ended up five feet across the hall from me in Kitzingen, Germany.

This was in 1963, when the Cold War was at its height. My first assignment was in an Honest John unit—a name now largely forgotten even by military types. The Honest John was a tactical nuclear weapon. The missile was fired by a rocket. East Germany was not too far away, and we had plenty of nukes to use if West Germany was invaded. On occasion, when I was the officer of the guard, I patrolled the bunkers where our bombs were stored.

While in Kitzingen, my Davidson friend and I roomed together "on the economy," meaning in German accommodations. We lived in Dettelbach in Frau Strobel's quite lovely basement apartment. Frau Strobel was a kind but Catholic landlady. When she met us at her door for the first time when we applied to rent the apartment, her very first words to us—before even a "guten Tag"—were "nitcht schaffen mit Frauleins" (no sleeping with girls). We hastily said, "nein, nein," and she rented us the apartment.

After a while—largely because I was a lawyer—I was transferred to the Third Infantry Division Inspector General's Office in Würzburg, Germany. (It also helped that the IG had attended Yale.) This was the perfect assignment for a noncareer officer. In my fourteen months in that position I was able to visit virtually every unit in the Third Infantry Division. My focus was on nonjudicial punishment and financial requirements. I worked hard at my tasks and was awarded the Army Commendation Medal.

I had a stroke of good fortune in Würzburg. I became the only American in a German tennis club—Tennis Club Weiss Blau. I spent my weekends playing tennis and basketball for club teams, drinking beer and Franken Wein and working on my German. I had one rule: Even though most of my German compatriots were or had been university students and spoke quite good English, I refused to speak English with them and insisted on communicating only in German. My friends and teammates appreciated this effort (although I am no linguist), and they all were happy to humor my feeble attempts.

As my army career was drawing to a close, I decided to spend a year at the London School of Economics (LSE) earning a master of laws (LLM) (which was officially granted by the University of London). I had enjoyed my time in Europe and was in no rush to return to the States. My British heritage and the joys of London were good reasons to delay.

At LSE I worked hard enough to receive a degree (an LLM), but the program was not demanding and I had considerable time for outside activities. London was cheap then; you could attend the Royal Shakespeare Company Theatre for under two dollars. Three or four nights a week I was at the theater, opera, ballet, or concerts. I spent all my savings from the military during my time in London, arriving home with $180 in my pocket.

I played tennis at the Globe Tennis Club—a somewhat run-down facility in Hampstead Heath made appealing by the fact that two-thirds of its members were not British. I also played basketball for the University of London and was awarded a half-purple necktie by the University's Warden of Purples, which signified that I was of "good university standard."

While playing for the university, I sprained my ankle quite badly. For a month I hobbled around London on crutches and a cane. One evening I ate at a cafeteria on Piccadilly Circus. Having selected my food, I placed my cane on my arm and, tray in hand, limped to the cashier fifteen feet away. The cashier was a hefty Cockney woman with a heavy accent. When she saw me hobbling toward her, she said, "Well, dearie, what happened to you?" In my southern accent, I replied, "I hurt my leg." To which she exclaimed, "Goodness gracious, malaria. That's awful!" The failure of communication was so great I didn't bother to explain.

At LSE I studied mainly in two locations—the Institute of Advanced Legal

Studies on Russell Square and the British Museum. The institute was an interesting venue. Two townhouses had been combined to create it. (It no longer exists in this form.) Tea was served every afternoon at 4:00 in a small room on the top floor. The student body came from all over the Commonwealth; it seemed to me that there were twenty languages spoken at teatime.

I also studied in the old main reading room of the British Museum, which has now been replaced by a modern structure. Back then it was a huge dimly lit smoky circular room with bookshelves rising several stories. The top shelves seemed obscured by mist.

I took breaks across the hall in a room that, at the time, housed the letters of Percy Bysshe Shelly, John Keats, and other Romantic poets. One day I struck up a conversation with the guard on duty. He was a large man with a handlebar mustache and a missing arm, which I assumed he had lost in the war. Knowing that Karl Marx had written *Das Kapital* in the main reading room, I asked the guard if he could tell me where Marx sat when he composed his consequential work.

"Yes, I can tell you that," he said, offering an explanation something like the following: "If you go through the main door and up to the circular center desk, and take a left and go down three aisles, then take another left, and it's the third seat on the left."

"That's very interesting," I said. "But I wonder, is there a plaque there to commemorate the fact that Marx sat there?"

The guard was incredulous, "A plaque," he said. "A plaque in the British Museum. Why, we can't put a plaque in the British Museum for everybody that comes here. Why the other day, Cary Grant was in here."

While at LSE, I traveled to the Isle of Iona, off the west coast of Scotland. As indicated, my mother's maiden name was Gilchrist. Around AD 550, her ancestors journeyed to Iona and were christened in Gaelic "Gille Criosd" (servant of Christ) by Saint Columba, who had sailed to the island from Ireland to convert the heathen Scots.

Because of her heritage, my mother was initially overjoyed that I was living and studying in London. But that was before she discovered the socialist tendencies that permeated LSE. At the end of one of her frequent letters, she casually asked, "By the way, Jimmy, who is this fellow Harold Laski?"[3]

When my year in London ended in September 1966, I returned to the States. Although in 1963 I had taken and passed the North Carolina bar,

I decided that Washington, DC, with its politics and unique brand of law, would now be more to my liking. So I headed there to practice law.

The two US institutions of higher learning I attended—Davidson College and Yale Law School—have a similar creed. Both imbue their students with the idea that they have societal obligations that reach beyond ensuring their own well-being. The students attending these institutions—even more so now than when I was there—are talented and receive a superior education not available to most. This mix of ability and educational privilege brings with it a responsibility to seek society's betterment.

I buy into this notion. It is especially pertinent for attorneys who, as officers of the court and bound by ethical rules, are obligated to provide zealous representation and to help the less fortunate. Had I not done something meaningful to promote the common good—at least my concept of what that is—I would not consider my career a success.

Some of my endeavors discussed in this book have, I respectfully submit, broadly benefited our country. For example:

- Leading the Senate Watergate Committee's investigation into the break-in and cover-up, which uncovered facts that brought down a corrupt president.
- Heading the vetting efforts for vice-presidential candidates for Al Gore, John Kerry, Barack Obama, and Hillary Clinton and for President Clinton's cabinet and Supreme Court candidates.
- Fending off Ken Starr and Brett Kavanaugh and winning the Supreme Court case establishing that the attorney-client privilege survives the client's death, a result that well serves clients, the profession, and the rule of law.
- Assisting, as a young attorney, the Lawyers' Committee for Civil Rights in establishing the right of non-Mississippi lawyers to represent Black clients in civil rights cases in that state.

I also submit that representing individuals who because of shortcomings, circumstance or happenstance, bad judgment, or partisan attack are in serious need of counsel also provides a societal benefit. This, after all, is what lawyers do and must do to allow our system of justice to work. I believe, for example, that the following legal work for individuals in trouble served the rule of law.

- Representing, before the Supreme Court, Vince Foster's family in a successful effort to keep photographs of his body taken after his suicide off the internet and out of the tabloids.
- Assisting former chair of the Joint Chiefs of Staff admiral Mike Mullen who, after he performed a public service in reviewing the Benghazi tragedy for the State Department, was subject to vile partisan attacks by a handful of House Republicans.
- Representing, at the request of the DC Bar, Marina Oswald, Lee Harvey Oswald's widow, who was called before a House Committee investigating President Kennedy's assassination.
- Representing beleaguered columnist Bob Novak after his reveal of a CIA operative's name subjected him to public opprobrium and a grand jury investigation.
- Representing my friend and former DNC cochair Don Fowler regarding investigations into various efforts to raise money for President Clinton's 1996 reelection campaign (a representation that inflicted a significant personal cost on me).

These and other matters are described in detail in this book. As I attempt to fill in gaps in history, readers will be able to make their own judgments about whether social good was achieved by my disparate endeavors. I start with Watergate because, for anyone significantly involved in that sordid but momentous series of events, it remains a career centerpiece.

2

The Senate Watergate Committee

The White House Tapes Uncovered

Few people have the chance to make a significant contribution in a matter of truly historical proportions. Watergate gave me that opportunity.

In the early hours of June 17, 1972, five men were arrested inside the Democratic National Committee headquarters in the Watergate complex in Washington, DC. Initially, only those five and two others were prosecuted for the break-in. Their trial began on January 8, 1973. Five pled guilty during the trial; two were convicted of conspiracy, burglary, and wiretapping on January 30. But questions lingered about whether others had participated in the crime.

Senators were not convinced that all was known about the scandal. On February 7, 1973, the Senate voted 77–0 to establish the Senate Select Committee on Campaign Activities to ferret out the full truth about the break-in. One may marvel today—when ultra-partisanship abounds and civility is an almost forgotten virtue—at the unanimity of that vote.

Senate majority leader Mike Mansfield chose Sam Ervin of North Carolina to chair the seven-person committee.[1] Ervin selected Sam Dash, a Georgetown University law professor and former prosecutor, as his chief counsel. Dash was friends with Charles Horsky, a respected, beloved partner at Covington & Burling where I was then working. Horsky recommended me to Dash, and I was hired as one of three assistant chief counsels who would run the required investigations. Dash was interested in my experience in large document-heavy cases. By good fortune I was assigned the responsibility of leading the investigation into the break-in and subsequent cover-up. That investigation evolved into the principal focus of the committee after one of the convicted burglars, James McCord, in March 1973 wrote the presiding judge, John Sirica, that there had been perjury at the trial, that political pressure to plead guilty and remain silent had been applied to the defendants, and that others besides those indicted were involved in the Watergate operation. At the time, my assignment was probably the best job in the United States for a young lawyer interested in investigative work and politics.

Congressional investigations have played a significant role in the US experience for most of the nation's history. Consider just a few of the major investigations of the last century—Teapot Dome, the House Un-American Activities Committee hearings, the Army-McCarthy hearings, Iran-Contra, the Keating Five, the Clarence Thomas Supreme Court confirmation proceedings, the Clinton impeachment. To recall these names is to remind us that congressional investigations are the stuff of our history.

But none of these other investigations, as momentous and important as they may have been, concerned more significant issues or commanded the attention of the nation more than the Senate Watergate Committee investigation. None dealt more with the fabric of what we are as a nation, and none was conducted with more success. There are a number of reasons why all of this was so.

Part of the reason, of course, was the magnitude of the wrongdoing being investigated. Watergate involved not only the break-in at the Democratic National Committee's headquarters in the Watergate Office Building and the subsequent cover-up but also massive illegal corporate contributions to President Nixon's reelection campaign; a wide-ranging series of dirty tricks, some quite puerile, designed to sway the 1972 presidential election; and an unlawful scheme to use the resources of the executive branch to reelect Nixon.

This latter endeavor, known as the Responsiveness Program, was the creation of White House operative Fred Malek, who later became a successful businessman and an ongoing influence in Republican politics. Malek escaped prosecution for his involvement in this scheme, but during the Reagan administration he had to withdraw from consideration for appointment to the board of the US Postal Service after senators condemned his conduct.[2]

The Responsiveness Program investigation produced my favorite document from my law career. There were many documents pertaining to this endeavor. The White House, realizing the peril the documents presented, had destroyed its batch. The Committee to Re-Elect the President, referred to by many as CREEP, was not so cautious and sent its set to the National Archives. That is where Gordon Freedman, a young staff member working with me on the investigation, found them. One of the preserved documents expounded in detail on the elements of the unlawful operation, which included use of federal grant money, legal and administrative decisions, and personnel appointments to re-elect Nixon. The author of this volatile document, recognizing the risk it presented, had written on the top of the first page, "Burn before reading."

Watergate involved a cast of characters worthy of fiction. There was President Nixon, as enigmatic as the best-known person in the United States could be. Nixon was a man of considerable ability, but as the release of the tapes of his conversations have revealed, he was beset by dark demons that overwhelmed his judgment and moral principles.

Watergate had the snarling duo of presidential aides John Ehrlichman and Charles Colson who were public relations nightmares for the Nixon administration. Ehrlichman could not speak to the committee without curling his upper lip in a sneer. It was notoriously reported that Colson said he would walk over his grandmother to re-elect Nixon.

Some would add President Nixon's Chief of Staff Bob Haldeman to this duo. But after spending hours with Haldeman in a prehearing interview, I found I rather liked him, which made me question both my own judgment and character. Haldeman, of course, had every reason to be agreeable toward me because I was heavily involved in investigating his conduct and would help shape the questions to him.

And then we had the Watergate burglars, which included four tough Cuban Americans with Bay of Pigs' and CIA backgrounds. Also involved in the burglary were the maniacal Gordon Liddy and the shadowy Howard Hunt. Hunt was a White House staff member and a former CIA agent. Liddy was a lawyer for CREEP. Neither Liddy nor Hunt seemingly had ever seen a clandestine, nefarious scheme they could not fondly embrace, no matter how bizarre and bound for failure it might be. Liddy did not testify at the public hearing, but his private session with the committee was memorable because of his demeanor. He revealed nothing and resembled a captured enemy soldier determined to provide only his name, rank, and serial number.

Leading the committee was a genuine folk hero, Sam Ervin, who, with his pungent humor, his rectitude, his southern drawl, and his iconic dancing eyebrows was the right man for this troubled historical time. Ervin was also a true constitutional scholar.

After the committee's work concluded, I wrote a book, *The Power to Probe*, about the laws that govern congressional investigations.[3] I asked Ervin to write the introduction to the book, and he graciously accepted on the understanding that he could first read the book. I agreed with trepidation because I knew I could acquire a critic with sweeping knowledge, keen insight, and pronounced views about my subject.

Several months later I sent Ervin the first two hundred pages or so. His response was not long in coming and went something like this: "I've read your book, enjoyed it, and think it's good. But, Jim, there's a mistake in it. In the book at page 147 in the footnote, you write that the *Groppi* case was decided under the Due Process Clause of the Fifth Amendment. As I'm sure you know, it was decided under the Due Process Clause of the Fourteenth Amendment."

Here was a seventy-eight-year-old man reading footnotes in a draft book and homing in on a mistake that surely would have escaped anyone not well-versed in constitutional niceties and the holding of an obscure court decision.

It is possible to disagree with some of Ervin's views on the Constitution (for example, his misguided views on civil rights). But it is impossible to dispute that he loved the Constitution, studied it with great care, and knew and understood its provisions and the decisions, explaining them far better than most lawyers and legislators.

Ervin remained a personal friend until his death in 1985. On my way to our family retreat in Montreat, North Carolina, Kristina and I would visit him at his home in Morganton, often chatting with him in his dark-wood bookshelf-lined library where he wrote his post-Watergate books. I attended his funeral, along with other Watergate Committee veterans, including Howard Baker and Sam Dash.

Ervin was revered in Morganton. I rode in the cortege to his gravesite, from which Table Rock Mountain—Ervin's favorite—can be seen. As the funeral procession passed, the town folk of Morganton stood on curbsides, hands on hearts, in last respect.

Another effective member of the committee was Dan Inouye (D-HI). Inouye was a war hero who enlisted in the army despite the mistreatment and internment of US citizens of Japanese ancestry during World War II. He lost his right arm in the Po Valley in Italy fighting in a renowned all-Japanese unit, and he received the Medal of Honor for his exploits.

After Dan had skewered the dissembling John Ehrlichman with proficient questioning, I slipped into the chair next to him and said, "Good job, Senator." In an unguarded moment, Dan replied into an open mic, "What a liar!"

The next day Ehrlichman's crusty attorney, John Wilson, who matched his client well in demeanor and churlishness, referred to Inouye, the war hero, as "that little Jap." Not surprising, this unseemly comment produced a stream of support and praise for Dan.[4]

Later I apologized to Dan for provoking his remark about Ehrlichman. His unperturbed response: "Don't worry about it. It was the only truthful thing said all day." He then observed that from now on he would make his private comments only in Hawaiian.

The Senate Watergate investigation was also successful because of good staff work. Chief counsel Sam Dash insisted on a rigorous, fearless investigation, and he received that from his staff. Dash also knew how to tell a story to draw the public into the investigation and convey its import, which is exactly what the hearings in the spring and summer of 1973 did. Those hearings were the best soap opera on television, and the nation was glued to the tube. One day around sixty million people heard White House counsel John Dean testify about Nixon's role in the cover-up and how he told Nixon that there was a cancer growing on the presidency.

Dean is remembered for his remarkable memory, and it was excellent. That said, much work was done to ensure that his testimony was accurate and credible.

Initially, Sam Dash, fearing leaks, met alone with Dean and his colorful attorney, Charles Shaffer. Then, as Dean's public appearance neared, I was brought in to help him prepare. I went over every line of Dean's draft statement with him, testing the accuracy and believability of his testimony. One morning I worked with him until 4:00 a.m. We believed Dean and wanted to ensure that the committee and nation also did.

At the hearing, Dean's statement lasted around seven hours. Then there were three days of sharp questions from senators and staff attorneys. Dean was cool under fire. Impressed, committee member Herman Talmadge remarked that Dean "was so calm he looked as if he could have performed heart surgery in the back of a pick-up truck."[5]

The working relationship between Senators Ervin and Baker was vital to the Watergate Committee's success. At the beginning of the investigation, Sam Dash and others felt that Baker and minority chief counsel Fred Thompson were Nixon allies and were improperly providing sensitive information to the White House. However, Republican committee member Lowell Weicker (who always was skeptical of Nixon) told me that as the evidence against Nixon mounted, Baker saw the light and appropriately pursued the facts. We all remember Baker's oft-asked question: "What did the President know and when did he know it?" Whatever the validity of Dash's views, the result of Baker's transformation was a remarkably nonpartisan investigation concerning a matter as controversial as any in US history.

Consider, for example, the following:

- The massive Watergate Final Report that condemned a Republican administration was unanimously adopted,
- The committee's decision to subpoena the president for the White House tapes was unanimous, and

- The committee's decision to sue the President when he failed to comply with the subpoena was by unanimous vote on a motion made by Senator Baker.

Senator Ervin paid tribute to Senator Baker in his book on Watergate. Ervin noted that Baker was a "stalwart East Tennessee Republican" with a "strong sense of loyalty to the Republican Party." "I suspect," Ervin wrote, "that the White House undertook to bring much pressure on him to influence his conduct as a member of the committee." "If it did," Ervin said, "it *failed* in its purpose." He added: "As vice chairman, Senator Baker rendered faithful service to the committee in its quest for the truth . . . and earned my enduring gratitude."[6]

This is not to say that there were not some tensions within the committee, partisan and otherwise. It would have been miraculous if there had not been given that the committee's intensely scrutinized endeavors affected careers as well as history. But as a Democratic staff member, I came to feel that the investigation was essentially a nonpartisan effort and that I was working for Senator Baker as well as Senator Ervin.

A personal recollection about Senator Baker shows that he also thought I was on his team.

In 1974, when we were wrapping up the investigation, in court against the president about the White House tapes, and beginning work on the Final Report, I came down with a bout of kidney stones that sent me to the hospital—an experience I would not recommend. One committee member took the time to visit me there: Senator Baker. I suspect he soon forgot that simple act of kindness. But I have not.

There is a final reason the Senate Watergate investigation was successful. We discovered the White House tapes that brought down a president.

There were clues that something like the taping system existed. John Dean testified that in an April 5, 1983, conversation with the president, Nixon went to a corner of an office in the Executive Office Building and, in a nearly inaudible tone, said that he was probably foolish to have discussed clemency for Howard Hunt with Chuck Colson. This gave Dean an inkling that the conversation was being taped. Ironically, it was later learned that the recording device in that office had run out of tape before the conversation occurred, and that it was not recorded.

Moreover, as Fred Thompson recounts in his book on Watergate, before Dean testified then-White House counsel Fred Buzhardt called Thompson and gave him in great detail the White House version of Nixon's conversations with Dean and others. Thompson prepared and distributed a memo of his conversation with Buzhardt, which at least suggested that there was a record of the conversations.[7]

In any event, on Friday, July 13, 1973, the committee's staff interviewed Alexander Butterfield. I gave the order to interview Butterfield because he had been an assistant to the president and in Bob Haldeman's ambit. But demonstrating my usual perspicacity, I decided not to go to the interview because I thought that he had nothing important to say.

At the end of the over three-hour interview, deputy minority counsel Don Sanders, who had Thompson's memo, asked Butterfield if there was any basis for the implication in Dean's testimony that White House conversations were recorded. Butterfield, an honest man, said yes and revealed the existence of the White House taping system.

I learned of this testimony early the next morning, Saturday, July 14, when Sam Dash called to tell me about it.

I now digress to discuss a *galling* incident.

As was well known, the Watergate Committee was plagued by leaks. Senator Baker once remarked that although the Senate Watergate Committee did not invent the leak, we elevated it to its highest art form. The running joke was that the Capitol Hill press corps would go out of business if a certain senator's Xerox machine broke down.

It is thus not surprising that, as they recount in their book *All the President's Men*, Bob Woodward and Carl Bernstein also learned about the tapes on Saturday, July 14, before many committee members and senior staff knew about them. Amazingly, however, *Washington Post* executive editor Ben Bradlee initially thought this was only a "B-plus" story not worthy of immediate attention, so nothing about the tapes was published by the *Post* until after Butterfield's testimony.[8]

Who leaked this information to Woodward and Bernstein, I don't know for sure. But the senior majority staffer in the session with Butterfield was later best man in Woodward's wedding.[9]

When Sam Dash called me early on Saturday, July 14, he said, "let's go tell John Dean what we've just learned." A little later, Dash picked me up and we drove to Dean's townhouse in Alexandria, Virginia.

John met us at the front door. John had a quizzical look on his face, for he did not yet know the purpose of our visit.

We went upstairs to their living room. John sat on a couch. Sam sat down to their left. I stood in front of John by a mantelpiece where I could look directly at him. I wanted to see his reaction when Sam told him what we knew.

When Sam finally did, John broke into a wide smile because he knew the tapes would confirm his damning testimony about Nixon. As John recounts in his book *Blind Ambition*, he then said to Dash: "Sam, do you know what this means, if you get those conversations? It would mean my ass is not hanging out there all alone. It means that you can verify my testimony. And I'll tell you this, you'll find out that I've undertestified, rather than overtestified, just to be careful."[10]

On Monday morning, July 16, Ervin, Baker, Dash, and Thompson met and decided to put Butterfield on the stand that afternoon. I was dispatched to summon him. When I told Butterfield that his presence was required that day, he was distinctly displeased. In fact, he refused to appear. He said he was preparing for a trip to the Soviet Union on Federal Aviation Administration business—he was then its chair—and that he was too busy to attend.

I relayed Butterfield's response to Senator Ervin. Ervin grew agitated. His eyebrows cavorted; his jaw churned. Then he said to me: "Tell Mr. Butterfield that if he is not here this afternoon, I will send the Senate Sergeant at Arms to fetch him."

If a lawful order or subpoena is ignored the Senate has the constitutional power to send its sergeant at arms to arrest the miscreant and to imprison him in the Capitol. This power has not been used since World War II, having essentially been replaced by application of the contempt of Congress statute that allows criminal prosecution for disobedience, or recently by civil suits. Nonetheless, the power still exists.[11]

But this power only can be exercised by a vote of the full Senate. Sam Ervin did not have the right, on his own, to dispatch the sergeant at arms to arrest Butterfield. Ervin, a constitutional scholar, undoubtedly knew that, but he nonetheless instructed me to deliver his message to Butterfield, which, having located him in a barber chair, I did faithfully.

That message changed Butterfield's mind. Later that afternoon Butterfield, now contrite and neatly coifed, arrived at the committee to give his electrifying testimony. The subpoena I served on him for that testimony hangs in my office.

Before Butterfield's testimony, Senator Baker approached Sam Dash and asked him to let Thompson open the questioning because minority aide Don Sanders had asked the fateful question to Butterfield. Dash thought about this request for a while and then, as he describes in his book *Chief Counsel*, reluctantly agreed because he thought it was only "fair."[12]

I have heard Thompson say that asking that question was a big boost to his political career. (He later became a senator from Tennessee.) I wonder if Sam, an ardent, unabashed liberal Democrat until the day he died, would have so graciously agreed to Senator Baker's request had he been prescient enough to realize the later political advantage it afforded. I'm certain Sam would have been pleased to assist Thompson in becoming a prominent actor, as he later did. But a Republican senator, probably not.

It was, however, a good thing for the committee that Thompson took the lead in questioning Butterfield. It demonstrated that Republicans and Democrats alike wanted all the facts to come out, no matter how dire the consequences were for the Nixon administration. Perhaps this also helped achieve unanimity in the votes to subpoena and sue the president.

After Nixon defied the committee's subpoena for certain tapes, the committee sued to obtain them. Special counsel Leon Jaworski also sued Nixon to obtain relevant tapes for use in the Watergate cover-up trial of several Nixon aides. Eventually, the Supreme Court ruled that Jaworski's need for the tapes in the Watergate cover-up trial outweighed Nixon's claim of executive privilege.[13] That ruling was Nixon's eviction notice. After the contents of a crucial tape showing his participation in the cover-up were revealed, he was forced to resign.

It is another irony of Watergate that the Senate Committee, although it discovered the tapes, never actually obtained them but had to settle for transcripts. The DC Circuit found that the committee's case involved not just a political question but also justiciable one—that is, it could be decided by a court—and that the president's executive privilege was not absolute but was subject to a balancing test. However, the Circuit Court held that the Watergate Committee could not make the strong showing of need for the tapes required to activate the balancing process for several reasons. It now had transcripts of the tapes, and the House Judiciary Committee, which was considering Nixon's impeachment, had the actual recordings. Their contents would become public whether or not the Watergate Committee obtained them.[14]

The ruling was frustrating. Precisely because the transcripts were public and the House had the actual tapes, the president had little confidentiality to protect. Nonetheless, useful precedent was established. That precedent, for example, was applied in the House Judiciary Committee's suit against George W. Bush White House officials Harriet Miers and Joshua Bolten. The US District Court for the District of Columbia, relying on the Select Committee's case, held in 2008 that the suit against Miers and Bolten could proceed, that the president did not have absolute executive privilege, and that the House had a right to the testimony and materials it sought that related to the firing of certain US attorneys.[15] I wrote an amicus brief in the *Miers* case supporting the House on behalf of, among others, Senator Dan Inouye. Nearly forty years earlier, I had written the briefs in the Senate Watergate Committee case against Nixon, proving, I guess, that in Washington we are all recycled.

The *Miers* opinion was only a very small part of the legacy of the Senate Watergate Committee. It also spawned significant legislation, for example, the central elements of the nation's campaign finance laws and the 1978 Ethics in Government Act, which included the misused, now discarded, but not lamented independent counsel statute.[16] Beyond that, the Senate Watergate Committee endures as a model of how to do things the right way, how to investigate thoroughly and fairly, and how to seek the truth in a nonpartisan manner.[17]

3

Senator Herman Talmadge

The Beneficent Overcoat

Washington, DC, has its highs and lows. Senator Herman Talmadge (D-GA) went from the high of being a star on the Senate Watergate Committee to the low of being investigated for financial improprieties by the Senate Ethics Committee and the Department of Justice.

During the Senate Watergate Committee hearings, I often sat next to Senator Herman Talmadge at the committee's green felt-covered table. Talmadge was no showboat but was content when his time came to ask concise, relevant questions in a lawyerly way.

After Talmadge heard John Ehrlichman's attempt at the Watergate Committee's 1973 hearings to justify President Nixon's right to burglarize and invade the privacy of private citizens, he engaged in this exchange with Ehrlichman:

TALMADGE: Now if the President could authorize a covert break-in, and you do not know exactly what that power would be limited [to], you do not think it could include murder or other crimes beyond covert break-ins, do you?

EHRLICHMAN: I do not know where the line is, Senator. . . .

TALMADGE: Do you remember when we were in law school, we studied

23

a famous principle of law that came from England and also is well known in this country, that no matter how humble a man's cottage is, that even the King of England cannot enter without his consent?

EHRLICHMAN: I am afraid that has been considerably eroded over the years, has it not?

TALMADGE: Down in my country we still think it is a pretty legitimate principle of law.[1]

This exchange brought Talmadge applause in the hearing room as well as national recognition and acclaim.[2]

I also tried to ask questions concisely and on point. I was the first Democratic counsel after chief counsel Sam Dash to interrogate witnesses at the public hearing. I recognized that my performance would influence how much public questioning lawyers besides Sam would be allowed to do. I thus interrogated the lead Watergate burglar, Bernard Barker, in around twelve minutes, eliciting the basic facts as to the Watergate break-in but leaving other probing questions (some of which I had prepared) for the senators.

Talmadge, I believed, approved of my restrained approach, concluding as he said in his 1987 memoir that I was a "mature and level-headed fellow." After I authored my book on congressional investigations, he wrote, too generously, that "Mr. Hamilton undoubtedly has written the most important book to result from the events known as Watergate."[3]

In 1978, allegations arose about financial misdealings by Senator Talmadge that eventually resulted in a Senate Ethics Committee investigation and a twenty-seven-day public trial before it. He asked me to represent him in those matters.

Herman Talmadge, to understate the matter, was a controversial, colorful figure. His father, Gene, a legendary Georgia politician, served three terms as governor of Georgia. Gene was elected in 1946 for a fourth term but died before taking office.

Recognizing that Gene was ill, his supporters maneuvered to have Herman chosen as governor. The Georgia Constitution provided that if the governor-elect died before taking office, the Georgia General Assembly would choose between the second- and third-place finisher for governor.

Talmadge loyalists thus arranged for write-in votes for Herman so he would be in the running.

When Gene died, three persons claimed to be governor: Melvin E. Thompson, the lieutenant governor–elect; Ellis Arnall, the then current governor; and Herman Talmadge, the write-in candidate chosen as governor by the General Assembly. All three concurrently attempted to run the state. For a while Herman Talmadge actually occupied the governor's office.

Eventually, the Supreme Court of Georgia ruled that Thompson was the rightful governor, concluding that the legislature could choose between the second- and third-place finishers only if no candidate had received a majority of votes (which Gene did). But in 1948, Talmadge took on Thompson in a special election and won. He served as governor until 1954 but was prevented by law from seeking another term.

Talmadge was elected to the US Senate in 1956, serving until 1980. He was a powerful member, eventually becoming chair of the Senate Agriculture Committee and a member of the Senate Finance Committee, which was responsible for the nation's tax laws.

Talmadge was a staunch segregationist early in his career, but his opposition to integration waned over the years. In 1975, he was named Georgia Man of the Year and awarded a doctorate of humane letters by Morris Brown College, a predominately Black institution. His widow, Lynda, relates that shortly before his death in 2002 he was visited at his home by singer James Brown. They prayed together.

Life went bad for the senator during the latter part of his Senate career. His son, Bobby, died by drowning in 1975. He and his wife, Betty, contentiously divorced in 1977. And his alcoholism, about which he has written extensively, worsened. In early 1979, after turning up drunk on the Senate floor, he was admitted to a federal clinic in California to sober up. He came back with a constant companion to keep him on the wagon, and he never touched alcohol again.

These tribulations coincided with the Senate Ethics Committee investigation.

The Ethics Committee investigation grew out of press accounts of a divorce-related lawsuit Senator Talmadge brought against Betty to recover the proceeds of a stock sale. These articles dealt with the sources of his spending money, inaccuracies in campaign reports regarding his 1974 re-election to the Senate, and allegations that the senator had received overpayments from the Senate based on inaccurate expense vouchers.

To explain his sources of spending money and why he rarely wrote a check, Talmadge advised the committee in a May 24, 1978, letter of "the long-standing practice of some of my friends in Georgia making to me small, personal cash gifts varying approximately from $5 to $20. . . . My use of the unsolicited gestures of friendship and affection has been solely to help defray my day-to-day incidental expenses."[4]

This practice had a history. The senator's populist father, Governor Gene Talmadge, had his pockets stuffed with small bills by his devoted rural constituents known as "wool hat boys" because of the hats worn by white farmers while working the fields.

The claim that Herman Talmadge had received excessive expense payments from the Senate had substance. On August 18, 1978, after auditors for Talmadge and the committee reviewed the senator's reimbursements, Talmadge repaid $37,125.90 to the Senate for excess reimbursements.

Nonetheless, the committee decided that substantial violations of rules within its jurisdiction had occurred and proceeded to try the senator for these purported violations, which, the committee decided, had to be proven by "clear and convincing" evidence.[5] The most serious charges were: (1) from 1972 to 1978, fifteen vouchers were submitted to the Senate in his name seeking improper reimbursement of $43,435.83 and that he had failed to sign as required by law and to supervise the preparation of those vouchers, and (2) a secret bank account at the Riggs National Bank in Washington in the name of "Herman E. Talmadge/Talmadge Campaign Committee" had been established to receive improper Senate reimbursements and unreported campaign contributions.[6]

In total, $39,314.67 had been deposited in this secret account. Of this amount, around $13,000 came from improper Senate reimbursements. Most, if not all, of the rest, the committee believed, came from diverted unreported campaign contributions.

The senator's chief accuser was Daniel Minchew.[7] Minchew had been Talmadge's administrative assistant, and, with the senator's recommendation, had been appointed chair of the International Trade Commission. Minchew claimed that Talmadge was aware of the phony vouchers. He also asserted that Talmadge knew of the secret Riggs account and that

Talmadge, his wife Betty, and his deceased son, Bobby, all benefited from that account.

Talmadge pushed back hard against these allegations. As to the overpayments, he asserted that he was not aware of them until 1978. He said he left voucher matters to his staff. When vouchers were presented to him, he asked if they were correct, and if assured they were he signed them without reviewing the details. He had more important demands on his time, and his conduct, he said, was no worse than negligent and certainly was not unethical. Some of the vouchers had been signed by autopen (an automatic pen used to affix a senator's signature).

Talmadge's defense to the secret Riggs account charge consisted largely of an attack on Daniel Minchew, on whose word the allegations mainly rested. The evidence showed the following:

- Minchew had deposited nearly $13,000 of Senate funds and about $26,000 of campaign contributions into that account.
- Minchew opened the secret account by forging Talmadge's signature.
- Minchew obtained the $13,000 in Senate funds by forging Talmadge's signature on phony vouchers.
- Minchew made all the deposits into the account, and he made all the withdrawals from the account by forging Tallmadge's name on checks made out to "cash."
- All bank statements were sent to Minchew's private residence.
- Minchew admitted to taking over $7,000 from the secret account for his own benefit.
- In June 1978, Talmadge, over Minchew's objections, ordered an independent audit that would have disclosed the secret account and the theft of Senate funds. (As Talmadge said, no reasonable person would have done this if he had previously known about the secret account and Minchew's stealing. He told the committee in testimony that "even my enemies don't claim I'm stupid.")[8]
- When Talmadge learned that two Senate checks had been processed at the Riggs Bank, he promptly reported that to the committee and the Department of Justice.
- Talmadge's wife Betty denied she had received money from the account, as did Bobby's widow and Talmadge himself.
- At the time when most of the money was taken from the account,

Minchew needed $40,000 to cover his personal financial obligations and thus had a powerful motive to steal.

A problem for Talmadge was that, as forensic evidence showed, there were two documents typed on the typewriter of his trusted secretary, Allyne Tisdale, suggesting that the senator knew that campaign contributions had not been reported as required by law and had been converted to his personal use. But these documents were fraught with controversy. Minchew claimed these documents were Talmadge office records, but they were not found in Talmadge's files. Rather, they came from Minchew's home, where he claimed they had been for four years. Moreover, Tisdale testified that she did not type these documents. Evidence showed Minchew had access to and, on at least one occasion, had used her typewriter. Evidence also showed that an event described in one of the documents never occurred. Talmadge testified that he never received the money the documents indicated he had received.

Minchew claimed he showed Talmadge these documents in June 1978, but Talmadge testified that he would have been a "fool" to instigate an audit that led to the discovery of the secret account had he known that Minchew held two incriminating documents.[9] Nonetheless, as we shall see, these documents influenced the committee.

The hearings were contentious and difficult, in part because of the substance, in part because of the players involved. The chair of the committee was Illinois Democratic senator Adlai Stevenson III, a shadow of his more famous father. Stevenson, a former banking lawyer, had limited knowledge of the rules of evidence, which in any event are not strictly adhered to in Senate ethics proceedings.

The vice chair was Republican senator Harrison Schmitt of Arizona, a former astronaut who walked on the moon. Schmitt was unaffectionately referred to by some on Capitol Hill as "Moon Rock." Not surprisingly, he also had little knowledge of evidentiary rules. He also had a distinct distaste for Talmadge.

Joining him in dislike for Talmadge was the committee's special counsel, Carl Eardley. Eardley was generally a decent fellow, with a Department of Justice and civil rights background. But at the time of the hearing, he was a senior citizen and, as we shall see, was not in his prime as a litigator.

The other Democratic members of the committee were Quentin Burdick of North Dakota and Robert Morgan of North Carolina. The Republicans were Mark Hatfield of Oregon and Jesse Helms of North Carolina. All four of these senators had been recently appointed to the committee.

Before those appointments, Talmadge implored Majority Leader Robert Byrd (D-WV) to designate members with some seniority who knew Talmadge and his stature in the Senate. I was in Talmadge's office when he had one such conversation with Senator Byrd over the telephone. At one point, Talmadge handed the phone to me to make the case to Byrd. After I introduced myself as Talmadge's lawyer, Senator Byrd said, "I will speak to Senator Talmadge about this matter but not with you." I think even Talmadge was taken aback by this imperious dismissal.

During the hearings, dealing with Senator Schmitt proved especially difficult. I sparred with him frequently over evidentiary and other matters. At some point, a reporter from a small Georgia paper—whose requests for leaks I repeatedly had refused, much to his irritation—commented on my frequent battles with Schmitt and asserted that I was "rude, arrogant and humorless." I didn't like being called rude and arrogant, but being branded humorless really irked me. Sometime later this same reporter asked me to consider representing one of his family members who might face criminal charges. I guess he thought a humorless lawyer would be effective. I declined.

By the conclusion of the hearing, Senator Schmitt may have mellowed a bit. He thanked counsel on both sides "for their diligence in this affair and general comity of activity." He then said: "Things get heated at times, but, nevertheless, I think in spite of the length of the hearings, we have all survived."[10]

The hearings were made more difficult because I sat for weeks between a cigar smoker, Herman Talmadge, and a pipe smoker, my law partner Ron Wertheim. I am a lifelong nonsmoker. My lungs suffered.

Talmadge also chewed tobacco. While representing Talmadge, I took my parents to his office to meet him. His office featured his father's famous red galluses, framed and hanging on the wall, and a bronze spittoon. The spittoon was between his desk and the couch on which my mother sat. His aim was good, but with every splash my proper mother shuddered.

The hearing began on April 30, 1979, when I rose and said, "Mr. Chairman, the opening argument of Counsel will be made by a distinguished lawyer from Georgia, Senator Herman E. Talmadge."[11] We had worked hard on the substance of that statement, and Talmadge, a natural orator, delivered it with flair and gusto.

Much of our focus at the hearing was on establishing that Daniel Minchew was a consummate liar. He was in the witness chair for the better part of eight days, much of that time under heavy cross-examination. At the end, his credibility was in tatters.

The evidence, for example, showed the following:

- Minchew lied to the Department of Justice when interviewed about the matters at hand, including the secret Riggs account.
- He lied to an FBI polygrapher, which he admitted in cross-examination.
- He lied to the IRS about when he sold real estate to avoid paying taxes in a certain year.
- He lied on financial statements to various banking institutions, which is a federal crime.
- He lied to the committee about his real estate investments.

Perhaps most egregiously he lied to and cheated one of his best friends. Minchew and Matthew Nimetz, counselor to the Department of State, had purchased a house together.[12] Minchew sold this house in 1974 and pocketed the proceeds.

In 1978, he sent Nimetz a check for "rent" money to conceal the sale of the property. Nimetz learned of this skullduggery in 1979 when my law partner Ron Wertheim asked him about the house they bought together and sold. Matt's response: "What do you mean 'sold?'"

Even special counsel Eardley could not stomach all this lying. He publicly acknowledged that Minchew had been "deceptive" and that his credibility had been "eroded."[13]

The most titillating testimony at the hearing had little to do with the specific charges against Senator Talmadge. Betty Talmadge testified that when they were in DC the senator kept an overcoat in a hall closet that was a cornucopia of cash. She testified that over the years she took thousands of dollars from this overcoat. Specifically, she testified that in January 1974 she

removed seventy-seven consecutively numbered $100 bills from this benefi-
cent item of apparel. That $7,700, she testified, was in two envelopes. The
inner envelope, which contained the cash, was a plain envelope with the
name Harry Anestos handwritten on it. The outer envelope was a Talmadge
"franked" envelope. In other words, it was an envelope with a facsimile of
Talmadge's signature where a stamp normally would be placed, which at the
time allowed a letter to be mailed without postage.

Other facts raised questions about Betty's testimony. The source of the
money was unclear. It did not come from Anestos, a Maryland lawyer who,
while he was a supporter of the senator, never gave him more than $250
at one time. The money also did not come from the secret Riggs account
but apparently had been distributed by the Houston branch of the Dallas
Federal Reserve Bank to a corresponding bank within the Houston area.
Exactly which correspondent bank had received the money was unknown.

The money also could not have been found in the senator's overcoat in
January 1974. The evidence showed that Rogers Wade, the senator's administrative assistant, had written Anestos's name on the envelope. But he did
not know Anestos or his name before 1975. He thus could not have written
that name on any envelope Betty Talmadge found in January 1974. Wade
also testified that he transmitted no funds to the senator in that envelope.

Betty had a motive to fabricate testimony against the senator. She had
learned from a television report that he was filing for divorce. Not surprisingly, the divorce proceedings, which she did not want, became bitter. Their
marriage had faced other difficulties, including the senator's alcoholism
and her depression. She also had lost a hotly contested property dispute
with him.

Betty's testimony to the committee was contrary to her testimony in the
divorce proceedings, where she said she did not "take" any money from
the senator. The $7,700 also was not included on a financial statement she
had submitted during the divorce proceedings, which she had testified was
"accurate."[14]

In any event, the time came for Special Counsel Eardley to question Talmadge about the cash and the envelopes. His dislike for Talmadge was pal-
pable, and he was, I think, looking forward to this moment.

In response to Eardley's questions, Talmadge testified that while he had
seen one-hundred-dollar bills before, he had not seen these particular seventy-
seven one-hundred-dollar bills.

Showing him the Anestos envelope, Eardley asked, "Sir, have you seen this envelope before?" Talmadge said he had "no recollection" of it.[15]

Then Eardley circled in, he thought, for the kill. He handed Talmadge a franked envelope. His eyes glistening in anticipated triumph, he asked: "Have you seen it before?"

Senator Talmadge, a smile growing on his face, said, "No."

Eardley then asked: "Is this the first time you have ever seen it?"

Senator Talmadge said, "Yes."

Becoming increasingly incredulous, Eardley asked, "It is one of your franked envelopes, is it not?"

Senator Talmadge responded: "No, it has Adlai Stevenson's name on it."

Eardley had given Talmadge the wrong envelope!

Hearing that, Senator Stevenson threw up his hands in exasperation and covered his expansive brow with them. Unable to restrain myself, I rose and said, "Mr. Chairman, we don't have any objection to admitting that [envelope] into evidence."[16]

The hearings concluded at 1:10 p.m. on Thursday, July 12, 1978. Senator Stevenson had planned to end the next day, but I told him that was not possible. I was being married on Saturday and had to be in New Canaan, Connecticut, on Friday evening for wedding festivities. Stevenson kindly pushed to finish on Thursday.

But I was not given much leeway. Supplemental briefs were due the next Thursday. Kristina and I postponed our honeymoon for three weeks, and I returned to DC to figure out how to bring the Talmadge matter to a satisfactory conclusion.

Even though the evidence was a mishmash, it was obvious that the committee was very concerned about Talmadge's conduct. Some significant sanction was going to result. Talmadge wanted to avoid a sanction of "censure"—which had befallen Senator Thomas Dodd a few years before—or being "condemned," which was Senator Joe McCarthy's fate. He would have preferred a reprimand or admonishment, but the committee was not going to agree to any such mild result.

After final briefs were filed, I sat down alone with Senator Stevenson in his private office to negotiate a resolution the committee would accept and that Talmadge would agree not to challenge on the Senate floor. Stevenson, I believe, realized that Talmadge had many friends in the Senate and that, particularly given the confused state of the evidence, he might prevail in a floor fight.

We eventually agreed that Talmadge would accept being "denounced." But that verdict would come with an explanation that this sanction was something less than censure or condemnation. The final resolution of the committee, although harsh, did just that.

Focusing on the phony Senate reimbursement vouchers and the secret Riggs account into which campaign contributions were deposited, the committee on October 4, 1979, submitted the following recommended findings to the full Senate:

> *Resolved,* it is the judgment of the Senate that Senator Talmadge either knew, or should have known, of these improper acts and omissions, and, therefore, by the gross neglect of his duty to faithfully and carefully administer the affairs of his office, he is responsible for these acts and omissions.
>
> *Resolved further,* it is the judgment of the Senate that the conduct of Senator Talmadge, as aforesaid, is reprehensible and tends to bring the Senate into dishonor and disrepute and is hereby denounced.[17]

The committee tempered those harsh findings with the following statement: "The facts in this investigation are distinguishable from those of earlier matters in which the Senate 'censured' or 'condemned' a Member. The committee therefore expresses its judgment and its recommendation with respect to the conduct of Senator Talmadge and the effect of that conduct on the Senate with words that do not depend on analogy to dissimilar historical circumstances for interpretation."[18]

Senator Schmitt filed extensive "additional views." He asserted that Talmadge should have been censured for his conduct. He argued that the words "reprehensible" and "denounced" should be viewed by history as the equivalent to "censured" in cases of financial misdeeds and where years of illegal activities by subordinates have been overlooked.[19]

To some degree, Senator Schmitt won that argument. Historical accounts have treated Talmadge's denouncement as tantamount to censure. Even the Senate parliamentarian was confused about the meaning of the term *denounced.* He said: "It's not censure and it's not reprimand. . . . Where it falls [between the two] I sure don't know."[20]

The Senate met on October 11, 1979, to consider the committee's report and recommendations. In an unusual move, I was allowed to go on the Senate floor with Senator Talmadge. Senator Stevenson reported on the investigation, stressing that the resolution did not attribute actual knowledge of wrongdoing to Talmadge. Senator Schmitt reiterated his argument that censure was the appropriate sanction.

At the end of the debate the resolution passed without amendment 81–15 with 4 abstentions. Talmadge then spoke. While he "humbly" accepted the judgment of the Senate, he stressed that there was no finding of intentional wrongdoing and that censure had not been sought.[21] When he concluded, various senators expressed their friendship and support. Perhaps the less than condemning attitude of the Senate is captured by an Oliphant cartoon that is reproduced on page 135. In his memoirs Talmadge wrote that he regretted not seeking full exoneration by the Senate.

Talmadge still faced two hurdles: one he surmounted; one he didn't.

Talmadge stood for re-election to the Senate in 1980. He had a tough primary race against Lieutenant Governor Zell Miller, winning in a runoff. Then he faced Republican Matt Mattingly. Talmadge's denouncement became an election issue, and Mattingly won. Mattingly also was part of the beginning of a Republican wave that would largely engulf the South and lead to Republican dominance in the South's congressional representation for years to come.

The other hurdle was the Department of Justice. Particularly given the conflicting testimony before it, the committee had referred the matters under investigation to the DOJ and made available all of its files. The DOJ was already fully aware of the matter; a DOJ lawyer had attended the committee hearings.

At an appropriate time, I made a visit to the DOJ Criminal Division to argue why Talmadge should not be indicted. There were ten to fifteen DOJ lawyers in the room, including Phil Heymann, then the head of the Criminal Division. I emphasized the confusing nature of the evidence. But mainly I argued that no case could be based on the testimony of Daniel Minchew, a proven liar.

I am told that five persons voted on whether to indict Talmadge. It was 3-to-2 against indictment. Heymann and two others voted no. I am told that

Reid Weingarten, who later became a friend and one of Washington's leading white-collar lawyers, voted yes, along with another colleague.

Daniel Minchew was not so fortunate. He pleaded guilty to one felony count for submitting a fake expense voucher for $2,289.99 to the Senate. That money had gone into the secret Riggs account. Minchew claimed to the end that he was a scapegoat for the conduct of his onetime "hero."[22] He was sentenced to four months in prison the day before the Senate denounced Senator Talmadge.

At last report, Minchew was giving private tours at the US Capitol.

4

Senator Dave Durenberger
The Fallout of Bad Advice

         I represented Senator Dave Durenberger, a moderate Republican from Minnesota, in two Senate Ethics Committee investigations. The first was resolved in a manner that caused little harm. The second, unfortunately, came to a sad end.[1]

Dave Durenberger served in the Senate from 1978 to 1995. He generally was known as a good senator. For eight years he served on the Senate Intelligence Committee, ending as its chair. He was on the Senate Environment and Health Committees and was viewed as an expert on the subjects within their purview.

    Durenberger was respected in Minnesota for his diligent work ethic and for the candor with which he expressed his views. His good looks and affability undoubtedly enhanced his popularity.

    But Durenberger began to have personal problems about which he spoke openly. In 1986, he announced that he had moved into a religious retreat (run by his spiritual advisor, Doug Coe) to explore why he was "unhappy in my relationship with my wife and with other people."[2] His staff said that he sought out a therapist because of marital difficulties. This strain and his inclination for candor led some to express concern about his emotional health and his readiness to handle classified information. As we shall see, financial difficulties eventually added to his pressures.

* * *

In March 1987, at two events in Florida sponsored by the American Israel
Public Affairs Committee (AIPAC)—a well-known pro-Israel organization—
Durenberger stated that the CIA in the early 1980s recruited an Israeli army
officer to spy for the United States. (The Israeli officer apparently was identified after Israeli officials saw information in the press that could only have
come from someone with classified Israeli military information.) This spying came about, Durenberger said, when CIA Director Bill Casey "changed
the rules of the game" and broke the agreement with Israel that neither it
nor the United States would recruit agents from the other country to spy
on it.[3]

Durenberger also said that the CIA urged the FBI not to pursue Jonathan
Jay Pollard, a US Navy intelligence analyst who recently had been convicted
and given a life sentence for spying for Israel. The Pollard affair had heightened tensions between the two countries. Durenberger was quoted as stating, "What I'm really saying to you is that this is not a one-way street. I can't
justify Pollard, but I can understand it."[4] The Israeli officer allegedly had
been recruited by the United States before Israel recruited Pollard.

The story about Durenberger's statements was first broken by Wolf
Blitzer, now a CNN anchor, who then was working for the *Jerusalem Post*.

Durenberger's comments produced a raft of negative reactions. Secretary
of Defense Casper Weinberger denied that the United States had done what
Durenberger claimed, adding that it was "very damaging and very wrong"
for the senator to make such a claim.[5] An unnamed, obviously vexed Senator told *New York Times* columnist William Safire, "This is censure stuff."[6]
Another irritated anonymous member of the Senate Intelligence Committee declared, "This is diplomatically and politically embarrassing . . . I think
Dave is a decent person, but this is distressing."[7] Other senators—Oren
Hatch, Rudy Boschwitz, and Mitch McConnell—came to Durenberger's defense. McConnell said, "I think Dave was a good chairman; he was very
scrupulous about maintaining confidentiality on these kinds of matters."[8]

Durenberger did not deny that he had made the statements attributed
to him. He initially said that he was just "relay[ing] . . . public speculations
that the United States may have had intelligence sources within the Israeli
government."[9] He later stated that he had spoken with an experienced aide
who said the information Durenberger relayed was based on press reports.

Durenberger also claimed he had indicated just that in his remarks to the AIPAC gatherings.[10]

It was not surprising that, in this context, the Senate Ethics Committee began an investigation into whether Durenberger had revealed classified information. Senate Resolution 400 explicitly states that "It shall be the duty of the [Ethics Committee] to investigate any unauthorized disclosure of intelligence information by a Member . . . of the Senate . . . and to report to the Senate concerning any allegation which it finds to be substantiated."[11]

To represent Senator Durenberger in this matter, I needed to examine the classified information he had seen. To do that, I required a top-secret code-word clearance. Amazingly—and perhaps because of a push from the Senate Ethics Committee, which wanted to get on with its investigation—I obtained that clearance in around two weeks.

After my clearance was granted I was given a briefing on US spying capabilities by a cautious CIA functionary. This fellow quickly went through a thick briefing book at a pace that left me unable to remember most of what I had seen. I concluded that he was either bored with his job or, more likely, he really didn't want some nongovernment lawyer like myself to have access to such highly classified information.

At the end of the briefing, he said to me, "Mr. Hamilton you now are in possession of most sensitive information. You must take steps to ensure that it doesn't fall into the wrong hands. For that reason, we want you to avoid all contact with foreign nationals."

Thinking about my beautiful Swedish wife I said: "But I sleep with one every night."

To which he replied: "Oh, yes. We know that, and because of that we have given you a special waiver."

My wife was quite pleased that I had received a special waiver that allowed me to continue to sleep with her!

Because the hearing on this matter involved classified information, it was held behind closed doors in a secure room on an upper floor in the Hart Senate Office Building. Two Durenberger allies attended the session: Senator Daniel Inouye of Hawaii, a highly respected Democrat who had served on the Senate Watergate Committee and who I thus knew well and trusted, and Senator Arlen Specter, a Republican from Pennsylvania. Specter, a bull-dog of a man, was particularly aggressive in his defense of Durenberger.

I will not reveal the contents of this classified session. But generally, as I remember it, the senators made several salient arguments. Inouye attested to Durenberger's character. Dave, he said, was not the sort of man who would intentionally harm the United States. Specter, who had educated himself on the evidence and was prone to insert himself vigorously in any argument, forcefully defended Durenberger on the facts.

There was also an elephant in the room: finding Durenberger culpable in the situation at hand posed risks for other senators. Senators often speak about information alluded to in the press that may still be classified. There was a danger that a finding adverse to Durenberger could serve as a prece-dent that might haunt other well-meaning but voluble senators who would speak about classified matters believing that the information had already been made public in some fashion.

The committee at this time consisted of three Democrats—Chair Howell Heflin of Alabama, David Pryor of Arkansas, and Terry Sanford of North Carolina—and three Republicans—Vice Chair Warren Rudman of New Hampshire, Jesse Helms of North Carolina, and Nancy Landon Kassebaum of Kansas. I was worried about the outcome of the investigation, fearing that Durenberger would be censured for several reasons.

There was precedent for that result. The first senator to receive the sanc-tion of censure was Timothy Pickering of Massachusetts, who in 1811 was censured for revealing secret papers regarding the 1803 Louisiana Purchase Treaty with France.

Another reason I was afraid of censure was Warren Rudman. From some-where, Rudman had received the gift of certainty; once he came to a con-clusion, it was difficult to persuade him otherwise.[12] In meetings with him it was obvious that he was troubled by Durenberger's conduct.

But the committee faced a conundrum. If it found Durenberger guilty of leaking classified information, it would be confirming that the information was true, contrary to what Casper Weinberger and others were saying. But if the committee exonerated Durenberger, it might encourage loose talk by other senators and negative press coverage for committee members.

The committee solved this problem in an ingenuous manner. It criticized Durenberger for giving "the appearance" that he was disclosing classified information. It said: "The ethics committee has determined that your state-ments gave the appearance that you were disclosing sensitive national secu-rity information and such appearance jeopardized the mutual confidence which must exist between the Congress and the intelligence community."[13]

There thus was no confirmation that the information Durenberger had relayed was true.

The committee added: "Because the committee has concluded that your actions were not intentional, deliberate, nor attended with gross negligence, and because of the particular facts of this case, we will not recommend that the Senate take institutional action against you. However, the committee wants to make it clear that it does not condone your actions."[14]

Durenberger continued to defend his actions in his own statement. He said he had discussed the matter with the former staff director of the Sen-ate Intelligence Committee, who at one time had been an assistant to the director of the CIA and an assistant to the chair of the Joint Chiefs of Staff. That person, Durenberger said, told him that his remarks were based on newspaper articles, as he had indicated at the time to the AIPAC groups. "I had no belief," Durenberger said, "that repeating such information would give any appearance that sensitive information was being disclosed."[15]

Senate minority leader Robert Dole, in his own statement, declared his confidence in Durenberger. Durenberger, Dole said, was "an excellent chairman [of the Intelligence Committee] during one of the most demand-ing and crucial periods for intelligence oversight."[16]

As we will see, Dole's regard and support for Durenberger proved crucial when his financial dealings came under investigation.

As remarked, Durenberger did not fare so well in his second Senate Ethics Committee proceeding, which, in major part, involved two matters.

The first was his arrangement with a fledgling book publishing company, Piranha Press. This arrangement involved an attempt to convert excessive honoraria for speeches into a "stipend" from that company for purportedly promoting books by the senator that it published. The name of the pub-lishing company, Piranha Press, is ironic because Durenberger's deal with it devoured his good name.

The second issue concerned a plan to obtain Senate reimbursement for "rent" paid to stay in a Minneapolis condominium that Durenberger had owned, when he was there on official business. This arrangement eventually resulted in Durenberger's plea to several criminal misdemeanor charges.

This was a sad affair for several reasons. As to both of these matters, Durenberger relied on horrendous advice from Minnesota lawyers who apparently had little notion of how these arrangements would be viewed in skeptical Washington. Moreover, in other respects Durenberger was an admirable senator and was considered a good man by many of his colleagues. It was painful to witness a tragic downfall.

A brief description of Durenberger's personal situation will place his transgressions into context. It also provides a cautionary reminder of the dangers faced by persons of limited means who engage in public service in a city where financial demands are substantial and political opponents and the media are motivated to probe for character flaws.

During the period when his publishing and condominium arrangements came about and were implemented, Senator Durenberger was under immense strains and pressures, personal and otherwise. Durenberger was not a rich man when he came to the Senate. His income thereafter came mainly from his Senate salary and speaking engagements. The reduction in the allowable honoraria limit, which was passed in 1983 and became effective in 1984, was a major financial blow; the senator had earned over $92,000 in honoraria in 1983. He thus had to borrow heavily. His wife, Penny, a homemaker and student, contributed only infrequently to the family income.

Although Durenberger's income was modest, his expenses were significant. He had four sons of college age. The costs of college and private preparatory schooling were high. Penny had pursued a master's degree in social work at Catholic University. Two of his sons had chemical dependency problems that required periods of expensive institutionalization. Durenberger himself underwent costly marriage counseling in Massachusetts. For a while he owned two homes—one in the Washington, DC, area, the other in Minneapolis—until in 1983 the expense became too great.

Added to the financial strain were family pressures. Senator Durenberger's first wife had died of cancer, leaving him with four young sons. Penny had lost her husband in Vietnam. Their subsequent marriage was never an easy one. The boys' discipline and drug problems heightened the tensions between the senator and Penny. The two separated for twenty months in early 1985. Senator Durenberger went to live at the Cedars, a religious retreat in Virginia run by Doug Coe, the head of a secretive Christian-oriented group known as the Fellowship, which in 2019 was the subject of an unflattering Netflix documentary.

Some of Senator Durenberger's problems were the unfortunate by-product of the prodigious hours he worked. He put his energies into his Senate tasks and into speaking, which to him was both a passion and a mission. His work schedule left him drained, with little time for family problems and even less for personal financial matters.

As a result, Durenberger came to lean heavily on staff, friends, and lawyers for financial advice and help. His original chief of staff and administrative assistant died in December 1983. At times in 1984 and 1985, his staffing situation was chaotic, with key jobs not filled or key aides on leave for extended periods. He thus came to rely with great frequency on Minneapolis lawyers. His Senate workload, his family strains, and his financial problems likely affected his judgment and made him all too susceptible to the questionable, politically insensitive legal advice he received.

Doug Coe, who perhaps knew Durenberger better than almost anyone outside of his family, submitted an affidavit to the committee that in poignant terms described the senator's personal travails:

Since I have known Dave, he has always had a very strong commitment to his Senatorial duties. This often leads him to put work ahead of his family and other personal matters. In my experience, I too often have seen the expectations of a public position destroy personal lives. . . .

During this difficult period when he was struggling in all the important areas of his life, Dave was not able to make good decisions. He seemed to lose his perspective, and his priorities became confused. He hit his lowest point during 1984–1985, and there were days when it was difficult for him to get out of the bed in the morning.

It was during this low point that Dave came to rely so heavily on others. He didn't have the time or energy to deal with all the details of his life; he had to conserve his resources to fulfill his Senatorial and family responsibilities. His frame of mind led him to trust others with too many of his business arrangements. . . .

I sincerely feel Dave is not a person to try to take advantage of people or to do things he knows are improper. I spend my life talking to public men, and I am convinced that Dave is not intentionally deceitful nor dishonest. However, Dave has not always made the best decisions. He has been naive and allowed himself to be put into bad situations when his personal problems caught up with him at home. But to me, to make a leap to thinking Dave has intentionally committed illegal or improper acts is unjust and simply wrong."[17]

As mentioned, in the mid-1980s the rules on honoraria for senators changed. A federal statute imposed a cap of 30 percent of a member's salary on the amount of honoraria they could earn.[18] The percentage shortly thereafter was raised to forty. The law also provided that no one honorarium could exceed $2,000. This meant that Durenberger had to find another way to supplement his income. The solution he reached was the deal with Piranha Press.

The law at the time made a distinction between an honorarium and a stipend. An *honorarium* was a payment for a single event where there was no ongoing relationship between the parties. A *stipend* was a payment for services on a continuing basis. Many members of Congress—for example, Senators Bob Dole, Alan Simpson, Charles Mathias, Ted Kennedy, Joe Biden, William Proxmire, and Daniel Patrick Moynihan—had legitimate stipendiary relationships.

Durenberger and Piranha Press entered into a contract under which Durenberger would give a series of speeches promoting his books *Neither Madam nor Messiahs* (which was about national security and defense policy) and *Prescription for Change* (about health care), both of which Piranha published. For this continuing service, Durenberger was paid $12,500 per quarter for a two-year period.

Durenberger received a written legal opinion from his Minnesota counsel that this stipendiary agreement was legal. That lawyer also sought an advisory opinion from the Federal Election Commission (FEC). That body concluded, on the information available to it, that "the arrangement . . . whereby the publisher will pay Senator Durenberger in quarterly installments over a two-year period for promotional appearances, creates a stipendiary relationship. Accordingly, payments made to Senator Durenberger under this agreement would not be viewed as honoraria and therefore would not be subject to [honoraria] limitations."[19]

During the two-year period, Senator Durenberger made 113 speaking appearances to businesses, trade associations, and colleges pursuant to the contract. For these appearances, Piranha received approximately $248,300 in speaker fees from the groups addressed. The amounts paid per speech typically varied from between $1,000 and $5,000.

The committee's special counsel was Bob Bennett, a well-known former prosecutor and DC white collar lawyer. Bennett had recently represented the committee in a proceeding resulting in the ouster from the Senate of Harrison Williams of New Jersey after he had been convicted of bribery and other criminal conduct. Bennett did not accept the proposition that Durenberger had received a legitimate stipend. Rather, he argued that the Piranha Press arrangement was simply "a means of converting into 'stipendary income' fees which would otherwise have been treated as honoraria."[20] Durenberger, Bennett said, had violated the statutory limits.

Bennett reached several specific conclusions:

- The speeches Durenberger gave were not intended to promote his books but to earn fees.
- None of the 113 speeches was the result of a request to promote his books. Rather, they were all based on invitations to deliver traditional honorarium speeches.
- After Durenberger reached his honoraria limit, his staff forwarded speaking requests to Piranha for treatment as promotional appearances.
- During his speeches, his books were often not mentioned or displayed.
- Twenty-six checks made out to Durenberger were deposited in the Piranha account. Most of these he had endorsed to Piranha.

Bennett contended that the FEC advisory opinion carried no weight. He noted that the senator's lawyer—*who had also served as Piranha's agent to negotiate and collect fees for the speeches*—had not informed the FEC that the groups Durenberger spoke to were paying Piranha a fee. Nor was the FEC told that the Piranha appearances came as a result of honorarium invitations to the Senate or that the speaking engagements were essentially identical to traditional honorarium events and were not book promotions.

Durenberger's condominium arrangements were also the product of bad judgment and atrocious lawyering by attorneys who included his counsel in the Piranha affair. The facts were complicated but essentially involved two separate but related transactions.

In 1983, Durenberger concluded that he could not afford to own two homes—one in DC and another in Minneapolis. He decided to place his Minneapolis condominium unit, #603, into an investment partnership owned by him and Roger Scherer, who had contributed another unit, #703, to the partnership. The senator then rented from the partnership his former unit, #603, when he was in Minneapolis on business (around one hundred days a year) at a rate of $65 a night. He submitted reimbursement requests for the rent to the Senate.

The partnership was supposed to be effective on July 28, 1983. However, the deed transferring Durenberger's unit to the partnership was not filed with the registrar of titles until May 14, 1984.

Originally the partnership was called the Durenberger-Scherer Partnership. Later the name was changed to the ##703/603 Association.

Durenberger was advised that he could seek per diem reimbursements from the Senate so long as #603 was not his official residence. He then changed his official Minnesota residence to his parents' home in Avon, Minnesota.

In August 1986, Scherer told Durenberger he wished to withdraw from the partnership, and it was terminated on March 31, 1987. Other arrangements had to be made.

Durenberger sold his interest "effective" April 1, 1987, to a company called Independent Service Company (ISC), owned by Paul Overgaard, for $52,804. Money changed hands but the legal documents for the sale were not given to Overgaard until October 1989 (after several protests by Overgaard about the incredibly sloppy lawyering), and they were never filed with the registrar of titles.

Durenberger rented the condominium from ISC for $85 a night and charged the rent amount back to the Senate. From August 1983 to mid-November 1989, he received over $40,000 from the Senate in reimbursements.

Special Counsel Bennett vigorously attacked these transactions, claiming that they were affected by back-dated documents and were intended to permit Durenberger to claim Senate per diem reimbursements for staying in what was essentially his Minnesota residence. Bennett noted that the parties had not executed the documents creating the partnership and transferring the condominium to it until early 1984. The legal title to #603 was not transferred until May 1984, even though Durenberger claimed per diem starting in July 1983. Even in May 1984, Durenberger held a 50 percent interest in the partnership and thus claimed per diem for rent paid to an entity he partially owned. Bennett also argued that the name change to the "##703/603 Association" was intended to hide the true ownership of the partnership from the Senate Disbursing Office.

Bennett's conclusion as to the sale to ISC was equally harsh. While the "effective" date of the sale was April 1, 1987, ISC was not identified as the buyer until the summer of 1987. The sale was made retroactive to April 1987, but the deed was not delivered to Overgaard until October 1989. Documents indicated that Overgaard would reconvey the condominium to Durenberger on demand. Because the necessary documents were not filed with the registrar of titles, ISC never had the legal title to the condominium. To Bennett, this evidence "strongly suggested" that Durenberger intended just to "park" the condominium with Overgaard so he could (improperly) collect per diem from the Senate. The sale, Bennett argued, was a "sham."[21]

We pushed back against these arguments as best we could. We argued that Durenberger had been advised by lawyers every step of the way. As to the partnership, one lawyer expressly advised him in writing that the partnership agreement should be dated before August 1, 1983, the beginning date for the reimbursement claims. We pointed out that under Minnesota law the intent of the parties is important regarding the effective date of a property transfer, which may be earlier than the date a deed is executed.

We noted that Deloitte & Touche had given an opinion stating that, for tax purposes, there was a partnership in July 1983. There was also a March 13, 1984, note in the files from the senator's bookkeeper stating that she had communicated with both the Senate Ethics and Rules Committees about the partnership. She wrote, "[I] spoke with my contacts in ethics and rules and no one has a problem with the partnership situation." This note, we contended, showed that there was no intent to hide the true ownership of the partnership.[22]

We observed that the other persons involved in these transactions were substantial citizens. Roger Scherer, the other partner, was at the time chair of the Minneapolis Chamber of Commerce. Paul Overgaard, the owner of ISC to which the condominium was sold, was in the Minnesota State

Senate and had run for governor. Neither of these men, we argued, would knowingly have engaged in a sham or facilitated unethical conduct.

As to the sale to ISC, we argued that although the transaction was handled in a uniquely careless fashion, it was a real one. Beneficial interest passed. Money changed hands. Overgaard made a down payment to Durenberger; Durenberger paid rent. Overgaard paid expenses and took a tax deduction for depreciation. He and Durenberger believed they had made a final sale. Overgaard's vociferous complaints about lawyer tardiness in completing the transaction showed he intended it to be completed.

We also argued that if Durenberger, Scherer, Overgaard, and a bevy of lawyers wanted to conspire to help Durenberger circumvent the reimbursement rules, they would have proceeded differently. They would not have left a bizarre, convoluted paper trail that defied comprehension. Durenberger's principal attorney in this mess admitted in a deposition that his conduct was "embarrassing and stupid . . . I don't think this is a model of how to do a transaction."[23]

The Ethics Committee held a hearing on the Durenberger case on June 12 and 13, 1990. In part because of financial restraints, Durenberger waived the right to an evidentiary hearing, which could have extended the hearing for a number of days. Instead, the committee heard arguments from Bennett and me based on the record before it. Durenberger also addressed the committee.

We approached the hearing with apprehension, fearing that the committee would sanction Durenberger with a censure or worse. With the evidence Bennett had, he was loaded for bear. We continued to fear that Senator Rudman's righteous streak would erupt and he would demand a severe sanction.

And then there was the political nature of the process. Senators are not federal judges with lifetime appointments and a habit of impartiality. They are politicians with an eye toward the next election. What a senator does in disciplining a colleague in a Senate Ethics Committee proceeding can become an election issue.

I had faith in the fairness of David Pryor, whom I later represented in the independent counsel investigation of Mike Espy, Bill Clinton's secretary of agriculture. The same was true of Terry Sanford, whom I came to know when he was president of Duke University and I was, for a time, in charge of organizing North Carolina for Senator Ed Muskie's presidential campaign. But I was not sure how political factors would affect the rest of the committee.

We took steps to guard against censure or something harsher. On May 16 we filed a lengthy brief with the committee dissecting the evidence and arguing against censure. The evidence showed, we contended, that while Durenberger had made mistakes, those mistakes were not intentional but were the product of his reliance on severely flawed legal advice. His conduct, we argued, may deserve a "strong reprimand" but not censure, which should be reserved for egregious, intentional misconduct such as that engaged in by Senators Tom Dodd and Joe McCarthy.

Filing a brief was not the only precautions we took. Durenberger and I had a private visit with Senate minority leader Bob Dole in his plush expansive office in the Capitol. Durenberger had great respect for Dole, addressing him repeatedly as "Leader." It was obvious that Dole had considerable affection for Durenberger, recognizing that in many respects he had been a commendable senator.

Dole was sympathetic to what we had to say—that Durenberger, while having erred, did not do so intentionally, that he followed flawed attorney advice, and that his personal problems had muddled his judgment. Whatever Durenberger's shortcomings, we argued, he did not deserve censure or expulsion. We mentioned that Senator Herman Talmadge had been only "denounced" even though the Ethics Committee had concluded that he "knew, or should have known" about certain criminal acts by his principal aide. While we thought denouncement would be too severe for Durenberger, we contended to Dole that this was the greatest sanction that should be imposed.

Dole listened attentively to our entreaty. When we concluded, he said he would speak to Senator Rudman about the matter.

Whether he did and what he said to Rudman, I don't know. I do know that, in Bennett's oral presentation and later written report to the committee, he recommended not expulsion or censure but denouncement.

The Ethics Committee adopted that recommendation unanimously. But it did so in sharp language.

As to the first major issue—Piranha Press—the committee found that Durenberger "did not proceed in good faith in instituting his arrangement" with that company. That arrangement, it found, "was simply a mechanism to avoid the statutory limitations on honoraria, and . . . the monies paid . . . were in reality honoraria."[24]

As to the second major issue, the condominium, the committee ruled that

- the partnership arrangement "was conceived and structured solely as a mechanism to enable Senator Durenberger to claim Senate reimbursement for overnight stays" in a condominium he actually owned, and
- Durenberger "subsequently structured a purported sale of the condominium to ISC, and knowingly participated in the backdating of the transaction . . . to justify claims" for Senate reimbursement, even though he "was in effect only temporarily 'parking' the condominium with ISC."[25]

The committee added: "Finally, the Committee finds that Senator Durenberger did encounter severe emotional strain from events in his personal life. The Committee further finds that the severe emotional and traumatic events in the Senator's personal life impaired his judgment. The Committee finds that these factors do not excuse the Senator's conduct."[26]

The committee's proposed resolution for the full Senate resolved that his conduct as to Piranha and the condominium (and certain other matters) was "reprehensible, . . . has brought the Senate into dishonor and disrepute" and was "clearly and unequivocally unethical."[27] The committee recommended that the Senate denounce him, that he reimburse $29,050 to the Senate with interest for condominium reimbursements, and that he contribute $93,730 in excess honoraria (less taxes paid) to charity. The committee also referred the matter to the Department of Justice.

Senator Durenberger did not contest the committee's resolution. On the Senate floor, Senator Trent Lott commented that the committee chose denouncement instead of censure because of mitigating circumstances and the lack of venal intent. A number of other senators remarked on Durenberger's worth as a senator and their friendship with and sympathy for him. Senator Alan Simpson of Wyoming had tears in his eyes as he watched the rebuke of his friend. But in the end the Senate passed the resolution denouncing him by a 96-0 vote.

I thus have the distinction of representing the only two US senators in history—Talmadge and Durenberger—who were denounced by the Senate. I hope that will not be my epitaph.

Dave Durenberger's troubles were not over because the Department of Justice now had the matter. I continued to represent him in that regard until a news article speculated that I would be named President Bill Clinton's deputy attorney general (which did not happen). The DOJ lawyers then told me that, in this circumstance, they would no longer talk to me about the case. I therefore asked my friend and noted white-collar lawyer, Tom Green, if he would consider becoming Durenberger's lawyer. He did so, and after years of legal wrangling, Durenberger pled guilty to several misdemeanors concerning Senate reimbursements for his condominium stays. He was sentenced to a year's probation. Durenberger previously had decided not to run for reelection in 1994.

In 1991, Congress banned the acceptance of any honoraria and stipends relating to a member's official position or duties. There thus will be, one hopes, no more fiascos of the Piranha Press ilk.

5

The Keating Five

Senator DeConcini Fights Back

Senators often need hefty campaign contributions to fuel their reelection efforts. Large contributors often solicit favors from senators they have favored. The issue presented in the Keating Five case was how far senators should go to assist those who have significantly funded their campaigns.

Charles Keating was a prominent Arizona businessman. His company, American Continental Corporation (ACC), at one time was the largest homebuilder in the state, employing around two thousand Arizona residents. In 1984, ACC bought Lincoln Savings and Loan Association. Keating quickly moved Lincoln into high-risk investments, and its assets over the next four years increased, on paper at least, from $1.1 billion to $5.5 billion.

In 1985, the Federal Home Loan Bank Board (FHLBB) promulgated a rule limiting "direct investments"—for example, investments in real estate and high-risk bonds—to no more than 10 percent of a savings and loan association's assets. This put a crimp in Lincoln's investment practices. In 1986, the San Francisco office of the FHLBB began an investigation and audit into whether Lincoln was abiding by the rule and other matters. It later appeared that Lincoln had grossly overvalued its real estate assets and sold ACC junk bonds that later turned out to be worthless to unsophisticated investors. In April 1989, ACC, which depended on Lincoln for cash infusion, filed for bankruptcy. A day later federal regulators seized control of Lincoln. The ultimate cost to the taxpayers for federally insured Lincoln's failure was over $3 billion.

Keating was convicted on both state and federal charges related to fraud and racketeering. He served four-and-a-half years on the state charges before both convictions were overturned by the Ninth Circuit Court of Appeals. Before retrial of the federal case, he pled guilty to several fraud charges and was sentenced to time served.

While running his enterprises Keating gave large contributions to politicians and organizations associated with them. He was not shy about asking politicians he had contributed to for political favors. This conduct was the genesis of the highly publicized political scandal known as the "Keating Five affair."

When Lincoln was being besieged by federal regulators, Keating called on five senators who had benefited from his largesse to help fend off the regulators. They did so to varying degrees. The result was a twenty-six-day televised hearing before the Senate Ethics Committee examining how aggressive should the senators have been in helping a constituent from whom they had received substantial political contributions.

The five senators in the dock were Alan Cranston of California, John Glenn of Ohio, Don Riegle of Michigan, John McCain of Arizona, and my client, Dennis DeConcini, also of Arizona. All except McCain were Democrats.

Cranston came to the Senate in 1968. He had been a journalist before World War II and had published a translation of Hitler's *Mein Kampf*, which included anti-Semitic parts left out in Hitler's sanitized version. Hitler sued him for copyright infringement and won, but a half million copies of Cranston's version already had been sold, exposing Hitler's despicable views. Cranston ran for president in 1984 but dropped out after finishing fourth in the Iowa caucuses.

Cranston participated in senior track events as a sprinter—at one time he held the world record for fifty-five-year-olds in the one-hundred-yard dash. He practiced for races by sprinting up and down hotel hallways while on Senate and political trips.

I knew Cranston socially and had found him particularly mild-mannered for a US senator from a major state. He was the featured speaker at the 1975 launch party for my post-Watergate book on congressional investigations.

John Glenn came to the Senate in 1974 and served until 1999. In 1962, as an astronaut, he was the first American to orbit the earth. In 1998, he flew again at age seventy-seven, making him then oldest person ever to fly in space. Glenn ran for president in 1984. (The movie *The Right Stuff*, which came out in 1983, starred Ed Harris as Glenn, who was favorably portrayed.) But he dropped out after the Super Tuesday primaries in March 1984.

Don Riegle was elected to the Senate in 1976, succeeding beloved senator Phillip Hart. Riegle began his political career in the House in 1966 as a twenty-eight-year-old Republican but switched parties in 1973 because of his differences with Nixon over Vietnam and Nixon's southern strategy.

John McCain served in the Senate from 1987 until his death in 2018 from a brain tumor. Before then, he had been a member of the House. He was a US Navy pilot and renowned war hero, having been shot down and badly injured during a mission over Hanoi in October 1967. He was a prisoner of the North Vietnamese until 1973. He was tortured but refused the out-of-sequence release offered him because his father was the admiral who commanded all US forces in the Vietnam theater. McCain was the Republican nominee for president in 2008 but lost to then candidate Barack Obama, after choosing Governor Sarah Palin of Alaska as his running mate.

Dennis DeConcini was elected to the Senate in 1977 and served until 1995. Before coming to the Senate he was the chief prosecutor for Pima County, Arizona. DeConcini was a moderate Democrat, a stance necessary to survive in conservative Arizona. The subtitle of his autobiography, "From the Center of the Aisle," reflects his political leanings. Dennis was known for constituent service. In 1993 and 1994, he chaired the Senate Intelligence Committee.

Keating and his associates had given a total of $1.5 million to the five senators and their political causes, most of which had gone to Senator Cranston and entities connected to him. DeConcini had received $31,000 for his 1982 Senate campaign and $54,000 for his 1988 campaign from Keating and persons related to him. Dennis returned those contributions in 1989.

Cranston received around $49,000 for his 1984 presidential campaign and his 1986 Senate campaign. But in addition, Keating companies gave some $945,000 to other Cranston-affiliated entities, including $850,000 in 1987 and 1988 to several voter-registration groups.

* * *

During the Keating Five hearing the chair of the Senate Ethics Committee was Democratic senator Howell Heflin of Alabama. Heflin had been chief justice of the Alabama Supreme Court and understood legal proceedings. However, he allowed the committee's lawyer, Bob Bennett, to flood the record with hearsay testimony.

My relations with Heflin were cordial, but after my closing argument when we were standing side-by-side in the men's room, he chastised me for exceeding my allotted time. That was the wrong place to respond in depth, but Heflin perhaps did not fully realize that I was speaking to four other audiences besides his committee: (1) the full Senate, which might be called on to rule on sanctions; (2) Dennis's Arizona constituents, who might judge him in the next election;, (3) the media, which was reporting copiously on the hearings every day; and (4) the Department of Justice, which was monitoring the hearings. (As far as I could tell, the department never seriously considered any charges against Dennis. As we shall see, that declination was fully appropriate given the evidence.)

The committee's Republican vice chair was Warren Rudman, who often presided at the hearings. Rudman had been the attorney general of New Hampshire. (He was succeeded by David Souter, whom Rudman later actively supported for the Supreme Court.) During the Clinton administration I served on the President's Foreign Intelligence Advisory Board (PFIAB) with Rudman. (More about that in chapter 15.) Rudman was a coauthor of the well-known Gramm-Rudman-Hollings Budget Act.

The two other Democrats on the committee were Terry Sanford and David Pryor. Sanford was a revered figure in North Carolina Democratic circles. A moderate, he had been governor of North Carolina and later served as president of Duke University. In the early 1970s I was for a time responsible for organizing Senator Ed Muskie's presidential campaign in North Carolina. Terry had been my principal source of information and advice.

David Pryor had been governor of Arkansas and was held in high esteem both for his political accomplishments and his decency. During the later highly controversial independent counsel investigation of Clinton secretary of agriculture Mike Espy, I represented Pryor, his wife, Barbara, and his staff.

Republican senator Jesse Helms of North Carolina was about as far from Terry Sanford as a man could be. Helms, who was elected five times to the Senate, was an archconservative, a contrarian, an opponent of civil rights and known as "Senator No" for his hostility toward liberal agendas. For many years he was chair of the Senate Foreign Relations Committee. Senator Cranston's attorney, Bill Taylor, sought to have Helms recuse himself because Helms, before the hearing, had commented that Cranston was "the leading water carrier" for Charles Keating.[1] Helms refused.

The newest member of the committee was Republican Trent Lott of Mississippi. An affable, effective politician, Lott eventually became Senate majority leader. In 2002, he was forced to resign that position after he praised segregationist Senator Strom Thurmond at Thurmond's one-hundredth birthday party.

The lawyers in the case were also persons of accomplishment. Bob Bennett, the Senate Ethics Committee's counsel, had previously represented the committee in its proceedings against Senator Harrison Williams, who resigned from the Senate in 1982 after being convicted of bribery in the Abscam scandal. As described in chapter 4, Bob also represented the committee in the proceeding that resulted in Senator Dave Durenberger's denouncement.

After the Keating Five matter, Bob gained even more prominence, serving as the lawyer for Secretary of Defense Casper Weinberger, Washington insider Clark Clifford, and President Clinton in the Paula Jones affair. To use Senator Rudman's term, Bob, a former prosecutor, was a "brawler." The respected Lloyd Cutler, when White House counsel, told me that Bob was chosen to represent Clinton in the Paula Jones sexual harassment litigation because he was known as a "streetfighter."

Cranston's lawyer was Bill Taylor. Bill started his career as a public defender. For a while we were in the same law firm, and he has worked with me on various vettings of potential Democratic officials. (See chapter 22.) After the Keating Five case, Bill represented Thomas Welch, the Salt Lake Olympic Committee chair, and more recently won a highly publicized jury trial for former Obama White House counsel Greg Craig, who was accused of lying to federal officials about his purported role in representing Ukraine.

Tom Green represented Senator Riegle. Tom, a former prosecutor, also for a while practiced at the same firm as me and Bill. He represented former assistant attorney general Robert Mardian before the Senate Watergate Committee. (I interrogated Mardian during the committee's public hearings.) Tom was the lawyer for Major General Richard Secord during the Iran-Contra hearings and later represented former Speaker Dennis Hastert, who pled guilty to a crime related to sexual misconduct with boys he had coached.

Senator Glenn's attorney was Charles "Chuck" Ruff. Chuck was confined to a wheelchair, the result of a disease contracted in 1964 in Africa as a young man. Chuck went on to become one of Clinton's White House counsel and was his lead defense lawyer in the impeachment proceedings against him. Chuck also served as one of my vetters over the years. Now deceased, he was an exemplary man and an excellent lawyer.

John Dowd was Senator McCain's attorney. He too has had a prominent career. He represented Major League Baseball in various investigations into betting and bribery, one of which resulted in Pete Rose being banned from baseball for life. For a time, he was President Trump's lawyer in the Robert Mueller investigation. While successful as a white-collar lawyer, in my opinion John could lapse into bluster and intemperance. More about John later.

The five senators had provided assistance to Keating and Lincoln in a variety of ways. Much of the focus of the hearing, however, was on two meetings in April 1987 that the senators had with FHLBB chair Ed Gray and officials from the Bank Board's San Francisco office.

The first meeting was on April 2 in Dennis's office. Dennis, Cranston, Glenn, and McCain attended. Although Riegle had suggested the meeting, he chose not to participate. Gray testified that someone in Dennis's office, whose name Gray could not recall, told him to bring no aides to the meeting. Dennis denied giving any such instruction.

Gray testified that the senators improperly pressured him on behalf of Lincoln and that Dennis offered him a quid pro quo—that Lincoln would make more home loans if the recently adopted direct investment rule were not enforced against it. Dennis denied Gray's claims. Gray's further contention that the campaign finance system was little more than bribery and "a case of too much money chasing too many politicians" angered committee members Sanford and Lott.[2]

At the meeting, Gray told the senators—untruthfully, the evidence showed—that he knew little about Lincoln and thus could not discuss it. He suggested that they meet with the San Francisco regulators handling the investigation. If Gray was as outraged by the meeting as he later claimed, one wonders why he sought to subject his underlings to similar pressures.

The five senators met with four regulators from San Francisco on April 9, again in Dennis's office. (Cranston appeared only briefly.) While what occurred at the Gray meeting was disputed, what transpired at the April 9 meeting essentially was known because one of the regulators, William Black, then chief counsel for the board's western region, had taken detailed notes and prepared a memorandum from them.

The regulators also said they felt improperly pressured. They asserted that Dennis was trying to negotiate a resolution for Lincoln.

Dennis, as he had with Gray—and consistent with his forceful engagement for other constituents—took the lead in the April 9 meeting. He opened with this statement:

> We wanted to meet with you because we have determined that potential actions of yours could injure a constituent. This is a particular concern to us because Lincoln is willing to take substantial actions to deal with what we understand to be your concerns. Lincoln is prepared to go into a major home loan program—up to 55 percent of its assets. We understand that that's what the Bank Board wants S&Ls to do. It's prepared to limit its high risk bond holdings and real estate investments. . . . Lincoln is a viable organization. . . . They have two major disagreements with you. First, with regard to direct investment. Second, on your reappraisal. They are suing against your direct investment regulation. . . . We suggest that the lawsuit be accelerated and that you grant them forbearance while the suit is pending. I know something about the appraisal values . . . of the Federal Home Loan Bank Board. They appear to be grossly unfair. I know the particular property here. My family is in real estate. Lincoln is prepared to reach a compromise value with you.[3]

However, Dennis did not thereafter attempt to "negotiate" an outcome. In fact, after the regulators told the senators that their office was making a criminal referral to the Department of Justice for file stuffing and other "imprudent actions"[4] such as bogus accounting, Dennis said: "The criminality surprises me. We're not interested in discussing those issues. Our premise was that we had a viable institution concerned that it was being over regulated."[5]

It was apparent that the ardor of all senators to advocate Lincoln's cause diminished after being informed that a criminal referral was in the works.

In declaring that the meetings were improper, Gray and the regulators did not seek to exonerate any of the attending senators. Nonetheless, Bennett and the Republican members of the committee reportedly were in favor of dropping McCain and Glenn from the proceedings. The Democratic committee members reportedly opposed this. I thought such a result would be disadvantageous for Dennis. Better to be part of the Keating Five than the Keating Three. In the end the hearing explored the conduct of all five senators.

The committee's hearing was a "preliminary inquiry," not an "investigation." This meant that no charges were being prosecuted—as was the case in the Durenberger "investigation." Rather, the purpose of the proceeding was only fact gathering.

This had an important ramification. Bob Bennett was a special counsel, not a special prosecutor. His assignment was to lay out the facts objectively so the committee could reach conclusions, not to attempt to prove a case.

Chair Heflin made this explicit in his opening statement:

Traditionally, the Committee has held hearings after it has concluded that there is some reason to believe that a Senator may have engaged in improper conduct. This is not true in this case because the purpose of these hearings is to find the facts. . . .

The role of our special counsel in this endeavor must also not be misunderstood. . . . The role of the Committee's special counsel is that of a lawyer for the Committee, not that of a prosecutor. His function is to help the Committee explore all the available relevant evidence, and the task must be carried out impartially.

Special counsel has been instructed to do everything he can to present the evidence fully and with an even hand. . . .

We have asked him to perform a delicate operation. To use the witnesses and the available records to recreate the past events which are at the center of this controversy, in a manner which is not prejudicial to any party, so that we and the American people will have the full story.[6]

As Heflin indicated, Bob was in a difficult situation. He had been a federal prosecutor and his prosecutorial instincts were strong. It was evident that he chafed under the restrictions placed on him.

At times Bob went beyond the prescribed limits. In his opening statement, when he was presenting his view of the evidence concerning Senator DeConcini, the following exchange between Bob and Senator Pryor occurred:

> MR. BENNETT: The evidence shows that Senator DeConcini was repeatedly asked by Mr. Keating to perform services for Charles Keating, and that Senator DeConcini almost always—not always—but almost always honored Mr. Keating's requests.
>
> The most obvious example of this is the meeting with Chairman Gray. The evidence will show that in response to Mr. Keating's request for help in his dispute with the Bank Board, Senator DeConcini orchestrated the meeting with Chairman Gray which was initiated by Mr. Riegle, and he ensured that it included a bipartisan group of Senators.
>
> He did so, I believe the evidence will show, with the intent of placing tremendous political pressure on Chairman Gray to achieve a specific outcome desired by Charles Keating. It will be for you to decide whether under existing standards such pressure is proper or not.
>
> SENATOR PRYOR: Counsel, I want to stop you right there if I might. . . .
>
> I have a sense that you have reached a conclusion there on that point, and on several of the other Senators involved, and in my opinion you are beginning to reach personal conclusions, and also you are deciding for us what is relevant and not relevant.
>
> I think that is our decision to make. I am really concerned a little bit about the conclusions that you are reaching. . . .
>
> I may reach the same conclusion, but I truly am a little concerned about the conclusions.

Bob's response was candid and revealing: "Well, Senator, I am sorry about that. I am at a decided disadvantage since I made conclusions to you in an extensive report, and I am here to present the evidence, and it is very difficult to do that."[7]

*   *   *

A critical issue in the hearing was the standard to be applied in judging the senators' conduct. S.R. 338 authorized the investigation of allegations of "improper conduct which may reflect upon the Senate" as well as violations of established rules.[8] I argued that under this Resolution there was a two-part test. There must be, first, "improper conduct" that, second, "may reflect upon the Senate." I argued that since there was no "improper conduct" by Dennis, the matter should be at an end.[9]

Bennett, however, advocated a different standard, one that he had invented for situations where no violation of specific rules had occurred. He contended that "a Senator should not engage in conduct which would appear to be improper to a reasonable, nonpartisan, fully informed person."[10] My response was that to adopt this standard would be to apply an ex post facto rule to the conduct of the five senators, which basic fairness principles would not permit. Moreover, I asked, where do you find such an exemplary, well-educated person?

In the end the committee did not adopt Bennett's standard. In his opening statement Senator Sanford was particularly critical of Bennett's appearance proposal. Sanford said: "The Senate and its Ethics Committee are morally and intellectually qualified to judge improper conduct without resorting to the suspicions or impressions of either reasonable or unreasonable persons."

Sanford added the following:

> If, indeed, there is an appearance of wrongdoing when, in fact, no wrongdoing is found, the problem is not that of the individual but rather of the institution. It is quite possible, . . . that the necessity for large sums [for] political campaigns . . . does raise suspicions of improper influence and improper conduct. . . . It would be . . . unfair to impose penalties for this appearance on individual Senators. The blame for this appearance and the remedy rests with the institution, not with the individual Senators.[11]

Both Dennis and I gave opening statements. For my part—recognizing the various audiences I was speaking to—I focused on what the case actually concerned.

> My immediate task is to have the Committee focus on . . . the basic

facts as to Senator DeConcini. To tell you what the case [as to] Senator DeConcini is about, and what it's not about. . . .

Let me begin by saying what this case, as to Senator DeConcini, is not about. . . .

It's not about a Senator who demanded or used intimidation to obtain certain Government activity or action.

It's not about a Senator who took a bribe to take an official action.

It's not about a Senator who accepted some form of compensation as payment for Government action.

And it's not about a Senator who received generous gifts or personal favors from a constituent. . . .

Rather, Senator DeConcini's case is simply about a Senator who did legitimate constituent services for a constituent whose company was a major employer and investor in his state, [when] that constituent . . . was also a campaign contributor and a fundraiser.

I concluded this portion of my argument in this way: "Mr. Chairman, with deference, I submit to the Committee that, if without more, conduct of this sort is unethical; if without more, it is improper conduct that may reflect upon the Senate, then a great many members of this body are at risk and the United States Senate is threatened with depopulation."[12]

Dennis presented a strong defense of his conduct. He pointed out how persistent he had been in his efforts to serve his constituents. In the fourteen years he had been a senator, his office had handled seventy-five thousand constituent cases. Some of the constituents served were Democrats, some not. Some were contributors, some not. Some had voted for him, some not. He gave several examples of his aggressive constituent service.

But much of his opening statement was an attack on Bennett for being a special prosecutor, not a fair presenter of facts. Dennis was not one to shrink from a fight, and he went after Bob with a full-throated roar. At the beginning of his statement, he said:

[A] Special Counsel is someone who is a lawyer's lawyer, who is an adviser, who presents facts to you; not makes judgments and offers conclusions. Not a prosecutor who tries to make a case.

And that's what this individual, this Special Prosecutor, did to this Senator, and I dare say to several others, as well.

Bennett says that the facts tilt. No, the facts don't tilt; he tilts them. And why does he do that?

Because he's like all of us. He's got something at stake here. And it's not just representing this Committee, gentlemen. He wants a victory. He wants to nail somebody. He wants to get somebody, I'm sorry to say. He wants another trophy on the wall, as someone who's represented the Committee and been able to nail up another Senator for ethical misconduct.[13]

The attack on Bob continued throughout the hearing. Dennis attempted to submit the affidavits of two former US attorneys who declared that, in their opinion, Bob had acted like a prosecutor during the hearings. The committee, over the telling dissent of Chair Heflin who found the affidavits relevant, denied their introduction into evidence.

In defending his conduct, Bob said: "Senator DeConcini and his counsel would like me to be a flower girl distributing the flowers at a wedding in equal shares to each Senator, without regard to the evidence. I won't do that."[14]

The image of Bob, a stocky former boxer, as a flower girl was arresting.

One of our better decisions was to call Senator Dan Inouye (D-HI), both as a character witness for Dennis and also to give his views on the propriety of Dennis's conduct. Dan, who had served on the Senate Watergate Committee and had been cochair of the joint Iran-Contra Committee, was one of the Senate's most respected members. I knew that he and Rudman were especially close. While once in Dan's private office, I saw a photograph of Rudman in an outdoor setting hanging on the wall. During Dan's testimony, Rudman commented: "I don't think that there is anyone in the Senate whose opinion I value more personally, Senator Inouye, than yours."[15]

In his testimony, Senator Inouye agreed that it would be "discriminatory" to deny constituent service to a contributor. He disagreed with the appearance standard Bennett proposed, stating that it would be "most difficult" to find a "reasonably well informed, non-partisan person" to make a judgment about whether conduct was improper. He affirmed the value of vigorous congressional oversight. He testified that a March 1987 letter from Arthur Young to DeConcini suggesting harassment of Lincoln by the regulators was a valid basis for action.

Inouye testified about the memorandum from Black describing the April 9, 1987, meeting between the senators and the regulators, which he previously had reviewed. He said that Dennis's conduct as portrayed in that memorandum "was proper" although "vigorous."[16] He did not think Dennis was negotiating for Keating in that meeting, but he said there was nothing wrong had Dennis done so.

As to DeConcini's character, Inouye testified that "I have always found his honesty to be beyond impeachment and his character of the highest nature."[17]

Inouye concluded his testimony on direct examination in powerful fashion:

I have had occasion to turn on the television set to watch the proceedings, and what I saw did not please me at all, sir.

It suggested that if a United States Senator should provide services to a constituent who has contributed funds toward his election or re-election, that service was placed under a cloud.

And it suggested that if we are to provide services to constituents, it should be of the mildest nature. . . .

If contributions are that evil, sir, then I think the whole system should be changed. . . .

But to suggest to me that, since one of my constituents contributed to me, I am forever estopped from providing services to him is ridiculous.

I have done that since 1959, sir. It might interest you to know that . . . my first constituent service in 1963, my first day in office as a United States Senator, was to intervene in behalf of a constituent corporation who was not the lowest bidder in the Saigon Waterworks. . . .

But I felt that my constituent was entitled to that bid, because it was an American company.

The lowest bidder was a company which later on we found out to be a subsidiary of the Taiwan Government.

I went to the Secretary of State. I pleaded with him. I finally threatened him. I said, I will expose this. Was I wrong in threatening the Secretary of State? I see my colleagues threatening the Secretary of State every other day.

(Laughter)

If everything turned out well, if we did not have this S&L crisis, if

Mr. Keating was able to once again revive, these men would be heroes to their constituents. They were able to save jobs.

So I think we are on trial here, the United States Senate.[18]

The hearings recessed for Christmas on Saturday, December 15. I had gone from the Durenberger hearings directly into preparation for the Keating Five proceedings. I had been working long hours for many months and in December was tired. But more than that, I was not feeling well.

Some telltale signs suggested to me that I had internal bleeding, so I went to the hospital for a checkup. Sure enough, I had a bleeding ulcer in my stomach. Stress is destructive.

I spent most of the time between Christmas and New Year's in the hospital. The ulcer required cauterization. Also, because I had lost considerable blood, transfusions were necessary.

The hearings resumed on January 2, 1991, and I was at my place at the table next to Dennis. I decided not to tell him then what had transpired because I did not want to cause him additional concern. He was vexed enough by the situation he was in. Also, no one on my team could fill in at the podium. Two talented associates worked with me, but neither had adequate trial experience.

I remember being somewhat wobbly during the first few days after the hearing resumed. I gripped the podium tightly to ensure I remained upright while cross-examining Senator McCain on January 4 on national television. Watching the proceedings at home, my wife, Kristina, who knew well my condition, was tense, fearing I would buckle. This was not an experience for the faint-hearted, but perhaps I proved that it was for the faint.[19]

Dennis and McCain were, of course, from the same state. Dennis was a Democrat, McCain a Republican. Not surprisingly, at times relations between them were fraught.

Nonetheless, when it came time for me to cross-examine McCain, I thought to myself: "I can ask questions that will hurt McCain, given his long relationship with Keating. But those questions will not help Dennis's cause. So I think I will pull my punches." As the transcript shows, Dennis allowed me to do just that.

My questioning of McCain was short, lasting only a few minutes. My questions were intended mainly to show that none of the senators had done anything inappropriate in approaching the regulators for a significant constituent. When I said I had no further questions, McCain looked surprised—and pleased. However, his counsel, John Dowd, did not approach his cross-examination of Senator DeConcini in a similarly agreeable fashion.

Dennis took the stand in January 1991, a few days after McCain. He was well-prepared for his testimony and gave it with his usual force. He held up well during Bennett's at times hostile cross-examination.

Even in the tensest of hearings, humor sometimes creeps in. During my direct examination, after Dennis referred to me as "Mr. Bennett" in response to one of my questions, these exchanges occurred:

MR. HAMILTON: I am only smiling because you called me "Mr. Bennett."

THE WITNESS: Excuse me, Mr. Hamilton.

　(Laughter.)

MR. BENNETT: I do not mind at all, Senator.

　(Laughter.)

THE WITNESS: My apologies, Mr. Bennett, or Mr. Hamilton.

　(Laughter.)

VICE CHAIR RUDMAN: Or both.

MR. HAMILTON: Just remember when you send the check, which one to send it to, please.

　(Laughter.)

THE WITNESS: Believe me . . . I know how to spell your name, Mr. Hamilton.

　(Laughter.)

THE WITNESS: And you know how to cash my checks, too.

　(Laughter.)[20]

John Dowd soon had his chance to cross-examine Dennis. Dowd attempted to demonstrate that Dennis, contrary to his assertions, was trying in various ways to harm Senator McCain. But Dennis was more than a match for him. I decided that, except for objecting to Dowd's too-frequent interruptions before Dennis finished an answer—a criticism also raised by Chair Heflin—I would not make additional efforts to protect Dennis. As the transcript indicates, Dennis concurred in this approach.

One exchange exemplifies Dowd's aggressive tactics. After an answer by Dennis that Dowd took as hostile to McCain, this followed:

DOWD: Getting it evened up again, Senator DeConcini?
DECONCINI: No, I am not evening up at all.
DOWD: Getting that shot in there, are you?
DOWD: No, I am not getting a shot in there at all, no more than you are trying to get a shot in, Mr. Dowd.[21]

At a break after Dowd's cross-examination, Dennis exited to the hall outside the hearing room to answer questions before the ever-present television cameras. I am told that a reporter asked Dennis if he was upset with Dowd's vigorous cross-examination. Dennis reportedly said, "No, not at all. I know John. In fact, I talked to him about being my lawyer."[22]

In January 1991, Dennis asked former attorney general Griffin Bell to testify about the propriety of a senator contacting regulators about matters under consideration by them. I had no doubt that Bell potentially had something useful to offer. In addition to having been attorney general, he had been on the Fifth Circuit Court of Appeals for a number of years, and he had been the vice chair of President George H. W. Bush's Federal Ethics Reform Commission, which had been charged with bringing all three branches of government under the same ethical requirements. Nonetheless, I had concerns about his testimony.

For starters, I didn't know exactly what Bell would say, and I would not have an opportunity to review his testimony until lunchtime before his afternoon committee appearance. Also, there were those who thought, right or wrong, that Bell on such a prominent stage would be more interested in protecting his reputation and demonstrating his probity than in assisting the senator for whom he was testifying. I had had my own prior experience with Bell that made me doubt his constancy.

At the beginning of the Carter administration, I was interested in joining Bell's Department of Justice. With help from Senator Herman Talmadge, I was granted an audience with Bell. (Both were Georgians.) Bell wanted me to come on board, but, he said, most high-level DOJ positions already were filled. He did, however, offer me the position of running the Law Enforcement Assistance Administration, which was tasked with giving federal grants to law enforcement agencies around the country. After considering the position and with some reluctance—it was an administrative and not a lawyering position—I accepted. The job did offer a chance for useful service, and I figured it might be a stepping-stone to something more in my baili-wick. Bell and I shook hands on my appointment. The press reported that it would come to pass.

Then nothing happened. Months later, Bell gave someone else the job. I was told that a very powerful senator wanted his guy in the slot. I was on to other interesting representations at the time, and, while irritated, I shrugged it off, well-aware that in Washington, reneging is not uncommon.

Several years later I ran into Bell in Senator Talmadge's office while I was representing him. Talmadge said to Bell, "Griffin, I think you know Jim Hamilton." "Yes," Bell said. "Jim and I are old friends." I suppose that was one way to put it.

I had about an hour to prepare Bell for his testimony before the commit-tee. I told him the questions I would ask. His answers seemed satisfactory, but as we walked out of Dennis's office to the hearing room, I said to Den-nis, "I'm nervous about this testimony."

Soon after I commenced questioning Bell, he began giving answers I hadn't expected, some of which were less than helpful to Dennis, albeit beneficial to Bell. After receiving several such answers, I left the podium, walked over to Dennis, and said, "I told you so."

After a few more unanticipated answers, I announced to Bell that I had no more questions even though one third of my planned examination re-mained unasked. Bell looked surprised. Certainly he was aware I was an-noyed because he had strayed from the testimony we expected after our lunchtime session.

Fortunately, however, the members of the committee, in their interroga-tions of Bell, elicited the essence of the testimony that my remaining ques-tions would have sought. Perhaps the abrupt halt to my examination caused him to focus on his reason for being there. In the end, his testimony was useful and was well received by the committee.

One line of questioning I initiated and that was followed up on by the committee was particularly successful. When Bell was attorney general, he had been contacted by Mississippi senators John Stennis, whom Bell called "one of the most ethical people I've known," and James Eastland, the powerful chair of the Senate Judiciary Committee.[23] Stennis and Eastland had learned that Litton Industries was going to be indicted for activities at its Pascagoula, Mississippi, shipyard. Litton was one of the largest employers in Mississippi, and the senators, concerned about the potential indictment, asked that Bell give the matter his personal attention. (Bell did so. Litton subsequently was indicted but was acquitted in a trial in Jackson, Mississippi.)

Bell saw nothing wrong in this contact by the Senators; it fit into his general view that under the First Amendment, "people had a right to contact me, to petition the Government with a grievance." He was "glad to help people, particularly people who'd been elected, about constituent complaints."[24]

This testimony was of special interest to committee member and Mississippi senator Trent Lott. Lott stated:

> You know, there's an invocation of the name of Senators Stennis and Eastland involving a project of building ships in Pascagoula, Mississippi, you strike very close to my heart. And Mr. Hamilton knows that.
> . . . And when you're talking about the shipyard of my home town [*sic*], where my father worked as a pipefitter, I get real teary-eyed, very quickly.
> So that was a very interesting question and your response, your description of that, that you didn't feel that was out of order at all was very important to me.[25]

Senator Lott then strongly suggested that, as a young congressman and like his predecessor Senator Stennis, he too had made a call to Attorney General Bell about the Pascagoula shipyard matter! Undoubtedly the individual experiences of Lott and the other committee members shaped their views of the propriety of the conduct of the Keating Five.

As Bob Bennett candidly admitted in his book *In the Ring*, the results of the Keating Five proceedings "were less than I had hoped for."[26] He had wanted Senators Glenn and McCain dropped from the hearing, which did not happen. He wanted the Senate to censure Senator Cranston and to reprimand Senators DeConcini and Riegle. Those outcomes did not come to pass. Bob blamed politics for the committee's conclusions. I would suggest that as to Dennis, the facts, as they should have been, were important to the decision.

Five members of the committee joined in a November 21, 1991, report setting forth its findings as to each senator. Senator Helms filed "Additional Views."

Generally, the committee recognized "that constituent service, even for contributors, is a legitimate and appropriate senatorial function." However, decisions about whether to intervene with the executive branch or independent agencies should be made without regard to political contributions. A senator must endeavor to avoid the appearance of being influenced by campaign contributions.[27]

The committee determined that each senator "had information that reasonably caused concern about the fairness of the [board's] examination of Lincoln . . . and which was sufficient to justify [their] contacting Bank Board personnel."[28] Each senator had "a legitimate interest which justified his involvement on Mr. Keating's behalf." Keating, a resident of Arizona, was Senator DeConcini's constituent.[29]

The senators' various "contacts with federal regulators . . . did not cause the eventual failure of Lincoln." Nor did "the evidence establish that their contacts affected the regulators' treatment of Lincoln."[30]

As to the April 2 and 9, 1987, meetings with Gray and the San Francisco regulators, the committee concluded that "when considered without regard to any contribution or other benefit, no Senator violated any law or Senate rule or engaged in improper conduct by attending these meetings." The committee continued: "The Committee concludes that the contributions received by Senators DeConcini, Glenn, McCain and Riegle were not improperly linked to the actions taken by each Senator. The fact that a Senator has received substantial contributions from an individual does not disqualify that person from receiving assistance."[31]

The committee made separate findings as to each senator. It concluded that Dennis had a basis for his actions for Keating independent of the contributions he received. Nonetheless, the committee stated,

Aggressive conduct by Senators in dealing with regulatory agencies is sometimes appropriate and necessary. However, the Committee concludes that, given that Senator DeConcini knew that Mr. Keating had not been forthcoming with him in the past and that he had accepted substantial campaign contributions from Mr. Keating and his associates, it was inappropriate for Senator DeConcini to be as aggressive as he was in pursuing Lincoln's cause without making a more thorough inquiry into the merits of Mr. Keating's allegations.[32]

The committee also said,

> While the Committee concludes that Senator DeConcini has violated no law of the United States or specific Rule of the United States Senate, it emphasizes that it does not condone his conduct. The Committee has concluded that the totality of the evidence shows that Senator DeConcini's conduct gave the appearance of being improper and was certainly attended with insensitivity and poor judgment. However, the Committee finds that his conduct did not reach a level requiring institutional action.[33]

As to Senator Riegle, the committee similarly concluded that his conduct "gave the appearance of being improper and was certainly attended with insensitivity and poor judgment."[34] Senators Glenn and McCain received lesser admonishments. Both were accused of "poor judgment" regarding their activities for Keating.[35]

The committee's treatment of Cranston was much harsher. At the conclusion of the hearing, it voted to proceed to an "investigation" of Cranston; that is, a trial on specific charges. Cranston agreed that the investigation could be conducted on the record already before the committee.

Based on that record, the committee ruled

> that Senator Cranston engaged in improper conduct that may reflect upon the Senate, pursuant to Section 2(a)(1) of S. Res. 338, 88th Congress. Based on the totality of circumstances including those surrounding four specific incidents in which Senator Cranston solicited or accepted contributions from Mr. Keating's companies, as well as evidence regarding Senator Cranston's fund raising and constituent service practices in general, the Committee finds that Senator Cranston engaged in an impermissible pattern of conduct in which fund raising and official activities were substantially linked.[36]

The committee concluded that Senator Cranston's conduct deserved "the fullest, strongest, and most severe sanction which the Committee has the authority to impose." Consequently, it said, in the name of the Senate it "does hereby strongly and severely reprimand" Senator Cranston.[37]

Cranston accepted the reprimand, but when it was presented on the Senate floor—and after he had retained the outspoken, attention-seeking Alan Dershowitz as counsel[38]—Cranston rose to defend himself, asserting that many senators had engaged in conduct not "fundamentally different" from that for which he was being reprimanded.[39] Rudman was enraged, responding that Cranston's contention that everybody does it was "poppycock."[40]

Senator Helms was not happy with the committee's report and filed his own "Additional Views." Essentially, with some crucial modifications, he submitted the draft confidential report Bennett had filed with the committee, drawing a rebuke from Heflin and Rudman for violating the committee's confidentiality rules. Helms responded that it was proper for him to use Bennett's draft in preparing his own report. However, while Helms advocated censure for Cranston, he did not join Bennett in calling for reprimands of DeConcini and Riegle.

Dennis DeConcini remained in the Senate until 1995 but decided not to seek reelection in 1994. Fallout from the Keating Five proceedings was likely a factor in his decision.

In August 1993, after gaining significant concessions, Dennis provided the crucial aye vote on President Clinton's 1993 tax bill, which resulted in a tied Senate vote. The tie was broken by Vice President Al Gore, allowing the bill to become law.

Clinton was in Dennis's debt. After Dennis left the Senate, Clinton appointed him to the Federal Home Loan Mortgage Corporation. Dennis's experience with Keating and Lincoln, painful as it was, at least provided him with useful background for this new role.

6

Lawyers for Mississippi

In the mid-1960s when I began practicing law, the civil rights movement was in full stride. I thought any lawyer worth their salt should be involved in it. I was delighted when, early in my career, I had the chance to participate in a case of considerable importance to civil rights litigants in Mississippi.

In the summer of 1963, President John F. Kennedy asked some of the nation's leading lawyers to form the Lawyers' Committee for Civil Rights Under Law. Kennedy's purpose was to bring the mainstream private bar into the fight against racial discrimination. An early committee focus was civil rights abuses in Mississippi.

In the mid-1960s, President Lyndon Johnson asked Gerard Gesell to join the committee. Gesell was a prominent litigator at Covington & Burling in Washington, DC. In the late 1960s, Johnson appointed him to the US District Court for the District of Columbia.

I joined Covington in the fall of 1966 and was assigned to work primarily with Gesell in his diverse litigation practice. Gesell, always concerned that his associates were having "fun," asked me to assist him on Lawyers' Committee matters.[1] That assignment exposed me to some of the nation's leading attorneys, involved me in a major civil rights case, and taught me a valuable lesson about how federal judges decide cases.

At the time, the Lawyers' Committee was chaired by Whitney North Seymour Jr., a leader of the New York Bar. Others on the committee were equally distinguished and well-known in legal circles and beyond. For example: Harrison Tweed, a founder of the Milbank, Tweed law firm; Bernard Segal, who would become president of the American Bar Association; former attorney general Ramsey Clark; Louis Oberdorfer, a former assistant attorney general for the Tax Division who would become a district judge; and Lloyd Garrison, a founder of Paul, Weiss, Rifkind, Wharton & Garrison. Gesell at times would send me to committee meetings in New York when he was otherwise occupied. Watching the ever-smooth Seymour control and even manipulate the high-powered intellects and egos in the room was itself an education.

Seymour was a patrician Republican who practiced at Simpson Thacher & Bartlett. During President Richard Nixon's administration, he was the US attorney for the Southern District of New York. For years on Independence Day, Seymour gathered his extended family on Cape Cod, where family members took turns reading aloud and discussing passages from the Declaration of Independence.

An issue of utmost importance to the Lawyers' Committee was the right of its staff lawyers located in Jackson, Mississippi—who were not members of the Mississippi Bar—to practice in the federal courts in that state. The problem was acute in the US District Court for the Southern District of Mississippi, where two judges, Dan M. Russell and William Harold Cox, presided. In September 1967, that court adopted a rule allowing pro hac vice appearance by out-of-state attorneys only on the following conditions, among others:

(1) A pro hac vice appearance by an attorney is permitted only if he is a nonresident of the State of Mississippi;

(2) A pro hac vice appearance by an attorney is permitted in only one case in any twelve-month period.[2]

This rule prevented appearances by both Lawyers' Committee and NAACP attorneys because they were either residents of the state or had been involved in another case in that court during the preceding twelve months. It was apparent that the purpose of the rule was to limit the ability of civil rights litigants to secure competent free legal representation.

The Lawyers' Committee tried to settle the dispute out of court. There was an extraordinary meeting in Houston, Texas, between the committee and members of the Mississippi Bar, which I attended. Seymour and several other committee representatives were present. There was a large contingent from the Mississippi Bar, headed by John Satterfield, who once had been president of the American Bar Association, the only such president ever from Mississippi. Satterfield had a long history of fighting desegregation. In 1962, when James Meredith attempted to enroll in the University of Mississippi, he served as Mississippi governor Ross Barrett's personal attorney. *Time* magazine once called him "the most prominent segregationist lawyer in the country."[3] He committed suicide in 1981 after a battle with Parkinson's disease.

The meeting of representatives of the Lawyers' Committee and the Mississippi Bar was not fruitful. Rarely has there been a more notable case of ships passing in the night. The committee made its points; the Mississippians stated theirs. The sides were far apart. There was little meaningful discussion and no chance of compromise. So we litigated.

I was asked to write a draft of the committee's brief to the Fifth Circuit Court of Appeals. For help I turned to an erudite attorney, Armand Derfner, who also was at Covington and had been a classmate at Yale Law School. Armand, who had finished many places above me in class standing at Yale—there were letter grades and rankings back then—was well versed in constitutional law. We put together a solid brief based on various constitutional principles—for example, due process, equal protection, and privileges and immunities. But the Fifth Circuit, where an order was sought directing Judges Russell and Cox to allow representation in civil rights cases by non-Mississippi lawyers, did not, at least ostensibly, rely on any of our well-thought-out constitutional contentions.

Jack Schafer, a dour but capable Covington partner, argued the committee's case. (Gesell, by then, was on the federal bench.) William Coleman III, a renowned African American lawyer who went on to become secretary of transportation in President Gerald Ford's administration, argued for the NAACP.[4] John Satterfield argued for Judge Cox.

Cox had disputed the claim that Mississippi counsel were not available to handle the types of claims the Lawyers' Committee and the NAACP were bringing. In a statement that is jarring today, he said:

> I don't think it's an accurate statement to intimate in this record that there are not local Counsel that are available to handle any kind of civil rights cases on either side. . . .

Only two or three months ago, I had a case that involved civil rights of the very worst kind. Matter of fact, it was a federal case against three colored boys for I believe about one of the most inflammatory charges that could be made against them, involved some white girls[,] and I appointed this very competent lawyer and he went right to bat for them. . . . People were tried before a mixed jury I think it had three colored people and nine white people on there and they were convicted but this fellow had no hesitancy and he didn't even wince at all, at my asking him to handle the defense.[5]

The Fifth Circuit, in a 1968 opinion, didn't buy this argument or the others the lower court judges raised in defending their rule.[6] Early in its opinion the court outlined what the case was and was not about:

The petitioners' position is simply that they have a federal right to retain counsel of their choice who are attorneys in good standing at their respective bars and are associated with locally-admitted counsel in non–fee generating school desegregation and civil rights cases in federal court. This case does not involve the right of non-lawyers to practice law. This case does not involve the right to practice in state courts. This case does not involve the right to general admission to a federal district court. This case does not involve the right of attorneys to be admitted pro hac vice without association with locally admitted counsel. This case does not involve fee-generating cases. This case does involve the need for free legal services in civil rights cases.[7]

The court then expounded on the problems experienced by persons with civil rights claims:

Out of twenty-two hundred lawyers in Mississippi, only twelve are negroes. Of course, all twelve are not always available. This is obviously an inadequate reservoir. Moreover, there is ample evidence in the record to demonstrate the burdens of counsel handling such cases . . . as well as the petitioners' inability to obtain representation, which, parenthetically, is borne out by literally hundreds of civil rights cases that have come to us in which out of state lawyers have had the laboring oar. It is no overstatement that in Mississippi and the South generally negroes

with civil rights claims or defenses have often found securing representation difficult.[8]

The court found no valid reason for limiting the number of pro hac vice
appearances to one a year or denying such privileges to attorneys who reside
in the state on a temporary basis. The court said:

> In these non-fee generating civil rights cases it is clear that only rea-
> sonably limits can be placed on a federal litigant's choice of counsel,
> and we find that the limits here established by the 'Rule as to Nonresi-
> dent Attorneys' are not reasonable. In our view the District Court must
> grant pro hac vice admissions in such cases upon a showing that an in-
> dividual lawyer is a member in good standing of the bar of some state.[9]

That said, the court exercised its supervisory power over the district court
and issued a writ of mandamus, declaring that the district court rule concerning nonresident attorneys was invalid. As noted, the court did so without expressly relying on any of the constitutional principles Armand Derfner and I had carefully laid out in the draft of the brief we had prepared,
even though those principles may have provided unspoken background. I
thus learned firsthand early in my law practice that if a court can avoid a
constitutional ruling and decide a case on other grounds, that is what it is
going to do.

More important, the Fifth Circuit's decision allowed Lawyers' Committee and NAACP attorneys to provide needed services to civil rights litigants
in Mississippi for many years to come.

7

"Otto the Terrible"

Even the most confident lawyers need to learn
to listen to the advice of others. The following account brings this home.

In his day, Louisiana Democratic congressman Otto Passman was famous
both for his pronounced hostility to foreign aid and his personal idiosyncra-
sies. Sadly for him, he also became famous for the scandal that engulfed him
at the end of a long career in Congress.

Passman was elected to Congress in 1946 and served until his primary
defeat in 1976. He was the son of sharecroppers and dropped out of school
at age thirteen, although he later graduated from high school and a business
college by attending night school while he worked. Before Congress he was a
successful businessman and a lieutenant commander in the US Navy during
World War II.

In Congress he rose in 1954 to be chair of the powerful House Foreign
Aid Appropriations Subcommittee. In that post he bedeviled Republican
and Democratic administrations alike that sought appropriations, earning
him the title "Otto the Terrible" from his critics.

Believing that foreign aid was wasteful of US money, he once said that it
"is the worst disaster to hit the Republic since the War of 1812."[1] Passman
had a particular dislike for the Peace Corps. He declared, "If I had three
minutes left to live, I'd kill the Peace Corps."[2]

Passman was a dapper dresser. At one time he claimed that his wardrobe
contained forty-eight suits. He also collected fine pocket watches, which he
displayed in the vest pockets of his suits.

Passman had a nervous twitch. When presiding over hearings, he would twist and turn in his chair. An aide once said that he "was the only man in the Congress to wear out his suits from the inside."[3] Perhaps that was why he had so many.

In 1970, Passman was involved in a sex discrimination suit that ended up at the Supreme Court.[4] The suit arose after he fired a female staffer, declaring that "it was essential that the [position] be [held by] a man."[5] The Court, 5-to-4, held that even though Congress had exempted itself from the Civil Rights Act of 1964, sex discrimination by members of Congress violated the equal protection guarantees found in the Fifth Amendment.

For years, Passman had been advised on various matters by well-known DC lawyer David Ginsburg, who in the late 1970s was my law partner. When Passman's problems with criminal law arose, I was asked to represent him.

Passman's legal problems involved his association with Korean businessman Tong Sun Park. That association resulted in two indictments in the District of Columbia. In the first indictment, filed on March 31, 1978, the United States accused Passman of violating conspiracy, bribery, and illegal gratuity statutes. The Department of Justice's Public Integrity Section asserted that Passman had used his office to pressure the Republic of Korea to purchase rice from US exporters through the Food for Peace program and commercial sales, in a manner ensuring that Park would be the agent for those sales and obtain substantial commissions. The indictment charged that Park had paid Passman $213,000 for his services.

The second indictment, filed on April 28, 1978, by DOJ's Tax Division, charged tax evasion relating to Passman's receipt of the money from Park. As we shall see, this indictment had significant consequences that the government did not intend.

Park also was indicted in 1976 for bribing members of the Congress with money from the South Korean government to ensure that US troops remained in South Korea. However, after he testified under a grant of immunity, those charges and subsequent ones were dismissed. But his testimony implicated Passman in alleged wrongdoing.

Two days before Passman's first indictment, he was admitted to the psychiatric unit at Touro Infirmary in New Orleans because of depression. As a subsequent court decision (discussed later) indicated, there was concern that he would take "extreme means." One doctor "ranked the suicide risk as high."[6] Passman remained at Touro until May 19, when he left the facility against medical advice.

Sometime after Passman was indicted I had a conversation with one of his confidants, Grover Connell. Connell was a prominent rice seller and exporter with substantial interests in Louisiana. I previously had represented his company, Connell Rice and Sugar—which at one time reportedly was the nation's largest rice exporter—in a lawsuit against the federal government, and I had good relations with him. (Connell later was indicted regarding his dealings with Tong Sun Park, but the case was dismissed after the government decided it could not rely on Park's testimony.)

During a conversation with Grover I speculated on directions Passman's case might take. I must have said something that displeased Grover or others with whom he spoke. Several days later, famed Louisiana criminal defense lawyer Camille Gravel arrived on my doorstep in Washington, announcing that he was now my cocounsel in representing Passman. I was surprised by this and irritated that I had ruminated about the case with Connell. But in hindsight, Camille coming on board was highly beneficial to Passman in several ways.

Because of Passman's mental condition, we moved to have him declared incompetent to stand trial. The judge in the case was Barrington D. Parker, an African American judge known as, according to his June 5, 1993, obituary in the *Washington Post,* "the most cantankerous federal judge in Washington."[7]

Parker had good reason to be cantankerous. In October 1965 he was hit by a car on a DC street. He was badly injured and his left leg was amputated. Every day he struggled to ascend to his seat on the bench, pain showing on his face.

While staying on Parker's good side took some effort, I succeeded in doing so. After the competency proceeding, he invited me to the DC Circuit's yearly Judicial Conference. He was not as favorably disposed toward Camille, whom perhaps he viewed as an interloper. In part because of Parker's sentiments I took the lead in the competency proceeding.

The test in a competency proceeding was stated by the Supreme Court in *Dusky v. United States.* It is "whether [the defendant] has sufficient present ability to consult with his lawyer with a reasonable degree of rational understanding—and whether he has a rational as well as factual understanding of the proceedings against him."[8]

Passman's competency hearing occupied four days in June 1978. Numerous medical and other witnesses testified. As the court said, "Direct and cross-examination of the witnesses was extensive."[9] All the medical witnesses agreed that Passman was cognitively impaired—that he suffered from "a genuine depressive state, largely related to his real life problems" and had a "mild to moderate chronic brain syndrome, either early Alzheimer's disease or cerebral arteriosclerosis." He had "some symptoms of senility."[10] The issue, however, was whether these conditions rendered him incompetent to stand trial.

Two medical witnesses were particularly noteworthy—Dr. F. W. Black, a neuropsychologist, and Dr. Richard Strub, a neurologist. These men where colleagues at the Touro Infirmary, where they had examined Passman. Moreover, they had written a book together on the mental status examination, which described tests calculated to reveal the extent of a patient's mental impairment. While Black and Strub agreed about the nature of Passman's condition, they disagreed about the effect of that condition on his ability to stand trial.

Dr. Black and two other doctors concluded that Passman "would be unable to participate intelligently in trial proceedings because the disease would so severely, and unpredictably, impair his memory and communication skills." Dr. Strub, however, concluded that Passman had "the ability to participate in a trial that is structured and monitored with an eye to his problems." A doctor Judge Parker appointed generally concurred with Dr. Strub.[11]

One lay witness at the hearing gave us fits. The government called a reporter for a Monroe, Louisiana, television station. She provided a videotape of a February 3, 1978, interview Passman had given in his room at St. Francis Hospital where he was being treated for exhaustion. In the video, Passman was sitting on his bed in well-pressed pajamas. As I remember it—and it is too painful to forget—he began the interview by saying something like this: "My lawyer tells me I should not give interviews to the press, but I'm going to talk to you anyway." I was not successful in explaining away this interview; Judge Parker concluded that Passman's "composure on videotape belies his claims of severe agitated depression."[12]

Having evaluated the testimony of all the witnesses and the documentary evidence, Parker concluded that Passman was competent to stand trial. As to the suicide issue, which clearly troubled Parker, he said:

A related question, which has justifiably preoccupied counsel, witnesses and the Court, is whether legal proceedings would substantially increase the risk of the defendant taking extreme means. The medical witnesses do not discount this possibility, both in light of statements attributed to the defendant and the statistical evidence that suicide occurs significantly more often in people of his age and condition than in the general population. [One doctor] ranked the suicidal risk as high, due not only to fear of legal proceedings but also to loss of bodily function and confusion. [Another doctor] with general consensus, testified convincingly that there is a greater probability that defendant would survive than commit suicide, basing this opinion among other things on the fact that Mr. Passman had read and discussed the indictments at the time of his second examination, though he had originally claimed that reviewing those documents would be disastrous. He further testified that the defendant has a personality quality which would keep him from giving up and does not exhibit the guilt feelings that appear almost invariably in people who are major suicidal risks. Indeed, considering Mr. Passman's frequent statements that he would seriously consider suicide only if found guilty, it is not unthinkable that the opportunity to prove his innocence at trial would have a positive effect on his depression.

Without presupposing to quantify anything as subtle as suicide potential, the Court finds from the testimony and evidence the impact of legal proceedings on the defendant would not be so great as to cause a substantial risk of self-destruction.[13]

During the competency hearing, Camille in essence said this to me: "Jim, I think we should move to consolidate the bribery and tax evasion indictments, without saying why we want that done. Then, after the judge does that, we should move to transfer everything to Louisiana for trial. The judge should grant that motion because a person has the right to be tried for tax evasion where he pays taxes, and Passman paid his taxes in Louisiana."

I thought Camille's idea was clever, and he was correct about the proper location for a tax evasion trial. But I initially resisted the idea. I thought Judge Parker, a known curmudgeon, would be offended and conclude we were being far too cute in seeking to consolidate the two cases without revealing why we asked for this and then, once that was done, moving to transfer. I also thought Louisiana could well end up being the venue for both trials even if the indictments were not consolidated because the tax case had to be heard there and it would have made little sense to have a separate bribery trial regarding the same alleged receipt of funds in DC. But Camille insisted and, despite my trepidations, I relented.

Golly was I wrong about Judge Parker. The judge was impressed with how the DOJ lawyers had been snookered. He transferred the consolidated cases to Louisiana.

New York Times columnist William Safire described the events in this way:

Here is how Mr. Passman's defense counsel, James Hamilton and Camille Gravel, made monkeys out of the Justice Department:

After a ruling by a tough D.C. judge that the ailing Mr. Passman was competent to stand trial, Passman's attorneys asked that the two cases (bribery and income tax evasion) be consolidated.

The Justice Department mulled this over and did not object. You cannot find anyone at Justice willing to take responsibility for that decision today. Since the prosecutors did not oppose the request to consolidate the two cases, the judge did so.

Then Mr. Passman's attorneys pointed to a law that requires that income tax cases be tried in the defendant's home district and asked for a transfer of the joined cases to Louisiana. The Justice Department lawyers gulped and tried to stop the transfer, but were then in the untenable position of asking for two trials on the combined cases.

Judge Barrington Parker chided the Justice Department for being "temporarily unmindful" of the consequences of coupling cases, adding that Justice may have been "finessed by the defendant's attorneys." He then sent the trial to Monroe, La.[14]

I spoke to Safire before his column ran. He was going to give me sole credit for this successful maneuver. I told him that would be most unfair, that this was Camille's idea. Fortunately, Safire included Camille's name in the article.

Camille, of course, represented Passman at his trial in his hometown of Monroe, Louisiana. The jury must have been impressed by Camille's florid, impassioned closing argument, which is now legend in Louisiana. The jury was out for less than ninety minutes before returning with a verdict of not guilty on all counts.

8

Marina Oswald
"Nobody I Can Turn To"

At times insight comes from unexpected sources.

In 1976 the House of Representatives established the US House of Representatives Select Committee on Assassinations to re-examine the murders of John F. Kennedy and Martin Luther King Jr. The reason behind this, at least as to Kennedy's death, was the burgeoning body of conspiracy theories and the concomitant decline of trust in the conclusion of the Warren Commission that Lee Harvey Oswald had acted alone in killing Kennedy. An African American congressman from Ohio, Louis Stokes, became chair of this committee.[1]

At some time after the committee's formation, Phil Lacovara—then president of the DC Bar and previously counsel to Leon Jaworski, the Watergate special prosecutor—asked me to represent Marina Oswald Porter, Lee Harvey's widow, on a pro bono basis. Never being able to turn down an interesting assignment, I said yes.

Marina Oswald Porter was born Marina Nikolayeuna Prusakover on July 17, 1941, in Mololovsk in the Soviet Union. In 1957 she moved to Minsk to study pharmacology. She met Lee Harvey Oswald—a former US Marine who had defected to the Soviet Union—at a dance on March 17, 1961. Six weeks later they married. A daughter was born in 1962, the year they moved to Dallas, Texas. Another daughter was born in October 1963.

Shortly thereafter, on November 22, 1963, Lee Harvey Oswald assassinated President Kennedy. Two days later Oswald was killed by Jack Ruby. Marina was a widow at twenty-one in a strange land.

Two years after Oswald's death, Marina married Kenneth Jess Porter. They had a son together. In the mid-1970s, the family moved to Rockwall, Texas. She was naturalized as a US citizen in 1989.

By age twenty-one, Marina had experienced far more than her share of tribulations. She came to this country, not speaking English, with a most unstable husband. Their marriage was difficult and marred by feuding; he beat her on occasion. Then, suddenly, she was the widow of one of the world's most notorious and reviled men. When I met her, I was struck by how she had endured all this. She had spunk and a sense of humor. She was a survivor.

Marina had been an important witness before the Warren Commission, testifying four times using an interpreter. The commission had relied on her testimony to formulate its views about Lee Harvey. Yet the Select Committee considered her testimony troubling, finding that she had given incomplete and inconsistent statements at various times to the Secret Service, the FBI, and the commission. I wanted to ensure that the Select Committee was convinced that she was now being fully candid.

Marina testified to the Select Committee for part of two days.[2] Her testimony was both chilling and revealing.

She believed Oswald killed Kennedy because of his "irrational" bid for prominence. "As long as [his victim was] somebody important, it probably does not matter what their political views are."[3]

She testified that she had taken the famous backyard photographs of Oswald holding the rifle used to kill Kennedy. In these iconic images Oswald has a pistol strapped to his waist and is displaying copies of communist publications. She said she had destroyed similar photographs after Lee Harvey was arrested.

On April 10, 1963, Lee Harvey came home very late, out of breath, and told her, "I just shot General [Edwin A.] Walker," a right-wing activist. She had found a note Lee Harvey had left her telling her what to do if he didn't come home. She was petrified. "Nobody I can turn to."[4]

She testified that on April 21, 1963, after the General Walker incident, Lee Harvey told her that Richard Nixon was visiting Dallas. He was about to leave their home with his weapons; "I am just going to look," he said. Alarmed, she lured him into a bathroom and held the door shut for a while. In the end he did not leave to see Nixon.[5]

Once, Lee Harvey suggested hijacking a plane to Cuba with her help. He said he would "teach" her maybe to "hold the gun." "Fidel Castro was his hero." She resisted his bizarre and dangerous suggestion.[6]

In response to the question of whether she believed Lee Harvey killed Kennedy, she said emphatically, "Yes. Yes, I do." "I do believe that the man was capable of doing such a crime." In answering the question, "Do you believe he acted alone?" she said, "Yes, I do." Later she added, "I have no doubt in my mind that Lee Oswald killed President Kennedy."[7]

She testified that she could not visualize Lee Harvey working with an accomplice. "He was not a very trustworthy and open person . . . I seriously doubt that he will confide in someone."[8]

Asked whether Lee Harvey was "mentally unstable or ill," she said: "I was only 21 when he died. I was not mature enough to recognize the symptoms, but I don't think anybody in their right mind can commit crimes like that. Right now I do assume the person was ill."[9]

She lied to the FBI and the Secret Service about various matters because "I was frightened of my well-being in this country" and "for my children." "I did protect Lee when he was alive because . . . I thought maybe he is innocent." "I did not have anybody in this country but Lee."[10]

In the end, the committee was more interested in its scientific analysis than in Marina's testimony. The committee concluded that Oswald fired three shots at Kennedy, that the second and third shots struck him, and that the third shot killed him. But it concluded that acoustic evidence—analysis of a police channel recording—"establishes a high probability that two gunmen fired at" the president. The purported fourth shot led the committee to conclude that Kennedy "was probably assassinated as a result of a conspiracy."[11] The committee's acoustic analysis is now widely considered to be discredited after reviews by both the FBI and the National Academy of Science.

Before Marina's public testimony, she traveled to Washington, DC, and spent a long day with the committee's staff. The staff went over her knowledge of pertinent events in great detail. She did her best, I believe, to answer their questions.

At the end of the day I said to her, "I know you don't want to come back to Washington to testify, but there is no way the Committee can hold a hearing into JFK's death without hearing Lee Harvey's widow testify." I told her that during the Senate Watergate hearings there had been a death threat on

John Dean, Nixon's White House counsel who was testifying against him, and that, consequently, we had arranged for round-the-clock police protection for Dean. I then asked her if she would like some police protection when she returned to DC to testify.

Marina thought about this for a moment and then said, "Yes, I think I would like some police protection when I come back. You know, there are a lot of nuts in the world and it only takes one."

How insightful this comment seems in our AK-47 world.

Marina did receive protection from the US Marshals Service and the Capitol Police. Chair Stokes thoughtfully allowed her to leave the hearing room before anyone else left their seats. There were no untoward incidents.[12]

In November 1996, Marina told Oprah Winfrey in an interview that she now believes that Lee Harvey was not Kennedy's assassin. She has made similar comments to others. Despite the better evidence, conspiracy theories abound.

9

Danger in Distant Palau

As this book illustrates, much of my career has been far removed from typical legal fare. But nothing I have done professionally was more unusual or exotic than my adventure in far-flung Micronesia.

On July 12, 1978, an election was held in the six island districts of the United Nations Trust Territory of the Pacific Islands (which the United States administered) to determine if there would be a Federated States of Micronesia. Four districts voted yes—Yap, Chuuk, Pohnpei, and Kosrae—and they now form that entity. Two districts—Palau and the Marshall Islands—voted no.

On August 16, 1978, a Palauan delegation led by its two high chiefs—the Ibedul and the Recklai[1]—sent a petition to the Congress of Micronesia, sitting in Kolonia, Pohnpei, asking that the election be invalidated because of various election improprieties. On September 4, 1978, the Congress of Micronesia established a Special Joint Committee on Referendum Review to examine the Palauan election results and the allegations of wrongdoing. I was hired to lead that investigation after being approached by a San Francisco attorney who had represented the Congress of Micronesia and knew of my Watergate work and my book on the law of congressional investigations.

The Congress of Micronesia invited the United Nations Visiting Mission, which had observed the referendum, to observe the conduct of my investigation. I readily agreed to this arrangement, which I thought could result in the UN's imprimatur on the results of the investigation and the methods by which it was undertaken.

I travelled to Pohnpei to familiarize myself with the allegations and Micronesian culture. Very quickly a problem arose—a death threat against the chair of the committee, Representative Julio Akapito of Chuuk. Akapito must have taken this threat seriously because he decided not to go to Palau for the investigation.

I concluded that it was prudent to go to Saipan to discuss the situation with the high commissioner of the Trust Territory. He was sympathetic, and when I arrived in Palau I was accompanied by the entire Micronesian Bureau of Investigation, which was assigned to protect me. The bureau consisted of two ex-CIA types with pistols strapped to their ankles.

Before I continue with this saga, a word about this part of the world. I saw much of it because to travel to the necessary places I needed to island hop. From Hawaii I went to the Marshall Islands, then to Pohnpei, then to Chuuk, then to Guam, then, after a side trip to Tinian, to Saipan, then back to Guam, then to Yap, and finally to Palau.

The Marshall Islands are composed of twenty-nine coral atolls and five low coral islands. These include Kwajalein Atoll, where the United States operated missile launch sites, and Bikini Atoll, where several hydrogen and atomic bomb tests were detonated. (I once assisted the Bikini islanders in their attempts to obtain compensation from the US government for the destruction of their homeland.)

Pohnpei is a high volcanic island. Its soil is fertile; some of the world's best pepper is grown there. (I brought home a large supply.) It also is the site of Nan Madol, a mysterious ruined stone city of canals that thrived from the twelfth to the sixteenth century.

The main part of Chuuk consists of fourteen mountainous volcanic islands. In World War II, the Chuuk Lagoon was Japan's main base in the South Pacific. On February 17, 1944, the United States launched an attack—"Operation Hailstorm"—that destroyed 12 Japanese warships, 32 merchant ships, and 275 aircraft. Chuuk Lagoon is now the world's biggest graveyard of ships and a diving mecca.

Guam is home to several important US military bases and a number of luxury hotels popular with Japanese tourists. Nearby is Tinian. After its capture from Japan in August 1944 and the devastation of the large Japanese garrison there, Tinian became the United States' largest World War II airbase. From its north airfield the aircraft *Enola Gay* and *Bock-scar"* carried the atomic bombs Little Boy and Fat Man that were dropped on Hiroshima and Nagasaki. When I visited Tinian in 1978, this airfield was deserted and overtaken by weeds poking up through cracks in the tarmac.

The battle for Saipan, of course, was one of the major military operations of World War II. It started on June 15, 1944, when US forces landed on the island's southwestern beaches. The sea there is shallow for hundreds of yards from the beach. When I was there in 1978, rusted hulls of landing craft and other vehicles rested on the sand, rising out of the water—grim, minatory reminders of a gruesome war.

US casualties were heavy, but the Japanese lost over twenty-nine thousand troops during the battle for Saipan. Around twenty thousand Japanese civilians died; over one thousand leaped to their deaths from "Suicide Cliff" and "Bonzai Cliff."

Yap has four major high islands and fifteen other islands and atolls. Yap is known for its huge stone money—doughnut-shaped disks up to twelve feet in diameter. The Yap airport runway is barely long enough to land a commercial jet. When I was there the "terminal" building was a thatched hut where old women, naked to the waist, sold and chewed narcotic betel nuts that turned their teeth red.

Palau is a strikingly beautiful place. The main Palauan group consists of hundreds of islands—some volcanic, some coral limestone. Many of these are "rock islands," which often rise like toadstools out of the sea. In the mud cliffs by the sea live fourteen-feet, sea-going, man-eating crocodiles. The Palauan rock islands are now a UNESCO World Heritage site.

The water in the coves and lagoons of the Palauan rock islands is unbelievably clear. You easily can see a crab crawling on the seabed twenty-five feet below the surface. Walking Palauan paths, you may come upon a downed World War II Japanese fighter plane lying untouched for many years in a secluded cove, gently lapped by the waves. Scuba diving is a Palauan passion. The "Big Drop Off" near Ngemelis Island is considered one of the world's best wall dives.

One art form of Palau is the storyboard. On these boards the legends of Palau are carved in intricate detail. Often the carvings are done by inmates in Palau's jail. I have several jail-rendered storyboards in my office and home.

I also bought Kristina, my wife-to-be, a Chuuk love stick. Amorous Chuuk men used to push their intricately carved love sticks under the walls of huts where the women they were pursuing dwelled. A woman could tell by the carvings whose love stick it was. If the suitor met with favor, she would pull the stick in. If not, she would push the stick away. Kristina's father was amused that the love stick I brought home arrived in a broken state.

In early October 1978 I arrived in Palau with my bodyguards, courtesy of the high commissioner. They surveyed the scene to see if trouble was afoot. At night, there also was a Palauan policeman posted on the patio just outside my hotel room door. I remember that he was only about four feet tall with a pistol that seemed nearly that height. However, I slept soundly, perhaps because I didn't consider the death threat on Chair Akapito to be that serious. Later events suggest that my attitude was too cavalier.

The investigation entrusted to me presented difficult challenges. I was in a foreign land and didn't speak the language. I came with no staff. I had no subpoena power. The side that won the election had reason to be hostile to my endeavor. Why would they even speak with me? I had to invent an investigation to fit the circumstance.

I assembled a small volunteer staff mainly consisting of Palauans to assist in the investigation. Notable among the staff was Arthur Ngiraklsong, a capable, agreeable fellow who later became the chief justice of the Palauan Supreme Court.

The Palauan election had been hotly contested, and the results were close. The yes votes for the federation and its constitution—by the "unionists"—were 2,720. The no votes—by the "separatists"—were 3,339. Thus, the vote for federation failed in Palau by only 620 votes.

The unionists had been led by the two high chiefs, the Ibedul and the Recklai, among others. The separatists were, in part, led by Roman Tmetuchl, a powerful politician who also was reputed to be the crime boss of Palau.

The separatists opposed union, which the United States long had favored, because other Micronesian districts were vast distances away and had different cultures and languages. (There were eleven distinct languages in Micronesia.) The separatists favored an independent commonwealth status and a "free association" with the United States. Famous Harvard economist John Kenneth Galbraith, a former US ambassador to India, had agreed to advise the new Palauan state.

Tmetuchl's advocacy for separate status was colorful. He contended that "it would be better to try to unify Canada, the United States and Mexico in a single nation. That would make more sense. . . . Separation is an act of God. Micronesia was made this way."[2]

The allegations of misconduct came in two broad categories—improprieties in voting and improprieties in the conduct of the election campaign. The most serious voting allegations were:

1. Ineligible voters were allowed to vote.
2. Numerous Palauans living in Guam were improperly refused registration.
3. Some eight hundred absentee ballots were mishandled.

The most disturbing allegations as to campaign misconduct were:

1. The opponents of union had engaged in bribery and bought votes and campaign support.
2. Persons had been intimidated by their traditional chiefs into voting no.

These allegations on their face were serious, and my team carefully investigated them. We told both sides that we were ready to speak to anyone who had pertinent information. Surprisingly, people from both camps came forth. We interviewed more than 50 witnesses (including Roman Tmetuchl) and considered over 120 affidavits and numerous other documents.

We reviewed every ballot cast, including absentee ballots, and every ballot stub to make sure it was properly numbered. We looked at registration affidavits and affidavits from persons not registered before election day or from those voting at a polling place other than where they were registered. We examined poll workers' work sheets, registration books, voter sign-in lists, and the election records found in every ballot box used in the election.

The UN Visiting Mission observing the investigation was complimentary. As to our interviews, it said: "The Mission was impressed by the thorough manner in which Mr. Hamilton and his team carried out their task. All allegations of misconduct were carefully investigated and cross-checked in interviews." The mission added that it "was also impressed with the thoroughness of the investigation of the voting process."[3]

The time eventually came to interview Roman Tmetuchl. We did this one evening in, as I recall, a cramped private room in a local restaurant. My two bodyguards were nearby. Tmetuchl was clever in his approach to the interview. While he spoke English well, he insisted that all my questions be translated into Palauan by one of his compatriots. This gave him additional opportunity to think about the questions. Then he would answer in Palauan and his answers were translated into English for my benefit. Needless to say, the interview took a while. I pressed Tmetuchl on the issues at hand—for example, bribery and voter intimidation. But, while he likely was irritated by my questions, he proved able in defending himself and gave no ground.

As admitted above, I was perhaps too casual about the death threat on my committee chair. Passions had run high during the election campaign, and my investigation could be seen as an attack on the victory for the separatists of whom Tmetuchl was a leader.

Tmetuchl himself had been the target of an assassination attempt in 1970. He ran for president of Palau in 1980 and 1984 against Haruo I. Remeliik, losing both times. In 1985, Remeliik was assassinated, shot by a rifle after he returned home from fishing.

And what persons were indicted and convicted of killing Remeliik? Three men, *including the son and nephew of Roman Tmetuchl.* Their convictions, however, were overturned by an appellate court, which, according to the *New York Times*, found that prosecution witnesses were "inherently incredible."[4] The murder never has been solved.

I submitted my report to the Congress of Micronesia on October 19, 1978. We indeed found shortcomings and misdeeds, but nothing sufficient to invalidate the election.

Eight hundred absentee ballots had been improperly stored overnight in the District Administration Office before they were examined by the UN Visiting Mission and transferred to a Palauan police station for safekeeping.

But adequate steps had been taken to protect the improperly stored ballots, and there was no evidence of tampering.

Certain Palauan residents living in Guam were denied registration, but properly so because the registration affidavits, signed in Guam, were notarized in Palau by a notary who did *not* witness the signatures. Election records also appeared to show that about half those Guam residents were able to vote on Election Day because they later submitted proper affidavits.

Some ineligible persons were allowed to vote. Twenty-five affidavits by absentee voters demonstrated that they were US citizens and not Palauans. Both referendum officials and representatives of the opposing parties observing the ballot counting had overlooked this important fact, which was clear from the affidavits themselves. Nonetheless, I concluded that the "existence of 25 improper ballots does not, standing alone, invalidate an election where the margin of victory was 619 notes."[5]

We reached several conclusions about bribery and vote buying. In most cases where money had passed hands, it was provided to defray campaign expenses and not to buy votes. One person told us he had been urged unsuccessfully by a union supporter to claim *falsely* that money had been given to him for his own use and not for campaign expenses.

In a few cases there was some evidence of bribery or attempted bribery. One chief admitted to us that he had taken money *to oppose union* but nonetheless had continued to campaign *for it*. Whatever the ramifications of such conduct were under the Palauan criminal code, it obviously did not affect the election outcome. All in all, we concluded that bribery was difficult to establish, and where it had occurred, it was on a small scale that could not have altered the results of the election.

Finally, we found that the allegations of intimidation by traditional chiefs opposed to union were not supported by hard evidence and appeared exaggerated. My report pragmatically concluded,

> Those familiar with Palau generally agree that the opinions of the traditional chiefs had significant influence on Palauan voters during the referendum. In fact, some believe the election was close because the two paramount chiefs supported the constitution. In any society, however, traditional leaders or men of esteem influence the votes of others. We believe the Palauan election should be nullified only if there is strong evidence that traditional chiefs, by specific threats, influenced

a substantial number of people to vote no. This sort of evidence is lacking here.[6]

The Special Committee of the Congress of Micronesia largely endorsed my report. It found that "weighing all the evidence before it, the Committee concludes that the validity of the 12 July 1978 constitutional referendum in Palau was not materially affected by any election irregularities or campaign abuses in connection with it."[7]

The UN Visiting Mission reached a similar conclusion in its report to Kurt Waldheim, the secretary general of the United Nations:

> The Mission considers that the investigation made in Palau on behalf of the Special Joint Committee on Referendum Review was carried out with commendable thoroughness and impartiality. The Mission was satisfied that all who wished to do so had the opportunity to present evidence or information to the investigators. . . . The Mission, having observed the investigations in Palau in detail, could record that it is aware of no reason to question the finding of the Special Joint Committee that the validity of the referendum in Palau was not materially affected by any election regularities or campaign abuses.[8]

Palau is now, as Roman Tmetuchl and other separatists desired, an independent republic in free association with the United States, which is responsible for its defense.

In 1988, Tmetuchl tried one more time to gain the presidency but failed again. He died in 1999, having become rich from business ventures after his political career. The Palauan international airport was named for him in 2006.

10

Debategate

In the days before the internet, a major news story could lie fallow for months or years. But when publicized, it could explode.

In 1983, Laurence I. Barrett published a book, *Gambling with History*, that dealt with President Ronald Reagan's 1980 election campaign. Barrett reported that the Reagan-Bush campaign had received a copy of President Jimmy Carter's debate briefing book before the October 1980 presidential debate—the sole presidential debate that election season.

On Tuesday, October 28, 1980, the day of the debate, Michigan congressman David Stockman, who was to become Reagan's director of the Office of Management and Budget, spoke to a not particularly august body, the Cassopolis (Michigan) Optimists Club. The next day his speech was reported by two lightly read newspapers—the *Elkhart Truth* of Elkhart, Indiana, and the *Dowagiac Daily News* of Dowagiac, Michigan. What Stockman had said was overlooked by the rest of the nation's media and essentially forgotten until Barrett's book appeared.

What Stockman had said was this: for the debate, which would occur later that evening, he had used a "pilfered copy" of Carter's debate briefing book to put Reagan through "eight or nine mock rehearsals."[1] According to both newspapers, Stockman said that he described five "white lies" Carter would use to attack Reagan and Reagan's responses. The October 29 *Elkhart Truth* stated, "Apparently the Reagan Camp's 'pilfered' goods were correct, as several times both candidates said almost word for word what Stockman predicted. The line of attack was exactly like the Michigan Representative said it would be."[2]

After Barrett's book emerged, the briefing book matter soon became a major news story. By late June 1983, it was front-page news and the subject of considerable editorial comment.

The media accounts were noticed by Congressman Dan Albosta (D-MI), then chair of the House Subcommittee on Human Resources, a subcommittee of the House Committee on Post Office and Civil Service. Albosta sent letters to various individuals who had been in the Reagan campaign and who were now high-ranking government officials—including Stockman, White House chief of staff James Baker, assistant to the president for communications David Gergen, and CIA director William Casey, who had been the Reagan-Bush campaign manager—asking about their knowledge of and participation in the briefing book matter. The justification for his inquiries was that the subcommittee was reviewing agency ethics programs and the implementation of the Ethics in Government Act. The allegations, he said, raised questions involving both theft of government property and violations of government ethical rules. Thus began the Debategate investigation.

On June 27, 1983, after extensive media coverage, President Reagan instructed the Department of Justice to conduct a "vigorous monitoring" of the incident. The White House asked anyone with relevant information, including White House aides, to provide it to the DOJ. Two days later, Reagan specifically instructed the department to "find out if there was any wrongdoing and take action." Thereafter, the DOJ announced that the FBI would conduct a "criminal investigation" into how the Reagan-Bush campaign obtained the Carter briefing materials and other Carter White House information.[3]

On June 28, the Reagan White House released hundreds of pages of documents Carter's staff had prepared for the debate that had been found in the files of David Gergen and Francis Hodsoll, then the chair of the National Endowment for the Arts, who also had been a campaign aide. These documents contained discussions of foreign policy and national security issues. Also found were briefing papers on those subjects put together for Vice President Mondale's debate with George H. W. Bush. The same day, Stockman informed White House counsel Fred Fielding that he had received materials that appeared to be Carter briefing papers about domestic issues.

On June 29, Albosta announced that his subcommittee would conduct an inquiry into the allegations about the unethical and unauthorized transfer of property from the Carter administration to the Reagan-Bush campaign. Shortly thereafter, I was hired as special counsel by the subcommittee to guide the investigations. The subcommittee's staff director was an astute young lawyer named Micah Green.

During the investigation the subcommittee interviewed over 250 people. It obtained 63 affidavits and an additional 150 signed answers to questionnaires from persons employed by the Carter administration. It gathered voluminous documents from individual files, from the FBI, and from the Hoover Institution of Stanford University, where Reagan campaign files were stored.

Although the subcommittee had subpoena power, the entire investigation was conducted *without issuing one subpoena.* This was made possible by President Reagan's pledge of cooperation with the subcommittee and because White House counsel Fred Fielding facilitated that pledge.

At this writing I have known Fred for over forty-five years. Until he became counsel to the firm, he was my law partner at Morgan, Lewis & Bockius. I could look out my window on the seventh floor of 1101 Pennsylvania Avenue directly into his corner office on the eighth floor of 1111 Pennsylvania Avenue.

I first met Fred when I interrogated him for six hours for the Senate Watergate Committee. Fred had been Nixon's deputy White House counsel under John Dean. Dean told us that Fred was a man of integrity and that he had purposely kept Fred apart from the wrongdoing perpetrated by many in the Nixon White House. Although Fred provided some interesting tidbits of information during the interrogation, I came away from the session convinced that he was honest and not involved in the Watergate cover-up or other White House misdeeds. The Senate Watergate Committee report made no accusations against him.

In late 1980 or early 1981, the FBI called me about Fred. He was, the agent said, being considered for a high-ranking government position. What was my view, the agent asked, of his character and conduct in the Nixon White House.

Given his role for Nixon, I assumed he was under consideration to be

Reagan's White House counsel. So I told the agent something like this: "Fred is an honest guy. Also, he would be perfect for the position he's being considered for because he knows where the potholes are."

As soon as I put down the phone, I called Fred and told him what the agent had asked and what I had said. Fred's response was "phew!" Shortly thereafter he was appointed White House counsel. He served Reagan—and later President George W. Bush—in that position with great distinction. CBS White House correspondent Rita Braver once told me that Fred was the best White House counsel she had dealt with because of his keen judgment.

My prior relationship with Fred was helpful as we negotiated issues regarding access to Debategate information. There was, for example, a dispute regarding subcommittee review of files at the Hoover Institution that contained transition as well as campaign materials. The issue was resolved in part by career professionals from the General Accounting Office who ensured that the subcommittee would see only campaign documents relevant to its investigation.

I negotiated the details of access to FBI files with Associate Attorney General Lowell Jensen. Eventually, the subcommittee was allowed to see all the information DOJ collected regarding its investigation, including documents that the FBI had gathered from the Hoover Institution. The subcommittee's minority counsel and I even were allowed to review relevant FBI 302s—the normally highly confidential FBI summaries of its interviews. While not unprecedented, this was quite unusual. As part of the compromise, the subcommittee consented to allow the DOJ to examine the records the subcommittee collected in its investigation.

The subcommittee's investigation produced mixed results. It reached definitive conclusions about some matters. The facts about other circumstances were less clear even though, as described below, the evidence strongly suggested wrongful conduct by several prominent individuals.

I thought it important that the subcommittee's report be precise as to what facts were beyond legitimate dispute and what conclusions were based on informed speculation. To reach that result I wrote or rewrote much of the report. I wanted an objective report, not one that read like a partisan screed.

As noted, the Reagan-Bush campaign had obtained foreign policy and national defense debate briefing papers prepared for President Carter and Vice President Mondale. The evidence also indicated that the campaign had acquired some version of the Carter briefing book on domestic matters. David Stockman in an affidavit stated that he saw materials of this type, as did Frank Hodsoll and a college student who had operated a copying machine at Reagan campaign headquarters. There also was some evidence that the campaign had obtained a more condensed version of Carter's foreign policy briefing papers.

The investigation established that the Carter briefing materials were used to prepare Reagan for the debate. Hodsoll stated that the Carter materials influenced what was in Reagan's own debate book. Stockman said he found them "useful," particularly in his role as a stand-in for Carter in the debate preparation sessions. Another campaign aide, William Van Cleve, stated under oath that Stockman told him that the Carter materials were of "great use" to him in that stand-in role.[4]

The big remaining questions were as follows: How did these briefing materials make their way to the Reagan campaign? Specifically, who removed them from the Carter White House? Who received them at campaign headquarters?

The subcommittee's investigation showed that Gergen and Hodsoll—in whose files Carter briefing materials were found—received those materials from James Baker. Baker recalled that he obtained those materials from William Casey, the campaign director. Casey vigorously denied this under oath.

In 1983, during the investigation, Baker was White House chief of staff and in the early stages of his illustrious career, which culminated in his becoming secretary of state in George H. W. Bush's administration. Baker understood the sensitivity of the issues under investigation and the danger to him of being at crossed swords with Casey, the director of the CIA. He proceeded with extreme care in responding to the committee's inquiries.

Baker submitted a detailed affidavit to the subcommittee. I remember talking with him on the phone for around two hours about what the subcommittee wanted addressed in the affidavit before he submitted it. He took pains to ensure that his sworn statements were accurate.

Baker swore to the following:

My best recollection is that I received the [Carter briefing] material . . . from William Casey, who suggested that it might be of use to the Debate Briefing Team. . . .

I do not remember whether or not Mr. Casey in 1980 identified the source of the material. . . . He might have suggested that it was from the Carter campaign, but I am in no way certain that he did. . . .

I believe I gave the material . . . to either David Gergen or Frank Hodsoll.

I believe I informed Margaret Tutwiler after I received the material . . . and before the election that I had received such material from William Casey, and that I had given the material to the debate team.[5]

Margaret Tutwiler was an aide to Baker during the campaign. She stated under oath,

During the 1980 campaign I had a conversation with James A. Baker, III, during which he told me, in essence, that he (Baker) had received Carter campaign or briefing materials from William J. Casey, which he (Baker) passed on to the Reagan debate people. . . .

Mr. Baker recently told me that he believed he had given the Carter material to Dave Gergen who was responsible for preparation of Governor Reagan's debate briefing book.[6]

Casey, however, was adamant that he had never seen the Carter briefing materials, had not engineered the Reagan campaign's obtaining of them, and had not passed any such materials to Baker. Casey told the *New York Times*, "I wouldn't tolerate it. I wouldn't touch it with a 10-foot pole." He said that the presence of Carter materials in the campaign could have "destroyed" the campaign and that the debate team was "remiss" in not bringing that to the attention of top campaign officials.[7]

Casey stated his unwavering positions under oath in an affidavit given to the subcommittee:

I have examined the Carter debate briefing materials that were released by the White House in June 1983 ("Briefing Materials"). . . .

I did not recognize these Briefing Materials as anything I had seen before. Indeed, as far as I can recollect, until June 1983, I did not know that materials prepared for President Carter's use in preparing for the debate had been in the possession of or been used by Reagan-Bush campaign workers. . . .

In June 1983, shortly before I received Chairman Albosta's first letter, Fred Fielding called to tell me that documents prepared for President Carter's use in the debate had apparently been in the possession of Reagan-Bush campaign workers and that James Baker seemed to have a recollection that he might have received them from me. I said I could not recollect anything like that. Shortly thereafter, James Baker told me that he thought I had handed him some papers in a binder saying, "This may be useful for the debate." I said that I had no such recollection. . . .

To the best of my recollection I did not receive or pass on the Briefing Materials nor did I authorize or direct any person to obtain the Briefing Materials. . . .

I have no knowledge of any intelligence operation established or authorized by the 1980 Reagan-Bush presidential campaign that was designed to obtain the Briefing Materials or any other similar materials.[8]

In a separate memorandum to Fred Fielding, Casey wrote,

If papers headed "Presidential Debates, Foreign Policy and National Security Issues" came in, I believe they would have caught my eye or would have been brought to my attention and I would not have forgotten, nor would I have forgotten if anyone came in and handed them to me. Until recent disclosures, I did not know that the campaign had any material from the Carter camp that was not publicly available.[9]

The Democratic members and staff of the subcommittee believed Baker over Casey. Baker was supported by Tutwiler, a credible witness even though she was known as a fiercely loyal Baker aide. Moreover, Casey had established what he called an "intelligence operation" to monitor whether President Carter would spring an "October surprise" and bring the Iranian-held hostages home before the election.[10] Numerous documents from the Carter White House, including those from an unnamed White House "mole," had crossed Casey's desk at the campaign headquarters. The minutes of a September 12, 1980, campaign deputies' meeting stated that Casey said he "wants more material from the Carter Camp and wants it circulated."[11] And there was evidence suggesting that a fellow named Paul Corbin had given Carter briefing materials to Casey.

Corbin was a shadowy, unsavory, and contradictory character. He once was a member of the Communist Party but had worked for Joe McCarthy. He had had brushes with the law and had an extensive FBI file. He was close to Bobby Kennedy and had worked on Ted Kennedy's 1980 campaign but was disliked and not trusted by others in the Kennedy circle. He was a long-time Democrat but disliked President Carter and went to work for the Reagan campaign. His propensity to lie was well known.[12] As the subcommittee's report too gently put it, his "reputation for veracity is uneven."[13]

In 1983 Tim Wyngaard was the executive director of the House Republican Policy Committee. Wyngaard was a long-time acquaintance of Corbin. In April 1983, in the course of an hour-long conversation, Corbin told him that he had obtained Carter briefing materials for the debate and given them to Casey. Shortly thereafter, Wyngaard reported this information to Congressman Dick Cheney (WY), chair of the Republican Policy Committee, and Wyngaard did so again in June 1983 after the briefing book matter became a subject of press interest. During the subcommittee's investigation, Cheney told Baker what Wyngaard had relayed to him.[14] Wyngaard was believable; he also was a respected congressional staff member with a solid reputation for honesty.

Corbin had been employed by the Reagan campaign, which paid him a total of $2,860 in 1980. His invoice indicated that the bulk of the money was for "research reports." No such research reports were located, and members of the Reagan campaign could not recall any. The affidavit he submitted to the subcommittee said the payment was for "political assessments and field trips," and in interviews he told the subcommittee and the FBI that he was paid to travel to Florida to pass out leaflets in condominiums around Palm Beach.[15] Those claims could not be verified; rather, a largely untouched collection of Reagan-Bush bumper stickers and campaign posters were found in his car. The subcommittee concluded "either that Corbin was paid for something else by the Reagan Bush campaign or that he neglected to perform the services for which he was paid."[16]

Corbin was in the Reagan-Bush campaign headquarters on at least four occasions in the fall of 1980, including on October 25 when he went to Casey's office. That appears to be the day that Gergen told another campaign staffer that someone had delivered Carter debate briefing materials to the Reagan-Bush campaign.[17]

It has been reported that Carter media aide Jerry Rafshood saw Corbin in the White House in the later stages of the 1980 campaign. That was surprising because his dislike of Carter was well known.[18]

Corbin was steadfast in denying that he had received any Carter briefing materials. In his affidavit to the subcommittee, he swore:

> I did not provide directly or indirectly any documents or information not readily available in this media from the Carter campaign or from the Carter Administration to the Reagan-Bush campaign. Specifically, I did not provide, or cause to be provided, any version or versions of debate briefing materials prepared for President Carter or Vice President Mondale for debates in the 1980 presidential election.
>
> I have no knowledge other than that which I have gained from the news media, about the transfer of Carter debate briefing materials, or other confidential Carter Administration campaign materials, to the Reagan-Bush Campaign.
>
> I did not tell Tim Wyngaard that I obtained briefing materials designed for use by President Carter or that I delivered such materials, or caused them to be delivered, to William J. Casey or to the Reagan Campaign.[19]

Casey admitted that Corbin had been in his office in October 1980 and said he was employed to contact labor leaders and political leaders in condominiums in Florida to seek votes for the Reagan-Bush tickets. But Casey denied receiving any Carter briefing materials from him. He did acknowledge receiving from Corbin a few pages of suggestions prepared by Adam Walinsky, "another Kennedy Democrat," to assist Reagan in the debate.[20] Baker, in his affidavit, offered the following: "On June 20, 1983, Casey indicated to me that Corbin might have been a source of material from the Carter Administration or the 1980 Carter-Mondale presidential campaign."[21]

The investigation required me to interrogate a variety of individuals, for example, Baker, soon-to-be Attorney General Ed Meese, Gergen, Stockman, Corbin, columnist George Will, and Casey. The interrogation of Casey was memorable, if not productive.

It took place one evening in a conference room in a House office build-ing. Casey arrived from the CIA with a driver in a government car. Con-gressman Albosta was there. The session lasted around two hours.

Casey was difficult to interrogate. One reason—he mumbled. I sat about five feet across the table from him but had difficulty hearing what he said. I have no doubt that his hard-to-comprehend, muffled sounds were intentional.

Casey, in my firm view, was not always truthful. Several documents had crossed his desk purportedly from a "White House mole." When I asked him who the "mole" was, his answer was something like this: "That was a detail. I was the campaign chairman. Many documents crossed my desk. I couldn't know all the details." This was a surprising and not credible answer from a man who had initiated an intelligence operation to ferret out infor-mation about a possible "October surprise" and had let it be known that he wanted more information from within the Carter White House.

Also, when asked a question about a suspect document for which he had a good nonincriminating answer, Casey would expound on "details" for several minutes.

Casey was lying. I knew he was lying. He knew I knew he was lying. But he kept on lying.

Eventually I exhausted my questions. Albosta had almost none; he also was frustrated with Casey's evasions. So I brought the session to an end.

When I did, Casey rose and said, "Mr. Hamilton I want to thank you for your courtesies—and for the intelligence of your questions."

I thought to myself, *Goddammit, I didn't touch this son-of-a-bitch.*

Also interesting was the interrogation of George Will, the *Washington Post* columnist. Will had participated in preparing Reagan for the debate, and he had reviewed Carter debate materials very briefly in David Stockman's DC home.

Will was hostile while being questioned, fearing was that the subcommittee would criticize his journalistic ethics because he had helped Reagan prepare for the debate. Will himself later branded his conduct "inappropriate."[22]

Will answered my questions with a number of polysyllabic words, such as those that frequently inhabit his columns. To show that I was also somewhat literate and not intimidated by this tactic, I started including polysyllabic words in my questions. I think I enjoyed the session more than he did.

Before the report came out, Will and I spoke again. He remained concerned about possible criticism of his conduct. I told him my interest was what he knew about the source of the Carter materials—he knew nothing—and that the report would not discuss his journalistic propriety. It did not.

The subcommittee eventually decided to rely on the many interviews it conducted and the affidavits it collected rather than holding a public hearing. In postponing a public hearing indefinitely, Chair Albosta said,

> Some time ago, I tentatively scheduled hearings into the matters under investigation for January 26th. However, recently I have become concerned that holding public hearings on the highly charged issues involved in a Presidential election year could have unwanted, undesirable and possibly counter-productive consequences. Because of the issues and the persons involved, there is potential for public hearings to degenerate into partisan bickering and a media extravaganza. If this occurred, the ultimate goals of the hearings—and objective presentation of the subcommittee factual findings and the development of proposals for administrative or legislative solutions—would be seriously impeded, if not defeated.[23]

There may have been unspoken reasons for declining to hold a public hearing. The hearing likely would have been inconclusive, serving mainly to highlight the disputes in testimony discussed in this chapter. Moreover, the chair of the full Post Office and Civil Service Committee, William Ford, may have had reservations about the ability of Don Albosta to handle the type of high-profile, controversial hearing that surely would have resulted. Albosta was a well-meaning, competent person, but he was a farmer, not a lawyer trained in interrogation skills. And in terms of demeanor, erudition, and personality, he was no Sam Ervin.

The Department of Justice's reaction to the evidence was disappointing. In declining prosecution, the department made several statements of dubious merit.

The department stated that "any seeming inconsistencies [in testimony] could be explained by differences in recollection or interpretation."[24] But Baker remembered receiving Carter materials from Casey, who said he didn't recall seeing the materials. Casey also wrote Fred Fielding that such materials "would have caught my eye . . . and I would not have forgotten, nor would I have forgotten if anyone came in and handed them to me."[25] Given Casey's statement, it is difficult cavalierly to dismiss the dispute between him and Baker as "differences in recollection."

The department also concluded that "no government documents are among the briefing materials that were obtained by the Reagan campaign."[26] This conclusion was contrary to the opinion of esteemed Carter White House counsel Lloyd Cutler, who stated in an affidavit:

> Our opinion was that material designed to defend a policy of the Administration or the President was Government material and that material designed to attack a position of Governor Reagan was campaign material. Therefore, the debate briefing materials were lawfully prepared by White House officials on Government time and were Government property to the extent they discussed or defended the President's policies. The majority of the briefing book materials fell into that category.[27]

Finally, the department concluded that there was "no specific, credible information of a federal crime."[28] But the subcommittee found that no one of authority in the Carter White House authorized the release of the briefing book materials and that their admitted use by the Reagan campaign was itself "specific, credible information" that some crime occurred.[29]

District judge Harold Greene also concluded that there was specific, credible information. In denying a motion to dismiss a suit to require the attorney general to appoint an independent counsel under a then-existing provision in the Ethics in Government Act (which action the subcommittee also had called for),[30] he said:

> The complaint in this case alleges, *inter alia*, that, according to information available on the public record, hundreds of pages of documents from the White House and the Executive Offices were removed or copied and then turned over to the 1980 Reagan campaign organization; that four of President Reagan's present or former aides have admit-

ted to possessing or seeing such materials; that at least some of these
aides knew that the documents had been taken from the Carter White
House; that an operation existed to collect inside information on the
Carter campaign through means of a "mole" and otherwise; and that
several high Administration officials appear to have made contradictory statements concerning these papers. Plaintiffs claim that the individuals involved in these activities may have violated one or more
federal criminal laws.

The government argues that this information is not specific or credible, and that plaintiffs have for that reason failed to state a claim upon
which relief may be granted. Indeed, the government goes so far as to
assert, more pointedly, that the term "mole" has no "criminal overtones"; that there are likewise no such "overtones" to an information
gathering apparatus employed by a Presidential campaign which uses
former agents of the FBI and the CIA; and that the statement of Budget Director Stockman—that briefing books were "filched"—may have
had a connotation other than theft. . . .

These contentions entirely lack merit. . . .

By the government's own admission, the Department has conducted
"a thorough and searching investigation of the transmittal of the briefing papers" in the course of which "over 200 interviews have been conducted and numerous criminal statutes have been considered, including those cited by plaintiffs. . . .

It is difficult to understand on what basis the government can conduct that kind of an investigation and yet assert at the same time that
when plaintiffs furnished evidence similar to that which generated the
Department's inquiry, they failed to provide information that is suffi-
ciently specific and credible to cause an Ethics Act investigation to be
conducted. . . .

For the reasons stated, the Court finds on the basis of the present record that plaintiffs have submitted information of sufficient specificity
and credibility to require the Attorney General to conduct a preliminary investigation provided for under the Ethics Act.[31]

The District of Columbia Circuit reversed Judge Greene, but not on the
merits. Rather, the appeals court found that "Congress specifically intended
. . . to preclude judicial review, at the behest of members of the public, of

the Attorney General's decisions not to . . . seek appointment of . . . independent counsel."[32]

In the end the subcommittee found that "the better evidence indicates that Carter debate briefing materials . . . entered the Reagan Bush campaign through its director, Casey." The subcommittee also noted the evidence that Corbin gave Carter briefing materials to Casey, but said, "It is unable to state how Corbin may have obtained those materials himself."[33]

On May 25, 1984, about a week after the subcommittee issued its report, President Reagan visited CIA headquarters. That day, the *New York Times* reported that Reagan walked "side by side" with Director Casey on the CIA campus and broke ground for an addition to CIA headquarters building. Reagan praised Casey's performance in his CIA role but did not comment on the subcommittee's report. According to the *Times,* White House chief of staff James Baker was not in the presidential party attending the groundbreaking.[34]

11

Impeachment Alaska Style

Washington is a dangerous place for reputations, but Alaska has its own set of hazards.

On July 1, 1985, an Alaska state grand jury took an unusual and controversial action. In a seventy-six-page report, the grand jury recommended that the Alaska Legislature be called into special session so that the "Alaska Senate may consider the evidence presented to and the findings of the Grand Jury for the express purpose of initiating impeachment procedures against Governor William Sheffield."[1]

On July 15, the Senate convened. In Alaska, unlike the US Congress, the Senate considers impeachment. If it votes for impeachment, the matter moves to the Alaska House for a trial to convict or acquit.

The Alaskan Senate referred the Sheffield matter to its Rules Committee. That committee hired Senate Watergate Committee chief counsel Sam Dash as its chief counsel for the impeachment proceeding. Sam asked me to be his deputy. It was hard to turn down my friend, particularly on an interesting case, and I accepted. But with a caveat. My wife, Kristina, was pregnant with twins, who were expected toward the end of September. I promised Kristina that I would be in Alaska for only two weeks. I told Sam that my service would be so limited, and he agreed. As will be described, I almost did not keep my promise to Kristina.

To some extent, this was Watergate revisited. The grand jury had been advised by Watergate prosecutor George Frampton. (I had known George since 1965, when we were both at the London School of Economics and played together on the University of London basketball team.) Phil Lacovara, who had been counsel to Watergate special prosecutors Archibald Cox and Leon Jaworski, represented the governor. Phil argued and won the critically important Supreme Court case requiring President Nixon to turn over the White House tapes by the Watergate cover-up trial. (As discussed in chapter 8, when president of the DC Bar, Phil had asked me to represent Marina Oswald Porter before a House Committee looking into the assassination of President Kennedy.) So, former Watergate compatriots and friends were pitted against each other in several respects.

Before he became governor, Sheffield had been a successful businessman, rising from repairing televisions to owning a significant hotel chain. During the impeachment proceedings, Dash and his team stayed at a Sheffield hotel in Juneau.

What had concerned the grand jury was intervention by the governor's office in the procurement of a $9.1 million lease for state office space in Fairbanks. The governor's chief of staff, John Shively, testified to the grand jury under a grant of immunity, which he asked for because, as he admitted to the grand jury, he had lied to the chief prosecutor's office and destroyed documents related to the lease matter.

Before the grand jury, Shively testified that he had directed that changes be made in a competitive "invitation to bid" for the lease.[2] He did so after the governor and a major fundraiser for and supporter of the governor, Joseph "Lenny" Arsenault, met on October 2, 1984, in the governor's office in Juneau. Arsenault was part owner of the Fifth Avenue Center building. Before this meeting, he had requested and received from Sheffield a draft of the not-yet-released competitive bid documents. At the meeting, Arsenault asked that the bid specifications be narrowed so that all potential bidders except the Fifth Avenue Center would be eliminated.

Shipley then took actions that caused the competitive bid process to be scrapped. A direct sole-source negotiation followed that resulted in the Fifth Avenue Center obtaining the lease. Eventually, the lease was canceled after the state attorney general, who the governor had appointed, declared that it was "tainted with favoritism."[3]

The grand jury also concluded that Governor Sheffield lied to it. Its report included nine pages describing what it considered to be false statements by Sheffield. For example, the grand jury found not credible the governor's statement that he had no recollection of the October 2, 1984, meeting with Arsenault. (Sheffield did testify that it was "highly probably that he [Arsenault]was there," adding that he had no "specific recollection of that meeting."[4]) Similarly, the grand jury doubted Sheffield's testimony that he did not specifically recall Arsenault's request to change the bid invitation to benefit his building or that such changes were subsequently directed by Shively. Sheffield also testified that he did not know that Arsenault had received a draft copy of the bid request, which testimony the grand jury disbelieved. Sheffield had added, however, that "I just assume he did."[5]

Before the hearing began, the Rules Committee made several decisions. First, it adopted a definition of "impeachable offenses." Such offenses, it said, encompassed "serious misconduct in office, such as treason, malfeasance, misfeasance, corruption or perjury."[6]

The committee decided that an impeachable offense must be found by "clear and convincing evidence."[7] It determined that it would consider only matters referred to it by the grand jury. It decided that all twenty senators and the governor and his counsel would be invited to participate in the hearings. Because of the magnitude of the interest in the proceeding, the committee authorized that the hearings be covered in their entirety on statewide television. The Rules Committee also decided to hold night sessions so that more people could view the proceedings.

From the beginning, Sam Dash focused on perjury. He concluded that given the state of the evidence, which showed, for example, that the lease was in the public interest, "it would be difficult to prove, by clear and convincing evidence, a violation of the official misconduct statute, or that the Governor violated his Constitutional responsibilities faithfully to execute the State's procurement laws. Impeachment on this charge is thus unlikely."[8]

Lacovara pushed back against the perjury charge, noting that the governor had not denied that the critical October 2, 1984, meeting had occurred. He also challenged the propriety of the grand jury's action in recommending an impeachment proceeding. He argued that the grand jury had gone "beyond its constitutional bounds. . . . The Grand Jury . . . was misled, either deliberately or negligently, about its lawful functions."[9]

This was an interesting argument, given that his friend and fellow Watergate prosecutor George Frampton had advised the grand jury. Moreover, the Watergate grand jury, with which both Phil and George had been involved, had sent a report on the conduct of Nixon and his aides to the House

Judiciary Committee for the Nixon impeachment proceedings. Phil's argument also seemed to me to be somewhat futile because the Senate had been presented with serious allegations with which it now had to deal. In its report, the Senate committee noted with approval the grand jury's power under the Alaska Constitution "to investigate and make recommendations concerning the public welfare or safety," but commented that "the Grand Jury should have been instructed that impeachment is a political process and not a substitute for judicial remedies."[10]

As the hearing proceeded, Sam Dash attempted to build a case for perjury. His examination of witnesses was prosecutorial in tone. Mine was less so. After I had questioned several witnesses, two senators visited me. They were, I believe, leaning against impeachment and were perhaps concerned with Sam's prosecutorial bent. They asked me to assume the task of questioning Governor Sheffield. Even though I thought impeachment unlikely, I declined. I thought the committee should ride the capable horse it had hired.

During twelve days of hearings nine witnesses testified; the printed record of the hearings was over three thoussnad pages. Voluminous grand jury records were received and reviewed. Numerous legal briefs and oral arguments by counsel were considered. The Dash-led committee was thorough in examining the facts.

In the end, the Rules Committee recommended against impeachment. To a large degree this was a recognition of political realities. The Alaska Senate at the time had twenty members. Eleven were Republicans and nine were Democrats. However, the senators often did not vote along party lines. Fourteen votes were needed for impeachment. Because all the Senate had participated in the Rules Committee hearings, the five members of that committee—four of whom were Republicans—had a good notion as to how the Senate would vote on impeachment.

The Rules Committee, bowing to reality, concluded that "it is the opinion of a majority of the Rules Committee that the evidence that an impeachable offense occurred, though substantial, does not rise to the level of 'clear and convincing evidence.' The Rules Committee also believes that sufficient support to approve one or more articles of impeachment is not available in the full Senate."[11]

The committee, however, was critical of the conduct in Sheffield's office, observing that "a lack of a recommendation to impeach the governor should not be interpreted . . . as in any way condoning the standard of behavior that has brought us here." The committee observed that there was lying and destruction of documents in the governor's office. It found "that there was clear failure on the part of the Governor . . . to declare standards of appropriate conduct for his appointees."[12]

The Rules Committee found that the manner in which the lease was awarded was "absolutely unacceptable." It declared, "There is direct evidence that at the Governor's request, a request for proposals was sent to a member of a partnership which was a potential bidder on the . . . lease, giving that bidder a definite competitive advantage over other potential bidders." This, it said, was "clearly contrary to the [applicable] standards and practices for contracting."[13]

Sheffield's lack of credibility received pointed condemnation. The committee found that "the Governor's total lack of memory of a key meeting precipitating [the change to a sole source contract], even after hearing detailed accounts of it by the other participants, raises serious doubts to this credibility."[14]

The committee concluded that "the whole pattern of the Governor's memory lapses is disturbing." It observed that "during his testimony, the Governor exhibited almost verbatim recall of conversations and events that were favorable to him and a substantial lack of recall of events that might reflect upon him unfavorably."[15]

Theese determinations by the committee struck me as practical frontier justice that was not particularly constrained by legal niceties. One Republican member of the committee said that he believed there was "'clear and convincing evidence' that [Sheffield] had lied to the grand jury but that the evidence did not warrant impeachment. 'You don't hang someone for shoplifting.'"[16] Before the hearing, a Democratic senator declared, "I've said there isn't anything there. . . . Somebody made some money, but somebody is always going to make some money. The Governor never hurt anybody. You got to remember that stupidity is not an impeachable crime."[17]

On my last day in Alaska I went flying with a bush pilot named Rick Halford. Rick was also the majority leader of the Alaska Senate. When the Senate was not in session, he made his living flying tourists to Mt. Denali and other scenic Alaskan designations.

We took off in Rick's somewhat antiquated four-seated pontoon plane in the early afternoon. There was a third passenger I will call Joe. For several reasons that I will not relate because they have little to do with this story, I was not fond of Joe. But to exclude him from what promised to be a pleasurable trip would have been selfish, so I acquiesced in his coming along.

We flew north from Juneau to Glacier Bay. On the way I marveled at how devoid of people the landscape below was. Alaska really was an untouched wilderness.

Glacier Bay is a spectacular place. The Fairweather Mountain range rises over fifteen thousand feet directly from the bay. Interspersed among the peaks are ten tidewater glaciers, seven of which thunderously calve blue-tinted icebergs that roil and then float in the bay. We flew low over these icebergs looking for seals and whales.

We then flew east to the Juneau ice fields. These ice fields are larger than Rhode Island. The ice in the valleys is thousands of feet thick and has been there for eons.

We headed south back toward Juneau. We were over a glacier near Juneau when the plane's engine stopped running.

In the army in Germany in 1964, I served in a tactical nuclear battalion. I had flown with an army aviator as we tracked the battalion's convoy, which was transporting weapons from our home base in Kitzingen to the Grafenwoehr training grounds. The army pilot was a cowboy. To scare me he turned off the plane's motor and let the plane fall five hundred feet before starting the engine again.

So, when Rick's engine stopped running, I said, "Rick, are you kidding me?"

For a while, he did not answer. Finally, he said, "I don't know what's wrong, but I'm going to get you in."

What was wrong was this: The plane's gas tank was a bladder in its wing. The cap to this tank had blown off, and the gas had been sucked out of the bladder. The bladder had been sucked up to the underside of the top of the wing, so the fuel gauge did not register that the tank was empty. We were 6,500 feet above a glacier with no gas!

Fortunately, Rick was an expert pilot and his plane had a ten-to-one glide ratio. That is, for every thousand feet it fell, it would glide ten thousand feet.

Fortunately, we were near Juneau. Rick steered the plane in a wide semicircle over Juneau and headed for a body of water called the Gastineau Channel between Juneau and Douglas Island.

I remember two thoughts as we descended. One, because I had confidence in Rick's abilities as a pilot, I became interested in how he was going to land the plane and surprisingly had no fear. My other thought concerned Joe. I remember thinking, "If I am going to die, I really don't want to die with Joe!"

A bridge crosses the Gastineau Channel. Rick steered the plane well and we missed the bridge by about five hundred feet. We landed on the plane's pontoons with a jolt. Then we bobbed up and down on the waters of the channel.

It was a beautiful late summer afternoon in Alaska. Twilight was coming. Salmon were jumping in the tributaries flowing into the channel. Fishing boats passed us going home for the evening as we bobbed gently in the dimming light.

I said to Rick, "Why don't you radio one of these boats to pull us to shore," which was several hundred yards away. "No," he said, handing me one of the paddles he kept on the plane for untoward events. "Let's just paddle the plane to shore."

With some effort, that is what we did. I confess irritation at being made to paddle after the pilot had come close to killing me.

The last thing Rick said to me as we parted after reaching the shore was, "Attorney-client privilege, you don't tell the press about this."

Sorry, Rick, I know something about attorney-client privilege, as chapter 12 of this book demonstrates. The fact that a plane you piloted on a recreational venture crash-landed in Alaskan waters is not protected.

In 2018, I saw Rick again at a congressional hearing in Washington, DC. I approached him and said, "Do you remember me?" He stared at me a moment and then asked, "Were you in that plane?" "You're goddamned right I was," I replied.

The day after our abrupt landing, I flew home to my pregnant wife bearing two small pairs of beaded Native Alaskan moccasins I had purchased for my unborn twins. Mine was a happy ending, but there is a sad postscript to this tale.

In 1992, I was involved in Bill Clinton's presidential campaign. His campaign finance cochair was Vic Raiser, a successful businessman. One day Vic told me that he and his son were off to Alaska on a fishing excursion. I related to Vic my harrowing flying adventure and suggested that he avoid small planes while in Alaska. "No way," he said, "we will be flying every day on small planes to different fishing spots."

Two weeks later, he and his son were dead, having crashed into a mountain.

12

The Foster Notes

Washington, DC, can be a cruel, unforgiving place. It is also a city where investigators can lose their moral compass and ignore time-honored overriding values in the rabid pursuit of their targets. The events set forth in this chapter underscore these observations.

Vince Foster was a splendid fellow. He was tall—6'4"—and handsome as a movie star. He grew up in Hope, Arkansas, where he was friends with Bill Clinton and Mack McLarty, Clinton's first White House chief of staff. Vince was intelligent and well-educated. He graduated from Davidson College (my alma mater) and was first in his class at the University of Arkansas Law School.

At the Rose Law Firm in Little Rock, he was Hillary Clinton's best friend and known as the firm's ethical soul. Many thought he was destined to be the president of the Arkansas Bar. But then he followed the Clintons to Washington to become deputy White House counsel—a fatal mistake.

I came to know Vince in early 1993. I had been counsel for nominations and confirmations for the Clinton transition, which placed me in charge of vetting Clinton's cabinet and White House staff. After Clinton took office, I was asked to lead the vetting of his candidates to replace Byron White on the Supreme Court after he announced his retirement. Vince and others assisted me in that enterprise (which is discussed in chapter 22). We spent hours together vetting Ruth Bader Ginsburg, Stephen Breyer, Bruce Babbit, and other High Court possibilities. In hindsight, I feel like a dunce because I missed the depression that soon would take Vince's life. Vince was excessively taciturn in these sessions. Even though he was the deputy White

House counsel, he deferred to me, letting me conduct the vast majority of the questioning.

Washington was the wrong place for Vince. He hated the press scrutiny and criticism he received. After his death, a handwritten note was discovered ripped up in the bottom of his old leather briefcase. It said in part that he was not meant for the "spotlight of public life in Washington."[1]

The public criticism Vince endured came mainly from the "scandal" involving the White House Travel Office—the office that handles arrangements for members of the press who accompany the president when he travels. The claim was that the Clintons had fired Travel Office staffers and replaced them with cronies. A further assertion was that they had misused the FBI to tar former staffers with allegations of financial improprieties to justify the firings.[2] Vince had been involved in the dismissals.

"Travelgate," as it came to be called, engendered intense press interest. Congressional investigations were likely. Senate minority leader Bob Dole (R-KS) called for an independent counsel. Two *Wall Street Journal* editorials criticized Vince by name for his role. The White House conducted its own investigation and issued a report on the matter, but that did not halt the criticism.

So, on July 11, 1993, a Sunday, at 10:00 in the morning, Vince visited me in my northwest DC home to discuss his and the White House's need for representation in the Travel Office matter. We talked for two hours. I took only three pages of notes on a legal-sized yellow pad in my somewhat large scrawly handwriting.

At the beginning of the conversation, Vince asked, "Jim, is this conversation privileged?"[3] Without much thought, I said "yes." Fortuitously, about the first word in my notes is the word "privileged."

Nine days later, on July 20, 1993, Vince took his life in Fort Marcy Park in northern Virginia, using an old pistol he had inherited from his father. Later that evening, first White House counsel Bernie Nussbaum and then Associate Attorney General Webb Hubbell asked me to represent Vince's family in the investigations that were certain to ensue.[4] Thinking that this assignment, which I initially and largely undertook on a pro bono basis, would be relatively short-lived, I readily agreed. My representation of the Foster family ended eleven years later after many investigations and two Supreme Court arguments.

The first investigation was conducted by the US Park Police, Fort Marcy

Park being under its jurisdiction. Then there were investigations by the FBI, two congressional committees, and two independent counsels, Bob Fiske and Ken Starr. Starr was appointed under the newly revived Independent Counsel Act by a panel of three federal judges after Fiske, who was Attorney General Janet Reno's appointee, already had issued a report on Vince's death. All investigations concluded that Vince's death was a suicide, a conclusion that a cohort of conspiracy theorists refused to accept.

It took Ken Starr three years to issue his report, despite all the work that had been done before. This delay infuriated the Foster family and Clinton loyalists because conspiracy theories asserting that the Clintons had murdered Vince for knowing too much about their various activities continued to swirl.

I gained enormous respect for the Foster family over the course of the investigations and litigations. While their grief was immense, they largely suffered in silence, rejecting many offers to comment to the press or on television about their sadness and the events that caused it. Lisa Foster, Vince's wife, made one exception: she gave an interview in 1995 to the *New Yorker* just before she remarried Arkansas federal district judge James Moody. The interview, I believe, was a form of catharsis, helping her to move on from a horrific event for her and her three children.

But even after the Fiske and Starr reports, there were conspiracy theories that needed to be debunked. So the family dispatched me to sit for a *60 Minutes* interview with Mike Wallace about Vince's death. I approached this with some trepidation. For years I had watched Mike savage people he thought were protecting wrongdoing or lying. I didn't know what Mike's views were about Vince's death and frankly did not trust him to be balanced in his approach.

Consequently, adopting a tactic I have frequently used successfully with the media, I said: "Mike, I will do the interview on camera, but off the record. When it is over, I will tell you if you can use it." At the end of the interview, I concluded that Mike had sought to reach the truth, and I allowed him to broadcast what I said. The piece was fair—that Vince had committed suicide came through; the family was satisfied.

*   *   *

Eventually I was interviewed by members of Starr's team—John Bates, later a federal district judge, and Brett Kavanaugh, now a justice of the Supreme Court. I told them I met with Vince shortly before he died about his and the White House's need for representation in the Travel Office mess, and that I had taken notes. They wanted to see the notes. I said no, they were protected by both attorney-client privilege and the doctrine that protects an attorney's work product.[5]

But that wasn't all Starr's team wanted. Their sweeping requests included all documents regarding conversations I had had with numerous people about Vince and his death, including the president, Hillary Clinton, White House counsel Bernie Nussbaum, and various other White House and government employees. Starr's team wanted other documents I had created or collected about Vince and the Travel Office, the Whitewater affair, and his state of mind before he died.[6] They made these requests even though there was an active grand jury investigation examining Vince's death in which I represented his family. In other words, Starr's team wanted me to be their eyes and ears into the White House on a number of matters. I declined what I considered their outrageously overbroad requests.

One specific request merits mention. Starr's team wanted to see all the documents I had retrieved from Vince's White House office, which included Vince's diary. I agreed to produce the diary without subpoena on one condition—that only Starr would review the diary, which contained personal information. This apparently infuriated Brett, who in a now-released October 25, 1995, internal memorandum to the file, which was uncovered by my friend Ruth Marcus while writing her fine book on Brett, wrote that the condition I imposed was "an implicit attack on my integrity and credibility."[7]

That was not the case. At that stage I knew very little about Brett. Lisa Foster, however, was concerned about leaks from Starr's office. I figured that if only Starr saw the diary, the chances of a leak would be reduced because if there were a leak its source would be certain.

The result of my recalcitrance was that on December 4, 1995—my birthday—grand jury subpoenas arrived for both me and my then law firm, Swidler & Berlin. Predictably, the subpoena sought not only the notes of my conversation with Vince but also hundreds of pages of notes and documents I had created and collected in my representation of the Foster family. Starr did this even though I had provided his team with a detailed legal analysis demonstrating that materials created and collected in representing someone in connection with a grand jury investigation are protected by the work-product doctrine.

My firm and I moved to dismiss the subpoenas. The chief judge of the US District Court for the District of Columbia, John Garrett Penn, ruled for us on every issue. Judge Penn inspected the notes in camera. He found that "Hamilton met with Foster to discuss possible representation of Foster," "that Foster spoke with Hamilton as an attorney and [that] a review of the notes supports that finding." He held that "one of the first notations on the [notes] is the word: 'Privileged,' so it is obvious that the parties, Hamilton and Foster, viewed this as a privileged conversation." He also found that the notes were prepared in anticipation of litigation and "reflect the mental impressions of the lawyer."[8] Judge Penn concluded that both the attorney-client and work-product privileges barred disclosure.

As to the trove of other documents Starr sought, Penn concluded, after reviewing them, that "all of the documents were prepared in anticipation of or with an eye toward litigation."[9] Penn said that "all but the most unsophisticated persons" would know that there would be an investigation into Foster's death.[10] Consequently, the documents were protected by the work-product doctrine.[11]

Showing at least a modicum of good sense, Starr appealed only the notes issue to the D.C. Circuit Court of Appeals. There he made a bright-line argument—that after the client's death, both the attorney-client privilege and work-product protection vanish in criminal (but not civil) proceedings. Kavanaugh argued the case for Starr in that court. After the argument, my law partner Andy Lipps—a fine attorney who later happily left the law to teach math at Washington's Georgetown Day School—said to me, "Jim, you did a good job, but your 12 year old daughter could have won this case." Then I lost it 2-1, which proves, I guess, either that Brett did very well or I should have allowed my daughter to argue.

Judge Stephen Williams wrote the opinion for the court. Judge Pat Wald joined, and Judge David Tatel dissented. I will never be able to understand how Wald, an eminent jurist, joined in an opinion that, as described below, was deeply flawed.

Judge Williams noted that "the parties agree that the communications at issue would be covered by the [attorney-client] privilege if the client were still alive" but concluded that "the client's death calls for a qualification of the privilege."[12] The "qualification" created by the court would permit "post-death use [of otherwise privileged communications] in criminal proceedings" where the prosecutor convinces the trial court that the "relative importance [of the communications] is substantial." The court declared that the prosecutor is entitled to obtain privileged communications that "bear on a significant aspect of the crimes at issue, and an aspect as to which there is a scarcity of reliable evidence."[13]

Judge Williams reasoned that the prospect of postdeath revelation in the criminal context would trouble a client less than in the civil context because after death "criminal liability will have ceased altogether" while civil liability "characteristically continues." The court recognized that a concern for survivors might stir a desire to protect the client's estate from civil liability but did not discuss whether the same concern might foster an interest in protecting the living from criminal penalties. The court also "doubt[ed]" that the client's concerns for postdeath reputation would be "very powerful; and against them the individual may even view history's claims to truth as more deserving." The court added that "to the extent . . . that any post-death restriction of the privilege can be confined to the realm of criminal litigation, we should expect the restriction's chilling effect to fall somewhere between modest and nil."[14]

In other words, Williams was saying that after death the client doesn't care much about his or her reputation or the fate of family or friends in criminal proceedings. Consequently, there would be very little or no effect on client candor if clients know that what they tell their attorneys could be revealed after their death.

This bold conclusion, I submit, is fundamentally at odds with human experience. People are concerned about what happens to their reputations and their families and friends after death. People write wills, establish trusts, buy life insurance and burial plots, invest in their children's education, establish foundations, endow chairs, and write memoirs—actions evincing concern for what happens to the well-being of others and their own reputations following death. Most of us also have family, friends, and associates we would not want to harm before or after our death. To argue that concern for others does not typically extend beyond death is to posit a callous self-centeredness that is inconsistent with common experience.

The court's assumption was particularly misguided as to Vince, who cared deeply about his own reputation and his family and friends. In May 1993, around two months before his death, Vince gave the commencement speech at the University of Arkansas Law School. He counseled the graduates that "there is no victory, no advantage, no fee, no favor which is worth even a blemish on your reputation for intellect and integrity."[15] His well-known note found in his briefcase said, with obvious reference to himself, "in Washington . . . ruining people is considered sport."[16] Both Bob Fiske and Ken Starr, in their reports, concluded that concerns about his reputation, which was under media attack, pushed Vince deeper into the depression that took his life.

Judge Williams's rejection of our work-product claim was even more bizarre. Normally, facts recorded by a lawyer receive heightened work-product protection because those facts reflect the lawyer's focus and process of selection. But this situation was different, Williams said, because "the interview was a preliminary one initiated by the client. Although the lawyer was surely no mere potted palm, one would expect him to have tried to encourage a fairly wide-ranging discourse from the client, so as to be sure that any nascent focus on the lawyer's part did not inhibit the client's disclosures."[17]

Because of William's conclusive presumption that, at this stage, the lawyer "has not sharply focused or weeded the materials," he found that the notes did not deserve the "super-protective envelope" normally afforded opinion work product.[18]

To put this another way, Williams essentially was asserting that, in the initial interview initiated by a client, the attorney is just a passive scribe who doesn't exercise professional judgment in deciding what to write down. I suspect that few, if any, experienced litigators would agree with this wildly uninformed conclusion. Before becoming a judge, Williams had been principally an academic.

His decision was also contrary to the facts before him. As noted, I had a two-hour conversation with Vince but took just three pages of notes. That was because I knew much about the Travel Office saga; I had read many press reports; I had studied and annotated the White House's report about it. What I recorded was selective, at times noting matters I thought should be pursued further. I was hardly a passive scribe. The notes, which the court had, made that plain.

Judge David Tatel, one of the stalwarts of the federal bench, dissented.

While conceding that concern for surviving friends and family or posthumous reputation "may not influence *every* decision to confide potentially damaging information to attorneys," he concluded that "these concerns very well may affect *some* decisions, particularly by the aged, the seriously ill, the suicidal, or those with heightened interests in their posthumous reputations."[19] Judge Tatel argued that after the court's decision such persons will not talk candidly with a lawyer after they received the following advice the court's opinion now requires lawyers to give: "I cannot represent you effectively unless I know everything. I will hold all our conversations in the strictest of confidence. *But when you die, I could be forced to testify—against your interests—in a criminal investigation or trial, even of your friends or family, if the court decides that what you tell me is important to the prosecution.* Now, please tell me the whole story."[20]

In his dissent to the court's refusal to hear the matter en banc, Tatel quoted my oral argument to emphasize that conversations with an attorney might not happen with a client contemplating death, unless the privilege pertained:

> I am not sure of a lot of things in life. I am not certain of why Mr. Foster took his own life, even though I think it's because of the taxing of his reputation and his fear about the trial of this investigation. . . . But I am totally certain, I am totally certain of one thing. . . . If I had not assured Mr. Foster that our conversation was a privileged conversation, we would not have had the conversation and *there would be no notes that are the subject of the situation today* (emphasis added).[21]

In his en banc opinion, Judge Tatel also dissented on the work-product issue. He disagreed with the court's conclusive presumption that attorney notes taken at an initial client interview do not reflect the attorney's mental impressions because there a lawyer does not "sharply focus or weed" the words of a client.[22] Instead, Judge Tatel argued, "lawyers bring their own judgment, experience, and knowledge of the law to conversations with clients." "Whether courts can require production of attorney work product should turn not on the stage of representation or who initiates a meeting, but on whether the attorney's notes are entirely factual, or whether they instead represent the 'opinions, judgment and thought processes of counsel.'"[23]

The notes, Tatel said, demonstrate that Mr. Hamilton "actively exercised his judgment when interviewing his client," because "in two hours, he created only three pages of notes," in which he "underlined certain words, placing both check marks and question marks next to certain sections." Consequently, he concluded, "the notes clearly represent the opinions, judgments, and thought processes of counsel."[24]

After the Court of Appeals for the DC Circuit denied our petition for en banc hearing, we petitioned for a writ of certiorari—that is, for review by the Supreme Court. Wanting to ensure that my firm continued to support this rather expensive endeavor, I entitled the case *Swidler & Berlin and James Hamilton v. United States of America*, rather than putting my name first. My cocounsel for the petition, as he had been in the Court of Appeals, was Robert (Bob) Zener, a brilliant appellate lawyer who, while at the Department of Justice, had argued over one hundred cases in federal courts of appeal. Many of the good ideas we had in this case were Bob's.

To increase the chances that the Supreme Court would exercise its discretion to hear the case, we did something unusual. We enlisted a variety of groups to file amicus curiae—friend of the court—briefs at the certiorari stage. Normally this occurs only after the Supreme Court has taken a case.

Among the various organizations we successfully enticed for amicus help were the American Bar Association, the American College of Trial Lawyers, the American Corporate Counsel Association, and the National Association of Defense Lawyers. Also, at Bob Zener's suggestion, we brought in the National Hospice and Palliative Care Association. Now, why did we do that?

One reason was that the hospice association's support bolstered our argument that the court of appeals' decision discriminated against the dying.

At oral argument I had the feeling that Justice Anthony Kennedy was leaning against our position. While one rarely knows exactly what sways a jurist at oral argument, I may have helped win his vote by this argument:

I think you can think of many hypotheticals where a client might be disinclined to reveal something to an attorney if the client knew that after death it might be revealed to the prosecutor. . . .

Let me just give you a specific one. . . . What if we have a father who is dying, and he wants to consult a lawyer about the criminal drug problems of his child. Now, in this circumstance the dying father will know that as soon as he passes away some prosecutor might be able to get to the information that he has imparted to his lawyer and, in that circumstance, I think that candor would be chilled.[25]

There was another reason we called on the hospice group for an amicus brief. Chief Justice William Rehnquist had recently lost his wife. Before she died, she had been in hospice care. Whether having the hospice association weigh in helped I will never know. I do know that Justice Rehnquist wrote the opinion upholding Vince's privilege.

After the Supreme Court decided to review the case, Starr, in his brief on the merits, returned to his bright-line argument. He did not ask the court to uphold the court of appeals' balancing test as to the attorney-client privilege because there was clear precedent against it. The Supreme Court, in rejecting a balancing test for the privilege, had declared that "an uncertain privilege . . . is little better that no privilege at all," because uncertainty will not promote candor.[26]

Starr also did not attempt to defend Judge Williams's misguided work-product decision. Rather, Starr asked the court to hold that the attorney-client privilege and work-product protection vanish upon the death of the client, and he requested that the court order production of the notes.

This was problematic because, as discussed, the court of appeals had not applied a bright-line test but had established a balancing process for determining whether the notes should be produced. And it remanded to the district court to apply that process. It had not ordered immediate production of the notes.

Starr thus was asking the Supreme Court to amend the judgment of the court of appeals. But that, as Starr should have known because he had been the solicitor general of the United States, he could not properly do unless he had filed a cross-petition for certiorari, which he had not done. In the first page of our reply brief (at Bob Zener's suggestion), we noted Starr's mistake, citing a recent opinion by Justice Ginsburg declaring that an attempt to amend a lower court judgment is improper without a cross-petition.[27]

Now why did we challenge Starr's attempt to amend the judgment? If the Supreme Court decides to amend a judgment, it will do so. We raised the issue to provoke sharp questions to Kavanaugh at oral argument that would distract him from his principal arguments, some of which, gave us heartburn. This gambit worked superbly. During his argument, which was the only argument he ever made before the Supreme Court, Justice Sandra Day O'Connor challenged his position. Then Justices Antonin Scalia, Rehnquist, and Ginsburg had their turn. Brett had to spend a number of minutes scrambling out of the hole he and Starr had dug. That Brett was imprecise about what the lower court had said and done, and about what he was asking the Supreme Court to do, did not help. I quote the following lengthy exchanges (which I have shortened somewhat) to demonstrate his difficulties and the success of our ploy.

JUSTICE O'CONNOR: And while I have you interrupted, how do you characterize the holding of the majority of the panel below that we're reviewing? They seem to adopt some sort of balancing test as applied to a specific case to see whether testimony should be—whether the privilege should be breached and the testimony compelled.

MR. KAVANAUGH: The court of appeals did require that the information be, quote, of relative importance, a standard that they said was plainly met in this case.

JUSTICE O'CONNOR: But it seemed to be some kind of a balancing test applied case by case. Do you support that approach? Is that the rule you suggest that we should apply?

MR. KAVANAUGH: We support that approach, but we also pointed out in our brief that it may be somewhat inconsistent with what this Court has done in cases such as *Branzburg*, where—

JUSTICE O'CONNOR: Yes, I think it is. This Court has rejected a sort of balancing approach. . . .

Well, it sounds like you're not arguing for affirmance of the test articulated by the panel below, but you didn't cross-petition.

MR. KAVANAUGH: We're arguing for affirmance of the judgment and we pointed out an alternative legal standard in support of the judgment below. We are not seeking to enlarge the judgment in any way, Justice O'Connor.

JUSTICE SCALIA: What was the judgment below? Was it that the district court consider the matter and come to a determination, or was it that the material had to be provided?

MR. KAVANAUGH: It reversed and remanded without specific directions as to what was going to happen on remand.

JUSTICE SCALIA: Well, did it tell the district court to apply the weighing test that it enunciated?

MR. KAVANAUGH: It simply said, reversed and remanded for further proceedings consistent with this opinion.

JUSTICE GINSBURG: Where—can you point out the portion of the opinion, because that's blurry in my mind. I don't remember the court of appeals having resolved the issue for the district court

MR. KAVANAUGH: On page 11a of the petition appendix, where the proponent has offered facts supporting a—

CHIEF JUSTICE REHNQUIST: Whereabouts on page 11a are you reading from?

MR. KAVANAUGH: The beginning of the first full paragraph, where the proponent has offered facts supporting a good faith reasonable belief that the materials may qualify for the exception, a standard plainly met here by the Independent Counsel, and the preceding paragraph—

JUSTICE GINSBURG: But what does it say after that? It says, the district court should, in its sound discretion, examine the communications to see whether they in fact do. That's hardly instructing the district court, go ahead and order the disclosure of this material. It says, examine the communications.

MR. KAVANAUGH: Well, we think the communications have to be examined to determine whether they're relevant to our investigation. There may be portions of the notes, again, that have nothing to do with the Travel Office and may be extraneous materials, and that's why the district court in the first instance has to look at it.

JUSTICE GINSBURG: And then the court goes on to say, to the extent that the court finds an interest in confidentiality—the district court—it can take steps to limit access, et cetera, so it's hardly an instruction to the district court to go ahead and order the divulgence of these notes.[28]

Later in Kavanaugh's argument, Justice Ginsburg returned to this topic, and Kavanaugh had to waste more time explaining his dubious position:

JUSTICE GINSBURG: But you're not urging that the law be what the D.C. Circuit—as I understand your position, you say, we think that death ends it, period. The D.C. Circuit said there's some kind of balancing.

Do I understand you correctly to say, we think the D.C. Circuit was wrong, but we'll take that as second best, so that your position is, death ends the privilege?

MR. KAVANAUGH: We don't think the D.C. Circuit was wrong. We do think the D.C. Circuit's articulation of the phrase, relative importance, has some inconsistency with what this Court has stated in cases such as *Branzburg*—

JUSTICE GINSBURG: Well, what is your first position, then? Is your first position is, death ends it, or is it—is it—

MR. KAVANAUGH: That is our first position. Our second position, alternative positions is that relative importance is a standard that we would be happy with.[29]

Starr and Kavanaugh expounded one argument that was particularly troubling for us. It went something like this.

Consider a defendant on trial for murder. He learns that a deceased client confessed committing the crime to his attorneys. The attorney says the conversation is privileged and refuses to reveal its contents. Under the Due Process Clause of the Fifth Amendment to the Constitution that guarantees a fair trial, the current defendant should have a right to break the privilege and learn what the deceased client had to say because the constitutional fair trial right outweighs the attorney-client privilege, which is only a common law right. To argue that the attorney-client privilege is absolute in that context would result in extreme unfairness to the criminal defendant, and a violation of his constitutional right to due process. And if this is so, Starr continued, a grand jury's constitutional right to evidence under the Fifth Amendment also outweighs this common-law attorney-client privilege.

That was not a bad argument. And there actually was an Arizona case where the state supreme court had refused to break the privilege in a similar context.[30]

So we had a conundrum. To assert that the privilege was absolute in the criminal defendant situation would allow the possibility of extreme unfairness down the road. But to admit that the privilege was not absolute in this circumstance could open the door to its relaxation in the grand jury context.

Bob Zener and I debated for several weeks how to respond to Starr's argument. We finally decided to concede that, despite the transcendent interests the attorney-client privilege serves, some rare circumstance might arise where applying it after a client's death would unconstitutionally disadvantage a criminal defendant. But, we said, that is not the issue here, and the court need not and should not decide it. Here we deal not with a defendant's right to evidence but rather with a prosecutor's attempt to gain information, and the law treats prosecutors and defendants differently.

There is, we argued, no principle equalizing the rights of grand juries and defendants to obtain evidence. Defendants have a due process right to obtain material exculpatory evidence the government possesses.[31] Prosecutors have no right to force incriminating testimony from defendants, and the Federal Rules of Criminal Procedure further limit prosecutors' pretrial discovery rights. Defendants have a right to exclude evidence prosecutors obtain illegally; prosecutors have no comparable right to exclude a defendant's evidence. Defendants have a special Sixth Amendment right to confront and cross-examine. Prosecutors, however, may obtain a court order immunizing a witness claiming a Fifth Amendment privilege, an investigative technique defendants do not enjoy. Given these diverse rights, we argued, there should be different rules for breaching the attorney-client privilege for prosecutors and defendants.

Our concession and argument, I believe, helped us win the case and saved us from being stuck in a position that was just too rigid and raised the possibility of unconstitutional harm to some putative defendant. When Kavanaugh sought to raise the potential unconstitutional harm to a defendant at oral argument, Justice Ginsburg observed that opposing counsel had conceded this point, and Brett should "curtail" his argument to the one I made for the privilege.[32] The court's majority opinion in a footnote noted our concession that in exceptional circumstances a criminal defendant's constitutional right might warrant breaching the privilege, but said: "We do not, however, need to reach this issue, since such exceptional circumstances clearly are not presented here."[33] The three dissenters (O'Connor, Scalia, and Thomas) thought we had given away the store by conceding that the privilege was not absolute but in some circumstances might be subject to balancing.

The Supreme Court issued its decision on June 3, 1998. Shortly before it came down, I received a phone call from a producer at ABC's *This Week*,

Cokie Roberts and Sam Donaldson's Sunday morning talk show. She said, "Mr. Hamilton, Sam and Cokie would like you on their show this Sunday—if you lose." Fortunately, my appearance was not needed.

The Supreme Court ruled that the privilege survived death.[34] It said:

> We think there are weighty reasons that counsel in favor of posthumous application. Knowing that communications will remain confidential even after death encourages the client to communicate fully and frankly with counsel. While the fear of disclosure, and the consequent withholding of information from counsel, may be reduced if disclosure is limited to posthumous disclosure in a criminal context, it seems unreasonable to assume that it vanishes altogether. Clients may be concerned about reputation, civil liability, or possible harm to friends or family. Posthumous disclosure of such communications may be as feared as disclosure during the client's lifetime.[35]

The Court added, "In the case at hand, it seems quite plausible that Foster, perhaps already contemplating suicide, may not have sought legal advice from Hamilton if he had not been assured the conversation was privileged."[36] My notes remained protected by the privilege.

The dissent agreed with the court of appeals' balancing process, not with Starr's bright-line position. But it rejected Williams's initial client interview theory, instead concluding that the work-product doctrine is inapplicable where this client is no longer a potential party to adversarial litigation. This latter conclusion overlooked the seemingly well-settled doctrine, which we had cited, that work-product protection can be asserted by the lawyer as well as by the client.[37]

Several postscripts to the Foster story are worthy of mention:

- After the Supreme Court's decision was issued, as I told the media, I received a "very gracious" phone call from Kavanaugh. Not to be a sore winner, I said, "Brett is a lawyer of great competence. He will be a force in this town for some time to come."[38] I was prophetic in ways I could not then have imagined.
- Starr recently published a book entitled *Contempt* about his inves-

tigations of the Clintons and Vince's death. His title signifies what he perceived to be the Clintons' contempt for our system of justice. It also calls to mind his extremely negative feelings toward the Clintons. Although his investigation of Vince's death and involvement in the Travel Office affair are recounted in great detail in his book, he fails to mention his efforts to obtain the notes and his loss in the Supreme Court. Perhaps he belatedly realized that, had he won the case, the profession, clients, and the rule of law would have suffered.

- I am often asked why, given that a lawyer who represents himself has a fool for a client, I argued the Foster case myself. Four reasons: 1) The Foster family wanted me to do so. 2) My firm did also, in part to avoid the expense of outside counsel. 3) Because only Vince and I participated in the conversation at issue, no one could persuasively challenge my appropriately limited description of what occurred. 4) Most important, I wanted to argue the case, which had enormous ramifications.

- Even in the saddest of events, humor may break through. A Mike Peters cartoon in the *Dayton Daily News Tribune* pictured a lawyer and a client. The client asks, "Is there any way to keep our lawyer-client relationship confidential?" The lawyer replies, "Marry me."[39]

- The day the decision came down, Vince's elegant sister, Shelia Anthony, sent me a poignant handwritten note, which I framed and keep in my office. It said: "Heartiest congratulations! Wherever he is, I know Vince is smiling too."

Listening to a witness at the Senate Watergate Committee hearing with committee members.

At the Senate Watergate Committee table with Senators Ervin, Baker, and Weicker.

Making a point to Senate Watergate Committee chair Sam Ervin and Chief Counsel Sam Dash.

With Senator Herman Talmadge on the first day of the Senate Ethics Committee's hearing into his financial affairs. AP Photo/Charles Harrity.

A Pat Oliphant cartoon after the Senate denounced Senator Herman Talmadge. The genesis of the cartoon apparently was a front-page Washington Post photo of Talmadge and me laughing on a walk back to Talmadge's office after the Senate action. Patrick Oliphant/Artists Rights Society, New York.

With Marina Oswald when she appeared before the House Select Committee on Assassinations. AP Photo/John Duricka.

With Senator Dave Durenberger during the Senate Ethics Committee's hearing into his financial conduct. Library of Congress.

With Senator Dennis DeConcini during the Senate Ethics Committee's Keating Five hearings. Library of Congress.

Arguing Senator Dennis DeConcini's case to the Senate Ethics Committee in the Keating Five case. Library of Congress.

Kristina and I with Governor Bill Clinton the night he was nominated for president by the Democratic National Convention.

My family and President Clinton's family at a White House Christmas party.

In the Oval Office with President Clinton, soon-to-be Supreme Court justice Stephen Breyer, and members of my team that vetted him.

With DNC chair Don Fowler at the Senate hearing into President Clinton's reelection fund-raising activities. Courtesy Library of Congress.

My son William and I with the Clintons, Wimbledon and US Open champion Stan Smith, his family, and US Davis Cup captain Donald Dell after a morning on the White House tennis court.

At the table to Al Gore's right the night he chose Joe Lieberman as his running mate. Also pictured: Warren Christopher, Bill Daley, and Ron Klain.

President Clinton's Foreign Intelligence Advisory Board. In the photograph are Chair Tom Foley, Vice Chair Warren Rudman, Admiral Bud Zumwalt, and Zoë Baird.

A Mike Peters cartoon before the Supreme Court decided the Foster Notes case. © Mike Peters 1996 King Features Syndicate, Inc.

Nina Totenberg interviewing me in front of the Supreme Court after my argument in the Foster Notes case. Associated Press/Wide World Photos.

Kristina and I with Queen Elizabeth, Prince Philip, Ambassador Phil Lader, and his wife, Linda.

Leaving the courthouse with Bob Novak after his testimony in the Scooter Libby trial. AP Photo/Pablo Martinez Monsivais.

Kristina and I with Vice President Biden and Dr. Jill Biden at a USO function at the vice president's mansion.

13

The Foster Photographs

A free press is one of the most important American inventions. We count on the press to ferret out corruption and other shortcomings in government and society. But the press, in its constant pursuit of information, at times overlooks the truth that certain aspects of human affairs should be kept from public scrutiny. Matters of national security. Grand jury materials. Information protected by the attorney-client, doctor-patient and spousal privileges. And, as this chapter illustrates, items whose release would constitute a serious invasion of personal privacy, which is a right of consummate importance that must be vigilantly protected in an internet world.

Alan Favish was a conspiracy theorist. Even though numerous separate investigations had concluded that Vince Foster died of a self-inflicted gunshot wound, Favish believed they got it wrong. He saw misconduct in the investigations and suggested there was a grand conspiracy to hide the truth among the Clintons, who he apparently suspected of having some role in Vince's death, and the investigators, presumably including independent counsel Ken Starr, the Clintons' nemesis. Given his fantastical views, it was fitting that he resided in Tarzana, California.

The US Park Police conducted the initial investigation into Vince's death because he had died in Fort Marcy Park, a federal facility in northern Virginia just south of Washington, DC. The Park Police took color photographs of the death scene, including ten photographs of Vince's body. The Park Police concluded that his death was a suicide by a revolver gunshot.

Subsequently, there were *five* more investigations—by the FBI, by Senate and House committees, and by two independent counsels, Robert Fiske and Starr. Each of those investigations reached the same conclusion: that Vince had taken his own life.

Favish believed these multiple investigations were "grossly incomplete and untrustworthy."[1] He requested 150 Foster death scene photographs from the Office of Independent Counsel (OIC)—that is, Ken Starr's office—pursuant to the Freedom of Information Act (FOIA). OIC rejected this request under FOIA exemption 7(C) which protects "information compiled for law enforcement purposes . . . [that] could reasonably be expected to constitute an unwarranted invasion of privacy."[2] Ultimately, Favish received all the photos requested, except those of Vince's body and one photo of his eyeglasses. Favish sued to obtain the rest in a federal district court in California.

The court initially rejected his suit. It held that Foster family members had a privacy interest that would be violated by release of the photos. That interest, the court concluded, outweighed whatever public interest there was in the release of the photos, except as to the photo of Vince's glasses, which the judge ordered released.

Favish appealed and received a better result from the Ninth Circuit Court of Appeals. That court agreed that the family's privacy interests had to be balanced against whatever public interest disclosure would serve. But the court remanded the case so the district judge could examine the photographs to see if they were "graphic, explicit, and extremely upsetting," declaring that "balancing without a knowledge of what the photos show would be an exercise in the air."[3] The court noted that, to prevail, the FOIA did not require Favish to show "knowledge of misfeasance by the agency" involved.[4]

On remand, the district court, as instructed, looked at the photographs. It then ordered five photographs released, withholding the other five because they were "so explicit" that they could not be released without "clearly violat[ing] the privacy of the survivors."[5]

The release of the five photographs horrified the Foster family. Their distress was vividly and poignantly described in declarations submitted by Vince's sister, Shelia Foster Anthony, and his widow, Lisa Foster Moody.

Shelia's declaration deserves quoting at length.

Our family has suffered a great loss under extremely tragic circumstances, compounded by the barrage of newspaper, magazine, and Internet articles, books and television programs and reports that followed
Vince's death. An intensely private matter drew national attention.
Reporters, as well as simply curious individuals, harassed my grieving
family in unbelievably insensitive ways. Conspiracy theorists imagined
and caused to be printed and published all sorts of wild and unsubstan-
tiated stories, alleging murder, treason, Swiss Bank accounts, high-level
and widespread cover-up of government wrongdoing, and other such
ravings. Political and commercial opportunists used Vince's death to
publish films and articles through media of tabloids, video, and on the
Internet to speculate about and sensationalize his tragic suicide and to
profit from it. . . . My now 86 year old mother and my sister received
middle-of-the-night calls from authors pretending to be Vince's friend
and seeking any personal tidbit of information about Vince from them.
We found flowers on his grave with handwritten notes from strangers
asserting that he had been murdered. I was sent a book authored by
a conspiracy theorist who stated that Vince had been murdered and
warned that my life could be in danger.

Our family was horrified and devastated by the photograph leaked
to the press and published on a national television network and in
newspapers of Vince's dear dead hand holding the gun he used to kill
himself. That photograph has been shown in national media again and
again, and every time I see it have nightmares and heart-pounding in-
somnia as I visualize how he must have spent his last few minutes and
seconds of his life. My mother has suffered unimaginable sorrow and
depression in losing her only son, but her grief (and ours) has been
compounded by the fear that she will see upsetting reports about him
on her television set or see headlines and photographs in the tabloids
on the grocery stores racks where she shops.

Undoubtedly, the photographs would be placed on the Internet for
world consumption. . . . I cannot adequately express how truly unjust,
unfair and cruel it would be to subject my family to more public scrutiny and the dissemination of these photographs via the Internet or by
other print and electronic media. Although I have struggled to read the
description of the photographs at issue here, I could not bring myself to
view them. The horror of actually seeing Vince's dead body and bloody

face and shirt would undoubtedly cause me extreme mental anguish. No member of my family should ever be concerned with the possible exposure of photographs of this nature.[6]

Vince's widow, Lisa, was similarly distressed:

I did not even open Vince's casket for fear of seeing him distorted by the autopsy. I surely cannot bear seeing him lying on the ground in Fort Marcy Park with blood stains on him, coupled with the indignity of the whole world's viewing these pictures in tabloids or on the Internet. My understanding of the photographs is that all of them would be extremely upsetting to the family and cause us no end of pain and sorrow. The shock of seeing the picture of Vince on the television with the gun in his hand is still a horrifying memory for me.[7]

Despite the vivid protestations of the Foster family, the Ninth Circuit confirmed most of the district court's holding. But it did so in a two-line unpublished opinion that released only four of the photographs, withholding one photograph of Vince's body that it apparently believed was too "graphic, explicit, and extremely upsetting" to be released.[8] The Foster family could not tolerate this extremely upsetting result and proceeded to seek Supreme Court review.

On its face, the case for Supreme Court review was strong. Nonetheless, the Foster family took steps beyond the ordinary to ensure that the Supreme Court would take this case.

Normally, the Supreme Court will consider reviewing a case where the opinion below conflicts with those from other circuit courts of appeal. That was manifestly the situation here.

One issue was what kind of preliminary showing a FOIA requester must make to overcome privacy concerns where the claim was (as in the Foster case) that an agency had engaged in misconduct. Several circuits had held that "compelling" evidence of government misconduct must be submitted. In contrast, in the Foster case the Ninth Circuit held that a requester is not required to present evidence of agency misfeasance and that a court is not required to assess any such evidence that is offered.[9]

A second issue was whether the requester must show a nexus between the claimed public interest and the specific records sought, as other circuits had required. The Ninth Circuit's failure to require such a nexus was particularly glaring in this case because Favish claimed public interest focused on alleged inconsistencies in different accounts of Foster's gunshot exit wounds. While the Ninth Circuit decided to release only photographs it found *not* to be "graphic, explicit, and extremely disturbing," it failed to explain how such photographs would resolve the alleged inconsistencies in the various accounts of his wound.[10]

A third issue was whether law enforcement records must be "graphic, explicit, and extremely upsetting" to implicate privacy interests. The Ninth Circuit stood alone in holding that records not meeting this test did not warrant privacy protection.

Moreover and uniquely, the Ninth Circuit's opinion was in *direct conflict* with a Court of Appeals for the District of Columbia Circuit case that had rejected access to the *same photographs*.

Prior to bringing his own action, Favish had been counsel to an organization in FOIA litigation in the District of Columbia seeking to obtain these death-scene photographs. In that case, *Accuracy in Media, Inc. v. National Park Services*, the District of Columbia Circuit unanimously affirmed the district court's denial of the FOIA request.[11] First, the circuit court held that

> protected privacy interests do extend beyond the interests of a document's subject while alive . . . obviously AIM [Accuracy in Media Inc.] cannot deny the powerful sense of invasion bound to be aroused in close survivors by wanton publication of gruesome details of death by violence. . . . While law enforcement sometimes necessitates the display of such ghoulish materials, there seems nothing unnatural in saying that the interest asserted against it by spouse, parents and children of the deceased is one of privacy—even though the holders of the interest are distinct from the individual portrayed.[12]

The court also examined whether "AIM has met the 'balancing' test under [Exemption] 7(C) by advancing 'compelling evidence' of illegal government activity and of the need for the photos to confirm or refute that evidence." AIM proffered evidence about "known contradictions in the published materials" as "adequate evidence of government foul play," but the DC Circuit found this evidence to be "considerably below the threshold" needed. "When multiple agencies and personnel converge on a complex scene and offer their hurried assessments of details, some variation among all of the reports is hardly so shocking as to suggest illegality or deliberate government falsification."[13]

Despite their powerful arguments for Supreme Court review, the Foster family recognized that such review was not a certainty. The court takes only a handful of the multitude of cases presented to it for review each year. Also, the Ninth Circuit's second opinion—the one actually granting release of the four photographs—was only a two-line unpublished opinion that gave us little to critique. So, what to do to enhance the chances of Supreme Court consideration?

While the Supreme Court reviews few cases offered to it, it takes many cases where the US solicitor general seeks review. The government was a losing party in the Foster case, having opposed the release of any of the photographs. So, our goal was to convince the Office of the Solicitor General that this was a case that merited Supreme Court examination.

We went about this in two ways. I met several times with members of the office—including with Deputy Solicitor General Ed Needler—to convince the office also to petition for certiorari—that is, for review. Needler was a career government lawyer with vast experience in arguing before the Court and a superb reputation as an advocate. We knew that his views would carry considerable weight.

Shelia Anthony, Vince's sister, took her own actions. Shelia had been a prominent government official—an assistant attorney general and a member of the Federal Trade Commission. She was respected and well-liked by both Democrats and Republicans. She approached a friend, Bill Webster, about assistance. Webster had been the head of both the FBI and CIA during Republican administrations as well as a federal circuit court judge. Shelia asked Webster to visit with Solicitor General Ted Olson to make the case for Supreme Court review.

In the end, the Office of the Solicitor General did seek review, as did Favish, who wanted more photographs than the Ninth Circuit had given him. The Supreme Court decided to hear the case. For the moment the Foster family could breathe easier.

We thought there was a significant possibility that the Supreme Court would find that survivors had privacy interests that warranted protection. Lower courts already had recognized the privacy interests of surviving family members under another FOIA exemption. In 1991, for example, a federal district court had upheld NASA's refusal to divulge a voice recording of the *Challenger* astronauts' final seconds before their spacecraft exploded, finding that "*how* the astronauts said what they did, the very sound of the astronauts' words, does constitute a privacy interest."[14] Another court withheld the autopsy photographs of President John F. Kennedy on similar privacy grounds.[15]

Nonetheless, we undertook to argue that not only the law but also long-standing traditions supported the family's right to object to release of the death-scene photographs. A death in the family is, we contended, a supremely important family event. The moments surrounding death typically are reserved for close family whenever possible. Even after death, both law and long-standing tradition recognize that the family has a right to the body in order to give it a private burial or other leave-taking consonant with the family's beliefs and traditions. Any conduct that puts the body on public display without the family's consent has been regarded as highly offensive since the origins of our civilization.

To make that point, we referenced *The Iliad*, which declares that after Achilles kills Hector in battle, he drags Hector's body in the dirt and leaves it on public display. Achilles is then told that "the gods frown" on his conduct and that Zeus is "angered," and so he returns Hector's body to his father for funeral rites according to the customs of Troy.[16]

We argued that publication of the photographs of Vince's body would be the modern-day equivalent of putting his body on display. To underscore this, we quoted the DC Circuit's opinion in the AIM case: "One has only to think of Lindbergh's rage at the photographer who pried open the coffin of his kidnapped son to photograph the remains and peddle the resulting photos."[17]

There was considerable interest in the Foster case, particularly among the media as demonstrated by those filing amicus (friend of the court) briefs. Teresa Earnhardt (widow of famous race-car driver Dale Earnhardt, who was killed during the Daytona 500 in 2001) supported the Foster family. Among the amici supporting Favish were the Reporters Committee for Freedom of the Press, American Society of Newspaper Editors, Radio-Television News Directors Association, Society of Professional Journalists, Association of Alternative Newsweeklies, National Press Club, Investigative Reporters and Editors, Inc., and National Freedom of Information Coalition. (I have on occasion been astounded and disturbed at how the media's insatiable drive for information blinds them to legitimate privacy concerns.) The media became the Foster family's most formidable adversaries.

Favish and his media coalition argued that Foster's widow and sister lacked a privacy interest in the photographs, contending that:

- Exemption 7(C)'s "personal privacy" exception relates only to one's own person and thus did not survive Mr. Foster's death;
- A family's right to privacy in the images of the body of a deceased family member did not exist at common law;
- Foster's surviving family had a "diminished" privacy interest since he was a public official who committed suicide during a high-profile political controversy; and
- Withholding Foster's death-scene photographs pursuant to a family privacy interest would create a slippery slope where the family privacy interest could evolve into broad general protection for survivors that would prevent disclosure of damaging revelations about a deceased.[18]

I argued the case with Patty Millet, then a lawyer in the Office of the Solicitor General. Patty is a brilliant constitutional lawyer. (Afterward, when she was in private practice, I called upon her to help me vet a prospective Supreme Court nominee, who was not chosen.) Patty is now on the DC Court of Appeals, appointed by President Barack Obama. At oral argument, Patty focused on the appropriate test to determine whether the FOIA exemption at issue should apply—that is, what type of showing a FOIA requester must make to overcome privacy interests. Her rebuttal argument, which met all the basic points the justices had raised, was one of the best I have ever heard.

For my part, I did something highly unusual in the Supreme Court. With both Shelia Anthony and Lisa Foster Moody in the audience, I essentially made a jury argument to the court. I homed in on why the privacy interests of survivors should be recognized and particularly why the privacy of the Foster family should be protected. Emphasizing the distress the family had been subjected to and the further suffering that would occur if any death-scene photographs were released, I offered this comment: "It has been 10 years and it is time to give this family some peace."[19]

I did, however, make a misstep. Before arguing, counsel received instructions from the clerk of court, General William Suter, an imposing fellow, who appeared austere in his morning coat but who treated lawyers with benevolence. The general often advised counsel not to make jokes during oral argument; jokes could waste time and could be misunderstood, particularly by persons reading a transcript.

I didn't follow this sage advice. When Justice Antonin Scalia asked about the claim by "conspiracy theorists" that "this conspiracy is so widespread," I responded that "it is a difficult argument to make that . . . Starr conspired with members of the Clinton administration to protect that administration."[20]

That response drew laughter, but it also provoked Justice Scalia, who perhaps saw humor as his personal turf. Scalia responded: "He might have been protecting Newt Gingrich. Did you ever think of that?"

Somewhat confused, I said, "I beg your pardon?"

Scalia persisted: "Mr. Starr might have been protecting Newt Gingrich. We really . . . we really don't know."[21]

Scalia achieved the desired laughter. Before I could respond to his bizarre and inane remark, Justice Anthony Kennedy, likely realizing that my time was being wasted, interrupted with a more pertinent and serious question.

The Supreme Court, in an opinion by Justice Kennedy, disagreed with all of Favish's arguments, condemning his "cramped" interpretation of Exemption 7(C).[22] It held explicitly that survivors have a right of privacy under the FOIA: "To say that the concept of personal privacy must 'encompass' the individual's control of information about himself does not mean it cannot encompass other personal privacy interests as well."[23]

The Court's conclusion was based on the "well-established cultural tradition" of a "family's control over the body and death images of the deceased [that] has long been recognized at common law." The court observed that "burial rites or their counterparts have been respected in almost all civilizations from time immemorial."[24] Justice Kennedy wrote:

The power of Sophocles' story in Antigone maintains its hold to this day because of the universal acceptance of the heroine's right to insist on respect for the body of her brother. See Antigone of Sophocles, 8 Harvard Classics: Nine Greek Dramas 255 (C. Eliot ed. 1909). The outrage at seeing the bodies of American soldiers mutilated and dragged through the streets is but a modern instance of the same understanding of the interests decent people have for those whom they have lost. Family members have a personal stake in honoring and mourning their dead and objecting to unwarranted public exploitation that, by intruding upon their own grief, tends to degrade the rites and respect they seek to accord to the deceased person who was once their own.[25]

The Court noted that "child molesters, rapists, murderers, and other violent criminals often make FOIA requests for autopsies, photographs, and records of their deceased victims. . . . Our holding ensures that the privacy interests of surviving family members would allow the Government to deny these gruesome requests in appropriate cases."[26]

The Court said that in determining whether a FOIA disclosure would be an "unwarranted" invasion of privacy violative of Exemption 7(C), "the exemption requires the person requesting the information to establish a sufficient reason for the disclosure." Requiring a FOIA requester to justify a request was unusual because such supplicants normally are not required to provide any justification as to why they request particular information. However, the Court determined that to "give practical meaning to [Exemption 7(C)], the usual rule that the citizen need not offer a reason for requesting the information must be inapplicable."[27]

Because Favish had asserted governmental negligence as his public interest justification, the Court required a more specific showing from him. It found, however, that Favish's conclusory assertions of governmental ineptitude lacked support. "Favish has not produced any evidence that would warrant a belief by a reasonable person that the alleged Government impropriety might have occurred to put the balance into play."[28] Because Favish had failed to assert a cognizable public interest, the Court did not need to balance the public's interest in the alleged misconduct against the Foster family's privacy interest.

Since the Favish case, lower federal courts have recognized that survivors have a right of privacy under the FOIA, the common law, and even the US Constitution.[29] This is a welcome result in this age of mass shootings such as those in Sandy Hook, Connecticut; Charleston, South Carolina; Parkland, Florida; San Bernardino, California; Las Vegas, Nevada; and too many other places to mention. It may be that, in those horrific situations federal authorities have obtained extensive photographs of the many slain bodies left by the gunmen involved. Presumably, family members of those victims would want such photographs of their loved ones protected from public view. And it is reasonable to assume that members of the media, or others with ghoulish interests, would want to obtain those photographs using the FOIA and if successful, pictures of corpses would soon be in tabloids or on some internet site dedicated to portraying death. The Favish opinion stands as a salutary bulwark against this kind of intrusion on family privacy.

14

The Clinton Impeachment

First, a few words to put this chapter in context.

I met Bill Clinton in the mid-1980s at a Renaissance Weekend event in Hilton Head, South Carolina.[1] All who heard his first speech to that group believed that, if political stars aligned, he could someday be president. When he was governor of Arkansas I visited Little Rock to advise him and a commission reviewing state ethics in government laws. (At the time, Arkansas legislators could be paid as lobbyists to lean on their peers in the legislature, a situation I thought, to say the least, was problematic.). Bill and Hillary hosted me at the governor's mansion.

I worked on Clinton's presidential campaign and attended the Democratic National Convention in New York in the summer of 1992. The night of his nomination, Kristina and I went to a party he and Hillary gave for their friends and family in the hotel where we all were staying.[2] Clinton had been nominated earlier that evening by New York governor Mario Cuomo in one of the finest political speeches I had then heard. Four years before, Clinton had bombed and lost the audience in his too-long nomination speech for Massachusetts governor Michael Dukakis. So I said to Clinton, "I have a line for your acceptance speech tomorrow: 'Last night Governor Cuomo taught me how to give a nomination speech.'" Clinton used it.

As discussed elsewhere in this book, I ran the vetting operations for Clinton's cabinet, White House staff, and Supreme Court candidates. He also appointed me to the President's Foreign Intelligence Advisory Board, which oversees the nation's various intelligence agencies. Clinton was a friend, although not an intimate one. I had great admiration for his intellectual capacity, empathy for the disadvantaged, and political and rhetorical skills. But other traits, which were not as laudable, became known.

In the fall of 1998, the House Judiciary Committee, armed with Ken Starr's inflammatory report about Clinton's relationship with intern Monica Lewinsky, began hearings into whether Clinton should be impeached for perjury, obstruction of justice, or abuse of power. Clinton's legal defense team presented his case to the committee on November 8–9, 1998.

Around ten days before those sessions began I was called by one of the president's counsel, Greg Craig. Greg asked me to testify in Clinton's defense. Given my Watergate experience, he wanted me to expound on why Clinton's conduct was not comparable to that of President Richard Nixon, who would have been impeached by the House had he not resigned.

Greg's call gave me some pause. I did not believe Clinton should be impeached, for reasons explained below. I also thought that, on balance, he was performing well as president. And as said, he was a friend—I wanted to help. But I also believed his conduct at issue was both legally and morally repugnant.

After thinking about Greg's request for a moment, I said in substance: "Greg, I will testify for Clinton, so long as I am free to say what I think about the situation." Greg agreed, and I set about preparing my testimony in the few short days before the hearing.[3]

The committee considered four articles of impeachment that alleged

- perjury in the grand jury about Clinton's sexual relations with Monica Lewinsky and related matters;
- perjury in the Paula Jones federal sexual harassment action about the same topics;
- obstruction of justice related to both the Paula Jones case and the grand jury investigation;
- abuse of power concerning lies about Lewinsky to the public, his cabinet, and his staff, as well as his recalcitrance in his dealings with the grand jury and the committee itself.

I gave my testimony to the committee on December 8. Before I did, I offered Greg the opportunity to read what I was going to say. I wanted him to be aware that I intended sharply to criticize the president's conduct. Somewhat to my surprise, he declined. In retrospect, I believe he expected that I was not going to pull any punches.

I remember being quite calm as I sat before the committee waiting to testify. That calmness was born of the recognition that my testimony would change few, if any, minds. Lindsey Graham (R-SC), then a young congressman but nevertheless a leading proponent of Clinton's impeachment, was positioned on the bottom row of the committee's dais, just a few feet in front of me. My recollection is that Graham paid scant attention to anything I had to say; he certainly asked me no questions during the spirited question-and-answer session that followed my testimony. Nonetheless, I thought it important to elucidate the basic standards for impeachment and why Clinton's conduct did not warrant that harsh result.

The Constitution states that a president may be impeached for "high crimes and misdemeanors." To Founder George Mason, who proposed that phase, it meant "great and dangerous offenses" against the state that amounted to "attempts to subvert the Constitution."[4]

As I told the committee:

The notion of "great and dangerous offenses" against the state captures the essence of what an impeachable offense should be. It must, as Alexander Hamilton said, "relate chiefly to injuries done to the society itself." A President should not be impeached to subject him to *punishment*, but rather to *protect* the state and society against "great and dangerous offenses" that might reoccur if he is allowed to remain in office.[5]

This last point demands emphasis. Impeachment is not designed to punish but rather to protect the nation against future crimes harmful to the nation.

I focused much of my testimony on Clinton's alleged perjury, which was the crux of the charges against him and was troubling. This was my take on Clinton's conduct:

Lying about private consensual sexual conduct seems more appropriately designated a low crime rather than a high crime. While reprehensible, it is not a "great and dangerous offense" against the state that demonstrates the necessity of removing the President from office to protect the nation from further abuses.

I readily concede that lies under oath about treason, bribery, the break-in at the DNC, or national security matters could be high crimes and thus impeachable, but the conduct at issue seems of a different character.[6]

To make the telling comparison between Nixon's and Clinton's conduct, I focused on the abuse of power allegations in Article II of the impeachment resolution against President Nixon that caused the Judiciary Committee to vote 28-10 to impeach him. The committee determined to impeach Nixon for essentially the following five abuses of power:

- Causing the Internal Revenue Service to audit and investigate Nixon enemies for Nixon's political advantage.
- Causing the FBI and the Secret Service to engage in unlawful wiretaps for Nixon's political advantage.
- Maintaining a secret investigation unit—the Plumbers—that, using CIA resources and campaign contributions, engaged in various unlawful covert activities, including the break-in of the office of Daniel Ellsberg's psychiatrist.
- Allowing conduct—for example, the payment of hush money—that impeded the investigations of the break-in of the DNC headquarters and the ensuing cover-up.
- Unlawfully interfering with the FBI, the Department of Justice's Criminal Division, the Watergate Special Prosecutor's Office, and the CIA for Nixon's political advantage, including his firing of Special Prosecutor Cox and attempts to abolish the Special Prosecutor's Office to stymie its investigations.

This conduct, I argued, constituted "great and dangerous offenses" demonstrating that Nixon was a danger to the nation. What Clinton had done, although "reprehensible"—and I used that term several times—did not reach that level of threat to the nation.

I concluded my prepared remarks with this statement:

Mr. Chairman, because this nation requires a strong, secure presidency, this Committee and Congress should be chary of making impeachment too easy. Long ago in 1691, Solicitor General, later Lord Chancellor,

Somers told the British Parliament that "the power of impeachment ought to be, like Goliath's sword, kept in the temple, and not used but on great occasions."

In a similar vein, Justice Joseph Story wrote that impeachment is "intended for occasional and extraordinary cases, where a superior power, acting for the whole people, is put into operation to protect their rights, and to rescue their liberties from violation.

Mr. Chairman, we must guard against turning our system into a parliamentary one where a national election can be negated by a legislative no confidence vote.[7]

In my responses to the committee's questions, I adhered to the same theme: the President's conduct was reprehensible, but he should not be impeached because he was not a danger to the nation.

Congressman Howard Berman (D-CA) asked this question:

Mr. Hamilton . . . I would like you, for the purposes of your answers, to make two assumptions. First, the President lied under oath. Second, as to his grand jury testimony, those lies were not to cover up a consensual sexual relationship, but to avoid conceding that he had testified untruthfully in the civil deposition.

The question is, to deal with the contention that this conduct justifies impeachment because coming from the President, it is so corrosive of the judicial system and it so erodes the rule of law.

I responded as follows:

Congressman Berman, clearly, lying under oath before a grand jury or in a deposition is reprehensible. I think the question is, does that rise in this circumstance where the lying is about private consensual sexual conduct, whether it rises to the level of an impeachable offense. Is it a great and dangerous offense against the State that indicates it would be a danger to leave the President in office.

My conclusion is that it is not.[8]

Similarly, Congressman Steve Chabot (R-OH), quoting me out of context, inquired: "Mr. Hamilton, in your opening you claim that the President's conduct should not be impeachable, and I quote, 'because other Presidents have not been candid.' Isn't this an argument for impeachments? Don't we want our Presidents to be honest, rather than giving them the opportunity, for example, to lie before a grand jury, or lie to Federal judges?"

I responded:

Congressman, I think I said that I don't find the President's conduct impeachable for a variety of reasons, principally because it is not a great and dangerous offense against the State.

But surely we don't want our Presidents to lie or our Congressmen to lie or our Senators to lie. But sometimes they do, and I think the question is, when we find that they have, do we want to initiate impeachment proceedings? I think there is some judgment that comes in here, some proportionality.[9]

The notion of "proportionality," however, led me to conclude that Clinton should not be let off the hook altogether. Rather, I said, he should be censured by Congress for his unacceptable conduct. A contemporaneous op-ed piece I coauthored in the *New York Times* with former White House counsel Lloyd Cutler, former federal circuit court Judge and White House counsel Abner Mikva, and former attorney general Nicholas Katzenbach also called for Clinton to be censured.

Eventually, the House Judiciary Committee recommended four articles of impeachment. Specifically, that Clinton be impeached for perjury in the grand jury, perjury in the Paula Jones case, obstruction of justice as to both those proceedings, and abuse of power in refusing to respond to certain requests for admissions propounded by the committee and for false responses to certain other such requests. The full House rejected two charges but impeached Clinton for perjury before the grand jury (by a 228–206 vote) and for obstruction of justice in the Jones case (by a 221–212 vote). Clinton, however, was acquitted of both charges by the Senate, where a two-thirds yea vote (from sixty-seven senators) was needed to convict. Only fifty senators voted to convict on the obstruction charge; only forty-five voted to convict on the perjury charge.

* * *

Shortly after I testified, I visited the White House. There I met briefly with Clinton. I remember that he wore a polo shirt and had an unlit, well-chewed cigar in his hand. Clinton was famous for compartmentalization—for blocking out unpleasantness while he attended to the business of state. But on that day he looked harried and distracted, which was understandable given that sordid details of his personal life were being discussed and dissected in the halls of Congress and on national television.

When he saw me, he gave me a tentative, perhaps reluctant, hug. Only in Washington does someone hug you after you have publicly denounced his conduct as "reprehensible."

15

DNC Chair Don Fowler

A Friend in Need

Of all of my cases, the one that took the greatest personal toll was the representation of my friend Don Fowler.

I first met Don Fowler in the early 1970s. He was chair of the South Carolina Democratic Party. I was in charge of the state for Senator Ed Muskie's (ME) presidential campaign.

Don stayed officially neutral in the contest for the Democratic nomination. However, he was helpful in suggesting people I should contact about supporting Muskie. With his advice I assembled a stellar group of South Carolinians to be on Muskie's state committee—including a number of Black activists, suddenly important in election politics due to the effect of the 1965 Voting Rights Act. Unfortunately, my work came to naught when Muskie faded after appearing to cry in the snows of New Hampshire following an attack on his wife by the New Hampshire *Union Leader*.

In 1995, Don became cochair of the Democratic National Committee (DNC), along with Senator Chris Dodd (CT). Dodd was often the committee's spokesperson; Don ran its day-to-day operations.

In his role, Don was involved in raising money for President Bill Clinton's campaign for reelection in 1996, although Harold Ickes, the White House deputy chief of staff, directed much of the fund-raising activities.[1] Charges of illegality arose about the various methods the Clinton campaign and the DNC employed to raise campaign funds. Don was a target of some of those allegations, and he asked me to represent him. This matter turned out to be troublesome for him, but it also had an unfortunate effect on me personally, as shortly described.

The Democratic fund-raising activities for the 1996 campaign became the topic of sprawling investigations by the Senate Committee on Governmental Affairs, the Department of Justice, and others. Among the matters investigated were illegal conduit[2] and foreign campaign contributions; favors to an Indigenous tribe that had made substantial contributions; a fund-raiser at a Buddhist temple; solicitation calls from the White House by the president and Vice President Gore; "perks" for large contributions such as overnight stays in the White House's Lincoln Bedroom; White House coffees (103 in number), usually with President Clinton; flights on Air Force One; seats in the president's box at the Kennedy Center; and use of the White House tennis court.[3] The illegal conduit and foreign contributions resulted in several federal convictions. The DNC returned around $2.8 million in illegal or improper donations after the 1996 election.

The Senate Governmental Affairs investigation had a Watergate flavor. The chair of the committee, Fred Thompson (R-TN), had been chief minority counsel for the Senate Watergate Committee. His chief counsel for its campaign finance investigations, Michael Madigan, had been one of Fred's deputies during the Watergate inquiries.

After I began to represent Don, a new allegation surfaced that caused problems for both of us. The assertion was that Don had made calls to the CIA on behalf of one Roger Tamraz, a Lebanese businessman who became a US citizen in 1989 and for years had supplied information to the CIA. It was alleged that Fowler had twice called the CIA seeking its help in having Tamraz—a substantial contributor to Democratic causes who was being blocked from attending White House coffees and similar events with the president and vice president—cleared for admittance to such functions. More about the specifics of those allegations, which were of considerable interest to both the committee and the DOJ, and Don's inability to remember these calls in a moment to the CIA.

These new allegations presented a problem for me because I was then serving on the President's Foreign Intelligence Advisory Board (which, in a town beset by acronyms, was known as PFIAB). President Clinton had appointed me to PFIAB in 1995 after I had been responsible for vetting his cabinet, White House staff, and Supreme Court nominees during the transition and early years of his presidency.

PFIAB was one of a small handful of premium boards to which persons not in government were appointed. I loved being on PFIAB, both because of its mission and the people on the board.[4] Its mission was to oversee all of the intelligence agencies—for example, the CIA, NSA, and Defense Intelligence Agency—and to give advice to the president on intelligence matters. Its work was highly classified, and board members needed top-secret code word clearances to participate. While I was on the board, Osama bin Laden was just becoming known as a threat and our intelligence capabilities in the Middle East were of utmost importance.

The board was populated by some prominent Americans. Former Speaker of the House Tom Foley was chair.[5] Former senator Warren Rudman (R-NH) was vice chair. Zoë Baird was on the board—a consolation prize after her unsuccessful bid for attorney general.[6] Also a member, to my particular delight, was Admiral Elmo "Bud" Zumwalt, the man who, as the youngest ever chief of naval operations, was responsible for the modern egalitarian navy.

Bud became a friend after we met at Phil and Linda Lader's Renaissance Weekend gatherings in South Carolina.[7] I admired few men as much as I did Bud. The only time I engineered being invited to the White House was when President Clinton presented Bud with the Medal of Freedom, the nation's highest civilian award. When his name was called, Bud, then in his eighties, bounded onto the stage with youthful alacrity. Clinton smiled and said, "Are you afraid I'll take the Medal back?"

Given PFIAB's oversight of the CIA, representing Don regarding his alleged contacts with that organization presented an issue. So, I informed the PFIAB staff that I would recuse myself from any PFIAB business that involved those contacts, although it seemed to me highly unlikely that they would concern the board in any way.[8]

But my offer was not good enough for Senator Rudman. He insisted that either I drop my representation of Fowler or resign from the board. I said I would do neither. Resigning from the board, I said, would suggest I had done something wrong, which was not the case. The Tamraz allegations had arisen sometime after I began to represent Don and were unknown to me when I assumed that assignment. I also believed my limited recusal was sufficient. Chuck Ruff, then White House counsel, and Steve Potts, then head of the Office of Government Ethics (OGE), agreed.[9] I also had worked hard on board matters and thought I had made a contribution.

Rudman's response to my refusal to resign was this. "Ok, but Hamilton must recuse himself from *all* PFIAB matters while the Fowler representation is ongoing. And, if he does not, I will resign from the board!" I thought this reaction was extreme, but it was consistent with Rudman's proclivity to take a position and doggedly stick to it. I thus had a dilemma—either give up representing Don or recuse myself totally until the Tamraz matter was resolved. The latter course, I was confident, would basically keep me from board activities for the duration of the Clinton presidency because Attorney General Janet Reno would have little incentive quickly to conclude a highly sensitive matter involving a prominent Democratic politician.

I chose to represent Don and to recuse myself from all board matters. Don was a friend and, more important, a client with an acute need for legal representation. I felt an ethical obligation to stand with him during his travails.

It made no sense to challenge Rudman on the recusal issue. Clinton admired Rudman and had unsuccessfully asked him to be secretary of the Treasury. I have on occasion advised my children and others not to pick fights you are not going to win. I followed my own advice. Chuck Ruff told me that, when he informed Clinton of my full-blown recusal, Clinton rolled his eyes.

Roger Tamraz was a controversial, aggressive businessman. He had an MBA from Harvard and was a significant venture capital investor in the oil and gas arena. But, according to the Senate Governmental Affairs Committee report, he was also the subject of an Interpol arrest warrant for embezzlement in Lebanon.

Tamraz was interested in obtaining US government support for a pipeline project to bring oil from the Caspian Sea region to Western markets. He sought exclusive rights to build such a pipeline. US government policy, however, supported multiple energy pipelines that would promote economic development in the region.

Tamraz was candid about the tenacious pursuit of his agenda with US government officials and his use of money to obtain his goals. He testified to the Senate Committee that, "If they kicked me from the door, I will come through the window."[10] Although he had not registered to vote, he made large contributions, first to Republican causes and then to Democratic ones, all intended to advance his business interests. When Senator Joe Lieberman (D-CT) asked him if he received his "money's worth" for the around $300,000 he gave to Democrats, Tamraz responded, "I think next time, I'll give 600,000."[11]

But Tamraz's largesse did not always gain him his objectives. He never did obtain US government support for his pipeline project. He never secured a formal private meeting with President Clinton. And although he attended six social functions at the White House, he was disinvited to a White House breakfast meeting with Vice President Gore in October 1985 after both Gore's staff and the National Security Council (NSC) raised objections to his attending. This rejection drove him to seek help in gaining White House access from DNC cochair Don Fowler.

Testimony to the committee and documentary evidence showed that Tamraz asked Don to call a mysterious figure known publicly as "Bob of the CIA" to obtain CIA support for Tamraz's clearance for White House events.[12] Bob, it was revealed in testimony, already had been lobbying the NSC on behalf of Tamraz's Caspian Sea pipeline project. Apparently, the CIA appreciated Tamraz's help to the agency over the years. According to evidence produced, Bob, at Tamraz's request, called Don. Don then called him back and, according to Bob's notes, they had two conversations on October 18 and December 13, 1995. Bob's memorandum as to the first call indicated that Don was attempting to arrange a meeting between Gore and Tamraz concerning his pipeline project but was aware of the opposition to that project. Bob's memorandum regarding the second call said that Don sought a CIA letter that would clear Tamraz's name with the president.

The oddity was that Don could not remember these calls. He was, he said, "flabbergasted" to read reports in the media about these calls. He testified that, "I have at midnight, at noontime, and almost every other minute of the day plumbed my memory in every way that I can, and I have no memory of ever having talked to anybody at the CIA."[13]

When shown one of Bob's memoranda, Don said, "I understand the implications . . . but it does not refresh my memory." He told Senator Thad Cochran (R-MS) that, "If I said to you I recall making those calls, I would be perjuring myself because I simply don't."[14]

The Republican committee report, which was not joined by any Democratic members of the committee, questioned Don's candor. But the Department of Justice never pursued any charges against Don for perjury, likely for several good reasons.

Don was a longtime respected participant in political affairs—and remained so until his death in 2020. His reputation as a man of integrity was shaped over many years in the public eye. He forthrightly did not shy away from the efforts he made on behalf of Democratic donors, stating, "It is fully appropriate for the head of a national political party to secure a meeting for a supporter with an administration official or even to advocate a worthy cause."[15]

Moreover, Fowler readily admitted that he approached the NSC about Tamraz. In a March 18, 1997, statement, he said:

Sometime in 1995 I was told by either a staff member of the Democratic National Committee or by Mr. Roger Tamraz that Mr. Tamraz would like to be invited to the White House for a group social meeting. I understood that there was some issue about his attending such a meeting.

In making an inquiry about this, I spoke with [NSC staff]. . . . In no sense of the word was it my intention to put pressure on anyone to do anything, much less anything that was improper. My purpose was to determine if it would be appropriate for Mr. Tamraz to be invited to a group social event. . . .

I made no request for a private meeting with the President or anyone else.[16]

Bob's testimony was somewhat helpful to Don. He said, "I was under . . . cover. I can't say for certain how he knew who he was talking to because CIA was never mentioned."[17] There was thus a reason Don could not remember calls with the CIA two years after they purportedly occurred.

There also was no good reason for Don to lie about calls to the CIA, especially after admitting his conversations with the NSC. Those calls were not illegal, whatever one might say about their wisdom. But lying about the CIA calls to a hostile Senate committee would have been both illegal and unwise. It would have been particularly foolish to lie about those calls in the face of the available documentary evidence. And Don was not a foolish man.

* * *

As I had predicted to myself, my recusal was the death knell of my participation on PFIAB. Attorney General Reno was in no hurry to exonerate Don. Her letter to us declining prosecution came in January 2001, in the waning weeks of the Clinton presidency.

After my recusal, I was invited back for one PFIAB function—the formal board photograph. It hangs in my office as a bittersweet reminder of my limited time on PFIAB and the Tamraz affair.

16

A Disgruntled
Prince Philip

I am, on my mother's side, of British lineage. But I was not, to say the least, accustomed to hobnobbing with the royal family.

In the winter of 2001, I traveled to London to conduct a Foreign Corrupt Practice Act investigation for an international energy company. Kristina went with me. Before leaving for London, I called my good friend Phil Lader, then the US ambassador to the Court of St James's, to ask if we could stay at Winfield House, the ambassador's residence. We had stayed with Phil and Linda Lader twice before—once on Holland Park, while Winfield House was being renovated, and once at Winfield House during a long event-packed weekend organized by the Laders for some of their close friends.

When I spoke with Phil, he asked: "What are you doing next Wednesday night?" I said, "Nothing." He said, "I'll get back to you."

Two days later his assistant called and said: "Mr. Hamilton, Ambassador Lader would like to know if you and Mrs. Hamilton are available next Wednesday evening for a small dinner party at Winfield House in honor of the queen."

For about a half an hour Kristina was furious with me for inviting ourselves to dinner with the queen. Then she went shopping. She was stunning in the long lime-green dress she purchased for this black-tie event.

There is rigorous protocol for dinner with the queen. How properly to greet and address the queen and Prince Philip is specified. You are told that they are to choose the topics of conversation. You are not to change the subject. You also are instructed not to say anything controversial. For the honor and fun of being there, we were more than happy carefully to abide by those restrictions.

The Laders, the most gracious and meticulous of hosts, threw some party. There were forty-eight people in attendance. It seemed to me that half the net worth of Great Britain was in the room—for example, several Rothchilds and Sir Martin Sorrell, then the head of the WPP group. We all had our photographs taken with the queen and Prince Philip.[1]

The queen was dignified as ever and had the ability to make even strangers feel comfortable in her presence. One could understand how, over her long reign, she rarely has taken a false step in public.

At dinner, Kristina sat at Prince Philip's table. He was entertaining, jaunty, and, living up to his reputation, irreverent.

After dinner, the prince and I had a long conversation. He was interested in my British heritage. I told him that my grandfather was from Manchester and my grandmother was from Goole. To be helpful, I added, "It's in Yorkshire."

To which the Prince replied, "I know."

Soon thereafter, the prince grew tired of standing and wanted to sit, which we did on a couch in Winfield House's exquisite green drawing room, with its antique chinoiserie wallpaper and huge Gainsborough painting. We sat there for ten or fifteen minutes. Ambassador Lader kept wandering by and listening in to ensure that I was not monopolizing or boring the Prince.

Philip was in high dudgeon over an act of Parliament that would outlaw foxhunting. An English sport of venerable age was being assigned to the compost heap of history.

Philip presented his arguments against the law. I have since learned that his support of foxhunting was well-known.[2] I knew nothing about foxhunting, but of course I could not change the subject.

"They say foxhunting is inhumane. But the dogs do it [kill the foxes]. People don't," he said, and then looked at me for a response. I thought this was a slanted way to look at the sport, but to say so would have injected a note of controversy into the conversation, so I said nothing.

Having received no response, Philip continued: "My wife has dogs. They chase animals. Under this law she could be arrested."

I had visions of the queen's corgis chasing rabbits, the queen chasing the corgis, and Scotland Yard chasing the queen. All this seemed quite improbable to me, but, although Philip again was waiting for a reply, I again remained silent.

Philip continued to press his case. "It's much better," he said, "for the dogs to do it. If people did it, they might just wound the poor animal!" Once more, he looked at me for a comment.

This time I had to say something. I desperately racked my brain for a response. Then I thought of the ubiquitous prints of foxhunting in stuffy law offices in New York City and DC. So I said, "Well it is true that over the years foxhunting has inspired a lot of art."

Philip gave me a look that said: "You twit. That is the most inane thing I've ever heard."

He was right, it was. But it was inanity born of desperation and faithful adherence to the evening's protocol. I had not changed the subject. I had not said anything controversial. I had not embarrassed my gracious hosts. And I had not damaged UK-US relations, at least not very much.

17

James Lee Witt

"Chicken Feathers"

James Lee Witt headed the Federal Emergency Management Association (FEMA) from April 5, 1993, to January 20, 2001—virtually all of President Bill Clinton's two-term presidency. Witt was one of the stars of the Clinton administration.

Witt, a nonlawyer, had been a county judge in Yell County in Arkansas, a post he was elected to six times. In 1988, Governor Clinton appointed him to lead the Arkansas Office of Emergency Services. In 1996, three years into Witt's federal tenure, President Clinton elevated the director of FEMA to cabinet rank, a compliment to Witt.[1]

Before Witt, FEMA was viewed as a "political dumping ground." Witt changed that. On February 12, 1996, an *Atlanta Journal-Constitution* editorial declared:

FEMA has developed a sterling reputation for delivering disaster-relief services, a far cry from its abysmal standing before James Lee Witt took its helm in 1993. How did Witt turn FEMA around so quickly? Well, he is the first director of the agency to have emergency-management experience. He stopped the staffing of the agency by political patronage. He removed layers of bureaucracy. Most important, he instilled in the agency a spirit of preparedness, of service to the customer, of willingness to listen to ideas of local and state officials to make the system work better.[2]

When the Bush administration came in 2001, a new crew populated FEMA. Thereafter, James Lee came under investigation in questionable circumstances.

While head of FEMA, James Lee received a magnificent headdress from the chief of the Choctaw Indian Nation in appreciation for his work after the Oklahoma City bombing. Witt kept the headdress, whose supposedly eagle feathers swept dramatically to the floor, in a cabinet he had specially made for it. But the new head of FEMA, Joe Allbaugh—who purged FEMA of many of Witt's appointees, with disastrous effect—saw something suspect about this gift and initiated an inspector general (IG) investigation into it and Witt's travel expenses. Witt asked me to represent him.

The investigation involved not only the FEMA Office of Inspector General but also the FBI. I recall a meeting with investigators from both bodies that I found unnecessarily hostile. Eventually nothing about Witt's travel expenses proved problematic, but there continued to be considerable interest in the headdress.

I could to some degree understand the IG's interest. Maybe, despite the fact that the gift of the headdress was transparent and well-known to FEMA's ethics official, there might be an issue under the gift rules that govern agency employees. But this didn't explain the FBI's involvement. What was the potential crime here?

Then two things happened. The first was 9/11. The FBI decided that the agent investigating the headdress matter had better things to do and reassigned her.

The other was the decision to send the headdress to the Department of the Interior's Fish and Wildlife Service. It turned out that the FBI's real concern was whether James Lee possessed a headdress containing eagle feathers. Under the federal eagle feather law, it is a crime for anyone but a Native American to possess such feathers. Anyone violating the law could go to jail for a year or be fined up to $250,000.

The Fish and Wildlife folks within minutes determined that the headdress contained not eagle feathers but either chicken or turkey feathers. The investigation was promptly dropped, much, I expect, to the dissatisfaction of Allbaugh.

I called James Lee to give him this news. Then I said, "James Lee, I want to give you my pithy legal analysis of this ridiculous case. This case, James Lee, involved chicken feathers and chicken shit!"

James Lee must have appreciated my legal summation because I represented him and his companies for many years thereafter.

18

Bob Novak and the
Valerie Plame Saga

As chapter 12 of this book demonstrates, law-yers are assiduous in protecting their clients' confidences. As I saw firsthand representing Bob Novak, journalists safeguard the identities of their confidential sources with equal fervor.

Bob Novak, a pugnacious conservative journalist, was a Washington, DC, institution. For fifty years, he was seemingly ubiquitous in the Washington media scene. In 1963, he and Rowland Evans began "Inside Report," which became the longest running political column in the history of American journalism, a column he continued after Evans died in 2001. The column was known for its unique insights and for the great variety of sources (often anonymous) who brought it information to which no other journalist had access.

Novak was often on television, working for CNN and appearing on, for example, *Capital Gang*, *Crossfire*, and *Evans, Novak, Hunt & Shields*. Because he was frequently dour and stirred up strife, he was known as "The Prince of Darkness," a sobriquet he happily adopted as the title of his autobiography.

I first came to notice Bob in 1973, when he began writing about the Watergate investigations. Bob wrote some 124 columns about Watergate and, despite his conservative leanings, supported Nixon's impeachment. Nonetheless, had someone told me then that I would represent this conservative journalist thirty years later in one of the most trying times of his professional life, I would have given that notion little credence.

Bob was raised in Illinois in a secular Jewish family. However, in 1998 at age sixty-seven, he converted to Catholicism. That sincere conversation, as we shall see, may have benefited him in ways other than spiritual.

Bob died in August 2009 from a cancerous brain tumor. The surgeon at Duke University who operated on him was the same doctor who operated on Novak's friend Senator Ted Kennedy, who also suffered from brain cancer.

On July 14, 2003, Novak published what he called "the most personally fateful column I ever would write."[1] Entitled "Mission to Niger," the column read in crucial part:

> The CIA's decision to send retired diplomat Joseph C. Wilson to Africa in February 2002 to investigate possible Iraqi purchases of uranium was made routinely at a low level without Director George Tenet's knowledge. Remarkably, this produced a political firestorm that has not yet subsided.
>
> Wilson's report that an Iraqi purchase of uranium yellowcake from Niger was highly unlikely was regarded by the CIA as less than definitive, and it is doubtful Tenet ever saw it. Certainly President Bush did not, before his 2003 State of the Union address, when he attributed reports of attempted uranium purchases to the British government. . . .
>
> Wilson never worked for the CIA, but his wife, Valerie Plame, is an agency operative on weapons of mass destruction. Two senior administration officials told me that Wilson's wife suggested sending him to Niger to investigate the Italian report. The CIA says its counterproliferation officials selected Wilson and asked his wife to contact him. "I will not answer any question about my wife," Wilson told me.
>
> After eight days in Niger's capital of Niamey (where he had once served), Wilson made an oral report in Langley that an Iraqi uranium purchase was "highly unlikely, . . . " CIA officials did not regard Wilson's intelligence as definitive, being based primarily on what the Niger officials told him and probably would have claimed under any circumstances.[2]

Novak's article spawned claims in the media that he had outed a CIA covert agent (Plame), and that someone may have violated the Intelligence

Identities Protection Act. Media stories also suggested that the revelation of Plame's name had ruined her career and was an act of revenge for Wilson's article that suggested President Bush had made a false claim in his 2003 State of the Union address. Certainly, this was Wilson and Plame's view. Bob's column also provoked a Department of Justice investigation into the leak of Plame's name.

That investigation and the accompanying news stories prompted Novak to call his longtime lawyer and my partner, Les Hyman, who was close to Bob personally and professionally. That led to my involvement. Here's how Novak described the initial interaction among us in his book:

> On Monday, September 29, I called my attorney, Les Hyman. He told me that I needed representation from his partner . . . , James Hamilton. I had never met Hamilton, but he was known to me as a Clinton lawyer and prominent backstage figure in national Democratic politics. Hamilton advised me to be quiet and ignore news media calls. I said I would shut up after writing a column and making some obligatory television appearances.[3]

Bob perhaps had reason to be skeptical of me given my Democratic connections, but he decided we could work together. In his book, he wrote:

> Les Hyman had been my attorney for three decades and was a personal friend. Jim Hamilton's words of advice were valued by his clients—including the Democratic Party. Hamilton had led the vice presidential searches for candidates Bill Clinton and Al Gore, and he had vetted judicial nominees in the Clinton administration. He had kept out of the headlines while representing famous Democrats, and he would keep out of the headlines representing a right-wing columnist.[4]

In his book, Bob has written at length about the advice I gave him. Consequently, the normal restrictions that apply regarding attorney-client communications are not fully applicable here, and I am freer than I otherwise would be to describe my advice to Bob and how his case was handled.

The additional column Bob referred to in the quote above was published on October 1, 2003. It read in part:

I had thought I never again would write about retired diplomat Joseph Wilson's CIA-employee wife, but feel constrained to do so now that repercussions of my July 14 column have reached the front pages of major newspapers and led off network news broadcasts. My role and the role of the Bush White House have been distorted and need explanation.

The leak now under Justice Department investigation is described by former Ambassador Wilson and critics of President Bush's Iraq policy as a reprehensible effort to silence them. To protect my own integrity and credibility, I would like to stress three points. First, I did not receive a planned leak. Second, the CIA never warned me that the disclosure of Wilson's wife working at the agency would endanger her or anybody else. Third, it was not much of a secret. . . .

This story began July 6 when Wilson went public and identified himself as the retired diplomat who had reported negatively to the CIA in 2002 on alleged Iraq efforts to buy uranium yellowcake from Niger. I was curious why a high-ranking official in President Bill Clinton's National Security Council (NSC) was given this assignment. . . .

During a long conversation with a senior administration official, I asked why Wilson was assigned the mission to Niger. He said Wilson had been sent by the CIA's counterproliferation section at the suggestion of one of its employees, his wife. It was an offhand revelation from his official, who is no partisan gunslinger. When I called another official for confirmation, he said: "Oh, you know about it." The published report that somebody in the White House failed to plant this story with six reporters and finally found me as a willing pawn is simply untrue.

At the CIA, the official designated to talk to me denied that Wilson's wife had inspired his selection but said she was delegated to request his help. He asked me not use her name saying she probably never again will be given a foreign assignment but that exposure of her name might cause "difficulties" if she travels abroad. He never suggested to me that Wilson's wife or anybody else would be endangered. If he had, I would not have used her name. I used it in the sixth paragraph of my column because it looked like the missing explanation of an otherwise incredible choice of the CIA for its mission.

How big a secret was it? It was well known around Washington that

Wilson's wife worked for the CIA. . . . Her name, Valerie Plame, was no secret either, appearing in Wilson's "Who's Who in America" entry.

A big question is her duties at Langley. I regret that I referred to her in my column as an "operative," a word I have lavished on hack politicians for more than 40 years. While the CIA refuses to publicly define her status, the official contact says she is "covered"—working under the guise of another agency. However, an unofficial source at the Agency says she has been an analyst, not in covert operations.[5]

Soon the FBI requested an interview of Bob. He was hesitant, but I advised that he speak with the FBI, knowing that if he did not do so voluntarily a grand jury subpoena would promptly be forthcoming. I also advised that he not publicly say that he was doing so. Bob followed my advice in both respects, but he was adamant that he would not reveal his sources to the FBI.

Protecting his sources was, to Bob, akin to a matter of religious faith, seemingly as important to him as the tenets of his adopted Catholicism. Les and I honored that imperative. We told him that, for now, we did not need to know who his sources were. I was confident, however, that soon he would be pressured to talk about them.

On October 7, 2003, the FBI interviewed Bob. The lead interrogator was Jack Eckenrode, a seasoned veteran of the bureau. Eckenrode set a friendly tone. It turned out that, like Bob, he attended St. Patrick Catholic Church in Washington, often sitting a few rows behind Bob. That was a happy circumstance; although highly professional, Eckenrode clearly was sympathetic to Bob's situation.

The interview lasted around two hours. Bob answered many questions, but when Eckenrode inquired about Bob's sources, he refused to reveal them. Eckenrode did not insist on an answer. It was certain, however, that this was not the last session with investigators.

On December 30, Attorney General John Ashcroft recused himself from the investigation, apparently because of his ties with senior White House aides, turning it over to Deputy Attorney General James Comey. Comey then appointed Patrick Fitzgerald, a US attorney in Chicago, as special counsel. (Fitzgerald was the godfather of a Comey child.) Fitzgerald had a sterling reputation, having successfully prosecuted a number of prominent politicians and other notables, including Illinois governors George Ryan and Rod Blagojevich.

Fitzgerald quickly informed me that he wanted to meet with Bob. Moreover, he told me that he had various waivers of confidentiality, including waivers from Bob's two sources in the Plame matter—Deputy Secretary of State Richard Armitage and White House official Karl Rove—who thereby gave Bob permission to talk to Fitzgerald. This news, to use Bob's words, was "a shock too severe for a seventy-one-year-old man."[6] I, however, was not shocked. High-level federal officials keep records of their personal meetings and phone calls. With a little effort, a prosecutor could determine exactly whom in the government Bob talked to in the days preceding his July 14, 2003, column.

Nonetheless, Bob said he wanted to protect his conversations with sources. If my memory serves me well, this, in essence, is what I told him:

Bob, you can refuse to talk about conversations with your sources. But if you do you will be called before a grand jury. If you refuse to answer questions about them there, you can be held in criminal contempt. You can be incarcerated until you talk.[7]

Of course, Bob, we can move to quash the subpoena, but precedent is against you and you will lose, after paying my firm several hundred thousand dollars. What's more, the ultimate court decision you will receive will be another negative precedent against the press.

So, Bob, what do you want to do?

Bob decided that he had no real choice. He would tell Fitzgerald what Fitzgerald already knew—who his sources were.

Fitzgerald and his team, including Jack Eckenrode, arrived at my law offices at 10:00 a.m. on January 14, 2004. He had the waivers from Armitage and Rove—and also one from CIA spokesperson Bill Harlow, who had suggested that Novak not reveal Plame's name. Fitzgerald questioned Bob for three-and-a-half hours. Bob revealed his sources and discussed what they had said to him about Wilson and Plame. He would not discuss his conversations with them beyond that subject.

Bob met again with Pat Fitzgerald, Jack Eckenrode, and others on February 5, 2004, at my offices. The topics were similar.

Fitzgerald asked Bob not to talk about these meetings. I urged Bob to comply with this request, even though questions about his actions were rampant in the press. Had he revealed his sources? Was he under subpoena? Was he indicted? Had he taken the Fifth? Had he agreed to a plea bargain?

Why was it so important to appease Fitzgerald? He was, in effect, a jury of one. I wanted to give him no reason to desire to indict Bob. Bob had done nothing legally wrong, but at age seventy-one, his memory was not always perfect. A misrecollection might be construed as a false statement by one inclined to do. While Eckenrode, Bob's fellow Catholic, expressed sympathy for the memory lapses of old age, Fitzgerald had a reputation for disliking and prosecuting prevaricators. In fact, the only person he prosecuted regarding the Plame affair was Vice President Cheney's aide, Scooter Libby, who was indicted for lying to the FBI and to a grand jury. I wanted to keep Fitzgerald friendly to Bob, especially in the situation where his revelations of Plame's name had caused resentment among many, perhaps including Fitzgerald.

On February 25, 2004, Bob appeared before the grand jury. He was afraid of this experience, knowing that he could be met by a horde of reporters before he entered the grand jury room and after he left.

I was determined to avoid that, having had distasteful experiences with the press in similar settings. During the Clinton administration I had represented a young White House staffer who was a witness before a Ken Starr grand jury investigating the Lewinsky affair. After his first grand jury appearance, my witness, who had a bad back, was physically jostled as we tried to make our way to a waiting car. After his second appearance before the grand jury and after I publicly chastised the assembled press for its previous rude and unruly behavior, he gave a statement to the press with a phalanx of US Marshals standing behind us, one of whom had biceps the size of a normal man's thighs. After we finished, the marshals escorted us to the car, keeping the ever-demanding press corps at bay.

To avoid such a spectacle, Jack Eckenrode and an FBI driver met Bob and me at my offices and took us in a window-darkened limousine into the federal courthouse garage. From there, a private elevator took us to a part of the courthouse where the grand jury was meeting and journalists were not allowed. After Bob's testimony, which I was not allowed to attend under grand jury rules, we exited the courthouse in the same manner. Happily, the press corps was oblivious to our presence.

Before Bob testified under oath, he read the following statement:

It is always a difficult position for a professional journalist when adherence to journalistic principles protected by the United States Constitution in retaining the anonymity of confidential sources conflicts with a citizen's responsibility to cooperate in a potential criminal case.

I had intended to decline to disclose the identity of my confidential sources in this case, whatever the personal cost to me. That was still my intention even after the government collected waivers signed by virtually all my potential sources, relieving me from any confidentiality in our relationships.

However, before I met with the special counsel, my attorneys were informed he would bring with him only two waivers—signed by the two officials who indeed were my sources. Since the special counsel knew who my sources were and these sources had waived confidentiality, I was protecting nobody's anonymity.

I concluded after receiving my attorneys' advice that had I still declined to discuss our conversations under these conditions, I likely would be challenged in court with poor prospects for success. In that event, I feared that this case could go all the way to the Supreme Court and actually chip away at cherished press privileges under the first amendment.

Nevertheless, I would like to say I am very uncomfortable in testifying here today, under subpoena, about conversations I had thought to be confidential and that I still believe deeply in the constitutional privilege.[8]

Having said his piece, Bob, under examination mainly by Fitzgerald, told the grand jury essentially what he had said to the investigators in my office. His testimony lasted two hours. The grand jurors were civil, although some appeared not to pay attention or dozed.

Bob was pleased about the confidential manner in which his grand jury testimony was handled, even though its nonpublic nature allowed continued media speculation about his fate. As he wrote in his book:

The federal courthouse in Washington is normally a wind tunnel of gossip and rumors, blowing straight onto the printed page and the TV screen. But not this time. Nobody knew that I even talked to the FBI, much less that I was cooperating and testifying before the grand jury. Pat Fitzgerald ran an extraordinarily tight ship (in contrast to leaky Independent Counsel offices I had covered over many years), Jim Hamilton was the tightest-lipped lawyer I ever saw, and I was not talking.[9]

Shortly after his grand jury appearance, Bob did something that did not please his lawyers—and undoubtedly made Joe Wilson and Valerie Plame increasingly unhappy. In a top hat and formal afternoon attire suitable for a diplomat, he portrayed former diplomat Joe Wilson in a Gridiron Club skit. To the tune of "Once I Had a Secret Love," he sang:

> Novak had a secret source,
> Who lived within the great White House.
> And one day his secret source
> Told him about my darling spouse.
> So, he outed a girl spy
> The way Princes of Darkness do.
> Cross the right wing you may try.
> Bob Novak's coming after you.
> Now John Ashcroft's asking who and how,
> Could be headed for the old hoosegow.
> And now his game is hem and haw.
> 'Cause Bob Novak's source is hiding from the law.[10]

I learned once again that lawyers can control their clients only to some degree!

On June 28, 2006, Pat Fitzgerald advised me that his "investigation concerning matters directly relating to Mr. Novak has been concluded" and that he would not continue to request that Bob "not . . . discuss this matter with others, including the media."[11] Bob, however, had one more role to play because Fitzgerald's trial of Scooter Libby for perjury and other offenses was still pending.

Libby's prominent lawyers—Ted Wells and Bill Jeffress (a friend who has done vice-presidential vetting for me)—asked Bob to testify. At the trial, Bob reiterated who his sources were and what they had said to him about Plame. He testified that Libby had not been a source. I was not convinced that this testimony measurably helped Libby, although his lawyers thought so. Libby was convicted of lying and perjuring about how he learned about the Wilson/Plame matter and for obstruction of justice. He was sentenced to thirty months in prison. President George W. Bush commuted his sentence but did not pardon him, to the reported annoyance of Libby's former boss, Vice President Cheney. Years later, Libby received a pardon from President Trump.

Bob Novak was a controversial figure and an interesting client. I did my best for him and the result, at least from a legal standpoint, was highly satisfactory.

Bob was appreciative. On the first page of his book *The Prince of Darkness*, the conservative columnist wrote in hand to an avowed Democrat: "To Jim Hamilton, with profound gratitude from his friend, Robert D. Novak."

19

A Stain on Baseball

> In law, as in other human endeavors, one must discern whom to trust.

In 2006, two *San Francisco Chronicle* investigative reporters, Lance Williams and Mark Fainaru-Wada, published *Game of Shadows*. The book laid out the widespread use of performance-enhancing drugs, such as human growth hormone and steroids, by Major League Baseball (MLB) players. Among the alleged users were several well-known players, including slugger Barry Bonds.

On March 30, 2006, Commissioner Bud Selig appointed former Senate majority leader George Mitchell (D-ME) to investigate the use of such substances by baseball players. I represented around a half-dozen then-present and former players in that investigation, some of whom were referred to me by the Scott Boras agency. Several were all-stars. Several were of lesser accomplishment. Some were pitchers; some were position players. Some were later mentioned in Mitchell's extensive report; some were not. For the purposes of this chapter, there is no need to reveal any of their names.

Mitchell's report, issued in December 2007, was the product of an extensive investigation. The report named eighty-nine players as users, including major stars such as famed pitchers Roger Clemens and Andy Pettitte. Many of the players involved had been supplied performance-enhancing substances by Kirk Radomski, a former New York Mets batboy and clubhouse employee. Radomski had extensive records—checks, money orders, mailing receipts, entries in an address book, and telephone records—identifying the players to whom he had supplied substances. Radomski talked to Mitchell

186

as a result of a plea bargain entered into with the US Attorneys Office for the Northern District of California. That office charged him with distribution of a controlled substance and money laundering; his plea deal required cooperation with Mitchell's investigation.

Despite Mitchell's efforts, few of the eighty-nine mentioned players spoke with him. In part this was because, in Mitchell's words, "The Players Association was largely uncooperative."[1]

After Mitchell requested that every MLB player with relevant information contact him, the Major League Baseball Players Association (MLBPA) sent out a memorandum discouraging that cooperation. The memorandum said:

> Commissioner Selig has not ruled out disciplining (suspending and/ or fining) players as a result of information gathered by the Mitchell investigation. Therefore, you should be aware that any information provided could lead to discipline of you and/or others. . . . Remember also that there are a number of ongoing federal and state criminal investigations in this area, and any information gathered by Senator Mitchell in player interviews is not legally privileged. What this means is that while Senator Mitchell pledges in his memo that he will honor any player request for confidentiality *in his report,* he does not pledge, because he cannot pledge, that any information you provide will actually remain confidential and not be disclosed without your consent. For example, Senator Mitchell cannot promise that information you disclose will not be given to a federal or state prosecutor, a Congressional committee, or even turned over in a private lawsuit in response to a request or a subpoena.[2]

Mitchell was frustrated that few players spoke with him. Nonetheless, because of the information he had from Radomski and others, many player names were mentioned and their situations discussed in the report. I saw no good reason to allow most of the players I represented to be interviewed by Mitchell. However, one player I represented did speak with Mitchell.

This player was far from an all-star. He was contemplating his life and career after baseball. He had, however, purchased performance-enhancing substances from Radomski, and Radomski had provided information to Mitchell substantiating that claim and naming him. But my client, for several reasons, had *not* ingested the substances.

My player was afraid that being mentioned in the report would be extremely detrimental to his career after baseball. My assignment, therefore, was to keep his name out of the report. But how to do that, given the incriminating information that Mitchell had from Radomski?

I had known Mitchell since the early 1970s when we both were involved in Senator Ed Muskie's run for president. (Muskie and Mitchell were both from Maine.) I had admired Mitchell's performance as a senator and majority leader, and I believed he was a person of fairness and integrity.

So this is how I proceeded: Knowing that Mitchell was anxious to talk with players, most of whom were stiffing him, I called his chief lieutenant, distinguished Baltimore lawyer Charlie Scheeler, and said something like this:

Charlie, I represent a player I will not yet name. He purchased substances but did not use them. I can establish his non-use by strong corroborating evidence. He is willing to meet and talk with George, under the condition that, if George believes him about non-use and credits his corroborating evidence, his name will not appear in the report. If George agrees, I will provide the player's name and make arrangements for him to speak with you.

Charlie said that he would relay my message to Mitchell and get back to me. A short time later, Charlie called and said Mitchell accepted the deal.

I brought in my player to meet with Mitchell and Scheeler. They spoke for a good part of the morning. In the afternoon, Mitchell and Scheeler considered the corroborating evidence I presented. As they informed me later, they believed my client and deemed the corroborating evidence credible.

Mitchell was as good as his word, as I had expected. His final report said only this:

I did not include in this report the names of three players to whom Radomski said he sold performance enhancing substances: two of them because the players had retired from Major League Baseball by the time of the alleged sales; and one of them because the player admitted that he had purchased and possessed the substances but denied that he had used them and his version of events was corroborated by other credible evidence.[3]

The name of the player I represented never surfaced.

Sometimes, the sweetest successes are not in court and go virtually unnoticed.

20

The Disgraceful Interrogation of Admiral Mike Mullen

I have long found offensive the manner in which some members of Congress treat witnesses, including those especially worthy of respect. The presence of television cameras seems to magnify boorish conduct; apparently, some lawmakers believe there are votes to be garnered by discourtesy and incivility.

Not all congressional investigations succumb to such tactics. During the Senate Watergate Committee's hearings, for example, Sam Ervin and Sam Dash, eschewing the practice of some committees, refused to compel witnesses asserting their Fifth Amendment privilege to do so in public session. No legitimate legislative purpose, they felt, would be served by subjecting such witnesses to the opprobrium resulting from publicly taking the Fifth. Thus, miscreants such as Gordon Liddy and Chuck Colson were allowed to assert their privilege in closed session.

The Watergate Committee's practice often is not followed. There are many examples of congressional abuse of witnesses. Perhaps the worst I have seen was the treatment of Admiral Mike Mullen, former chair of the Joint Chiefs of Staff, by congressional pit bulls such as Representatives Jim Jordan (R-OH) and Trey Gowdy (R-SC) during a hearing about the tragedy that occurred in Benghazi, Libya.

*   *   *

On September 11–12, 2012, terrorists launched attacks on two US facilities in Benghazi, Libya—the Special Mission Compound and a CIA Annex. Four Americans, including US ambassador to Libya John Christopher Stevens, were killed. The well-armed assailants employed small-arms and machine guns, grenades, rocket-propelled grenades, mortars, and arson. As required by statute in such circumstances, Secretary of State Hillary Clinton convened an Accountability Review Board (ARB) to examine the attacks and loss of life. She appointed Ambassador Thomas Pickering as chair of the ARB and retired Admiral Mike Mullen as its vice chair.

The ARB's report was sharply criticized by House Republicans, who branded it a "whitewash" and a "cover up," because it did not implicate Clinton in any misconduct or dereliction of duty. There were multiple separate hearings into the Benghazi events, including one by the House Oversight and Government Reform Committee chaired by Darrell Issa (R-CA). His hearing focused on the ARB's report. Pickering and Mullen were called to testify.

Recognizing that the hearing required legal representation, Mullen reached out to my then partner, Mike Levy, an experienced, effective white-collar lawyer. Because of my familiarity with congressional investigations, Mike asked me to participate, which I gladly agreed to do.

The representation promised to be interesting. Much of what the ARB had reviewed was classified. Because we needed to examine the same material, Mike, I, and others involved required top-secret clearances. Mine was expeditiously procured, in part because I previously had such clearances— most recently for my work during the Clinton administration on the President's Foreign Intelligence Advisory Board, which oversees the nation's intelligence agencies.

Among Mike's first decisions was to represent Mullen on a pro bono basis. Mullen had served on the ARB free-of-charge, and Mike concluded that he should not be forced to incur hefty legal expenses because of his volunteer service. I thought Mike's decision was both generous and appropriate.

Pickering and Mullen were among the most distinguished Americans in public life. Pickering had been the US ambassador to Russia, India, Israel, El Salvador, Nigeria, and Jordan, as well as the ambassador to the

United Nations. He also had been the under-secretary of state for political affairs, and he held the rank of career ambassador, the highest level one can achieve in the US Foreign Service. He had received a dozen honorary degrees.

Admiral Mullen was the seventeenth chair of the Joint Chiefs of Staff, serving two terms in that position from October 1, 2007, to September 30, 2011. He also was the commander, US Naval Forces Europe and the commander, Allied Joint Forces Command Naples. He is pictured in the iconic May 1, 2011, photograph with President Barack Obama, Secretary of State Clinton, and other members of the Obama national security team as they watched the raid in Pakistan that took out Osama bin Laden.

Admiral Mullen and I got along well. Part of the reason, I think, was that I was then (and am now) on the board of the United Service Organizations (USO), the stellar organization that serves our troops and their families around the world. As chair of the Joint Chiefs and since, Mullen has been a strong proponent of the USO. While chair, he participated in ten USO Christmas tours that entertained our forces in thirteen countries.

Despite the esteem in which Pickering and Mullen generally were held, certain members of Issa's committee treated them with disgraceful disrespect. I viewed those members as Lilliputians pricking at the heels of men of stature.

My assignment in preparing Mullen for this hearing was to ask him tough questions to simulate what he might expect from the committee. This is a role I often have played, and it is standard practice in preparing for a hostile committee hearing. Knowing the committee's composition, I did my best to be disagreeable and disrespectful in the practice sessions. As we shall see, my attempts at vituperative emulation were not entirely successful.

The ARB report was hardly a "whitewash." Rather, it harshly criticized the State Department and certain senior officials, conclusions the ARB reached after interviewing over one hundred people, reviewing thousands of pages of documents, and viewing hours of video footage. For example, the ABR found that "systemic failures and leadership and management deficiencies at senior levels within two bureaus of the State Department resulted in a Special Mission security posture that was inadequate for Benghazi and grossly inadequate to deal with the attack that took place."[1]

In particular, the ARB concluded that the Diplomatic Security Bureau "showed a lack of proactive senior leadership with respect to Benghazi, failing to ensure that the priority security needs of a high risk, high threat post were met." Benghazi staffing "was at times woefully insufficient." Moreover, "given the threat environment, the physical security platform in Benghazi was inadequate."[2]

Reliance on Libyan security forces was "misplaced." One group of Libyan guards left a pedestrian gate unlatched after seeing the attackers and fled the scene. Also, "[t]he Libyan government's response [was] profoundly lacking on the night of the attacks, reflecting both weak capacity and a near total absence of central government influence and control in Benghazi."[3]

The ARB recognized that Ambassador Stevens himself made the decision to travel to Benghazi on the anniversary of the September 11, 2001, terrorist attacks in the United States. "The Ambassador did not see a direct threat of an attack of this nature and scale on the U.S. Mission. . . . His status as the leading U.S. government advocate on Libya policy, and his expertise on Benghazi in particular, caused Washington to give unusual deference to his judgments."[4]

The report was explicit that the US military was not at fault:

There simply was not enough time given the speed of the attacks for armed U.S. military assets to have made a difference. Senior-level interagency discussions were underway soon after Washington received initial word of the attacks and continued through the night. The Board found no evidence of any undue delays in decision making or denial of support from Washington or from the military combatant commanders. Quite the contrary: the safe evacuation of all U.S. government personnel from Benghazi twelve hours after the initial attack and subsequently to Ramstein Air Force Base was the result of exceptional U.S. government coordination and military response and helped save the lives of two severely wounded Americans.[5]

However, the ARB also noted the intelligence community's shortcomings: "The Board found that intelligence provided no immediate, specific tactical warning of the September 11 attacks. Known gaps existed in the intelligence community's understanding of extremist militias in Libya and the potential threat they posed to U.S. interests, although some threats were known to exist."[6]

The board found that one group that had been providing security for the US compound was "made up of many different militias with differing ideologies, some of which are extremist in nature."

Finally, the board returned to its criticism of State Department personnel:

> The Board found that certain senior State Department officials within two bureaus in critical positions of authority and responsibility in Washington demonstrated a lack of proactive leadership and management ability appropriate for the State Department's senior ranks in their responses to security concerns posed by Special Mission Benghazi, given the deteriorating threat environment and the lack of reliable host government protection.[7]

The board recommended that two individuals be removed from their positions. It found that the performance and leadership of two others fell short of expectations. After the report, the State Department reassigned these four persons to different positions, and there were several resignations. Later, the assistant secretary for diplomatic security resigned. However, because no employee engaged in misconduct or willfully ignored responsibilities, the board recommended no disciplinary action.

Admiral Mullen's opening statement to Issa's committee focused on areas we knew would be subject to hostile questions. At the beginning of his statement, he emphasized the board's independence.

> From the beginning, the State Department emphasized that it wanted full transparency about what happened in Benghazi and what led to those events. We had unfettered access to State Department personnel and documents. There were no limitations. We received the full cooperation of all witnesses and of every State Department office. We interviewed everyone we thought it was necessary to interview. We operated independently, and were given freedom to pursue the investigation as we deemed necessary.
>
> This independence was particularly important to me. I would not have accepted this assignment had I thought that the Board's independence would be compromised in any way.[8]

We were certain that the board's independence would be attacked. While it had, as Mullen said, "assigned blame at the level where we thought it lay," in accordance with what the ARB statute intended, Hillary Clinton had not been interviewed and was not criticized in the report.[9] After one of the officials criticized the report, Charlene Lamb, the deputy assistant secretary for international programs in the Bureau of Diplomatic Security, was interviewed by the board; Mullen had advised Cheryl Mills, Clinton's chief of staff, that Lamb would be a poor witness before Congress. These facts provided grist for hostile questions.

We also knew that the US military would be attacked for not doing more to prevent the Benghazi tragedy. To counter such attacks, Mullen testified:

> We also concluded that there was nothing the U.S. military could have done to respond to the attack on the compound or to deter the subsequent attack on the annex. The actions of our military, which moved many assets that night, were fully appropriate and professional. The military could not have moved assets into Benghazi the night of the attack in a timely enough way to have made a difference.[10]

Later, Mullen testified that he personally had gone back a second time to reexamine the military situation to ensure that the military had not been at fault.

Mullen's opening statement did little to insulate him from the barrage of attacks from committee members that followed. I recount these attacks at some length to demonstrate the outrageous, partisan treatment he received at the hands of Republicans on the committee who sought to politicize a tragedy.

Early on, Mullen was questioned by Congressman John L. Mica (R-FL). Mica, who was defeated in 2016, never served on the Armed Services Committee, but he apparently thought he knew more about military capabilities than Admiral Mullen.

MICA: But the military is the one that could have saved the day. . . .
   I tend to differ with you—I am not the greatest military strategist, but Mr. Issa and I were, in January, we were at least at one post. I know of at least three other posts, we could have launched an attack.

The attack started at 9:45. We might not have been able to save the
first two, the ambassador and his colleague, but the Seal should never
have died. It was 9:45. It was a 5:15 to 5:30 when they died. You testified a few minutes, 2 and a half to 3 hours. There is no reason that
we couldn't launch from at least three locations I visited and been told
that we have in place people monitoring the situation, particular and
specifically in Africa and North Africa. And if we are not, shame on us

MULLEN: What I said was 10 to 20 hours to get there.

MICA: That should not be the case.

MULLEN: That is the way it was.[11]

Mullen was questioned on the independence issue by Congressman Jim Jordan (R-OH), a former NCAA wrestling champion. Jordan brought wrestling
aggression, untempered by grace, to his questioning of Admiral Mullen. On
multiple occasions, he did not allow Mullen to answer a question before he
interrupted.

JORDAN: Later in that same response to the committee's question about
you updating the State Department in the course of the ARB, you
said this: "So, essentially, I gave Ms. Mills, Cheryl Mills, chief of staff,
counselor to the Secretary of State, a heads up. I thought that her
appearance, Charlene Lamb, could be a very difficult appearance for
the State Department."

MULLEN: Correct.

JORDAN: Now, here is what I'm wondering. My guess is a lot of people
are wondering. If this is so independent, why are you giving the State
Department a heads up about a witness coming in front of this committee?

MULLEN: We had just completed—within a day or two of that phone call,
the—

JORDAN: So you had a phone call with Ms. Mills? Is that what we are
talking about?

MULLEN: Yes. I mean, I think that is what my statement said.

JORDAN: Okay.

MULLEN: But no, we had just completed the interview with Ms. Lamb.
And as someone who—

JORDAN: That raises an important question.

MULLEN: Can I answer your question?

JORDAN: Yes, you can.

MULLEN: So my—as someone having run a department and spent many, many times trying, as a leader of a department, to essentially—

JORDAN: Let me ask—my time is winding down.

MULLEN: To—let me answer this, would you, please?

JORDAN: Well, let me ask you this, because this is important. The ARB was formed on October 3rd; correct?

MULLEN: Correct.

JORDAN: All right. Charlene Lamb came in front of this committee October 10th.

MULLEN: Correct . . .

JORDAN: Seven days later.

MULLEN: Right.

JORDAN: So why was she one of the first people you interviewed?

MULLEN: She was—

JORDAN: Why not—

MULLEN: She was one of the first people interviewed because she was the one in control of Diplomatic Security decisions.

JORDAN: Okay. How did you know she was on the list? Who told you she was testifying in front of Congress?

MULLEN: It was public knowledge that she was—

JORDAN: That is not usually made public until 2 days before.

MULLEN: Well, by the time I knew it—

JORDAN: So what day did you interview Charlene Lamb? Do you know?

MULLEN: Between the 3rd and the 10th.

JORDAN: Okay. Then when did you talk to Cheryl Mills? Right after that?

MULLEN: No, not right after that. I would say within 24 hours and specifically to give her a heads up that I didn't think that Charlene Lamb would be a witness at that point in time that would represent the department well, specifically. And I had run a department, worked a lot, worked a lot historically to get the best——

JORDAN: But, again, we have been told that this—the ARB is an independent review. In fact, you said it. You have said it twice.

MULLEN: Correct.

JORDAN: You said it in front of the committee staff; you said it in your statement today.

MULLEN: Correct . . .

JORDAN [This is the same] Cheryl Mills in that same time frame you are giving a heads up to, and yet we are supposed to believe this report is independent.

MULLEN: I actually rest very comfortable that it is independent.

JORDAN: Let me ask you one last question because my time is out. Did Cheryl Mills—two last questions, if I could, Mr. Chairman. Did Cheryl Mills get to see this report before it went public?

MULLEN: We had a draft report when it was wrapped up. We specifically briefed the Secretary of State for a couple of hours and Ms. Mills was in the room.

JORDAN: So, both Cheryl Mills and Hillary Clinton got to see this report before it went public?

MULLEN: The report was submitted to her. The Secretary of State made a decision—

JORDAN: So before December 18—

MULLEN:—to release it.

JORDAN:—they both got to see it.

If I could, one last question. Let me just ask this, Admiral Mullen. So if an inspector general—if you learned that an inspector general in the course of an investigation informed its agency leadership that a witness scheduled to testify before Congress would reflect poorly on the agency, would you have concerns about an inspector general doing the same thing you did?

MULLEN: The intent of—

JORDAN: No, that is yes or no. If an inspector general did what you guys did, would you have concerns about that?

MULLEN: The intent of what I did was to give the leadership in the State Department a heads up with respect to Ms. Mills. That was—

JORDAN:—see the final report until it went public.[12]

This lengthy testimony demonstrates the disrespect and lack of basic civility with which Jordan interrogated a distinguished military leader. And to what beneficial purpose? The same information could have been elicited by far less aggressive means and far more efficiently, without Jordan's constant impolite and belligerent interruptions, including interruptions after he promised to allow Mullen the opportunity to answer a question. Unfortunately, the printed record does not fully convey the disdainful attitude with which Jordan approached his task.

Congressman Jason Chaffetz (R-UT), who resigned in 2017 to become a Fox News contributor, questioned Mullen on the US military response and the failure to call on NATO for help.

> MULLEN: Everybody in the military wanted to move forward. Everybody in the military wanted to do as much they can. There were plenty of assets moving. It became a physics problem, and it's a time and distance problem. Certainly that is who we are, to try to help when someone is in harm's way.
>
> CHAFFETZ: And the fundamental problem is they didn't. They didn't get there in time. . . . It is an embarrassment to the United States of America that we could not get those assets there in time to help these people. We didn't even try, we didn't ask for permission, we didn't ask for flight clearances, we didn't even stand up the assets we had in Europe. We didn't even try.
>
> MULLEN: I disagree with what you're saying. . . .
>
> CHAFFETZ: You just told me that they did not even get to the ready. They were never asked. You presided as the Chairman of the Joint Chiefs when we bombed Libya for months [and] we did so in connection with our NATO partners and you never asked those NATO partners to help and engage. . . .
>
> MULLEN: I actually commanded NATO forces, and the likelihood that NATO could respond in a situation like that is absolutely zero.[13]

And then there was South Carolina congressman Trey Gowdy, who left Congress after the 2018 election and also became a Fox News contributor. He interrogated Mullen as to why Hillary Clinton was not interviewed.

> GOWDY: I want to read you a quote, and I want to ask you if [you] know the author of that quote, okay? "The independent accountability review board is already hard at work looking at everything, not cherry-

picking one story here or one document there, but looking at everything." Do you know who the author of that quote was?

Secretary Clinton. How could you look at everything when you didn't even bother to interview the person who is ultimately responsible for what happens at the State Department?

MULLEN: I think we've explained that . . . we found no evidence that she was involved in the decision making and no need, therefore, to do that.[14]

Gowdy then returned to the Cheryl Mills/Charlene Lamb matter.

GOWDY: Admiral, my colleague, Jason Chaffetz, asked you about Cheryl Mills and a conversation you had with her. And I noted two different times you said you wanted to give her a heads up. And make no mistake she's the lawyer for Hillary Clinton. She used to counsel for the State Department. You wanted to give her a heads up. A heads up about what?

MULLEN: I specifically said that having interviewed Charlene Lamb and knowing that she was going to appear in Congress that I thought she would not, that she would be a weak witness.

GOWDY: Were you concerned that she would tell the truth or not tell the truth? When you say not be a good witness, what was your concern?

MULLEN: I wasn't concerned about whether she would tell the truth or not. That had nothing to do with it.

GOWDY: My question was a heads up about what? Were you concerned that she would tell the truth or not tell the truth?

MULLEN: No. That had nothing to do with it. I would never question the integrity of Charlene Lamb.

GOWDY: Did you think she was just not going to be an effective witness?

[RANKING MINORITY MEMBER ELIJAH] CUMMINGS: Would the gentleman just let him answer?

GOWDY: I'm trying to help him.

CUMMINGS: He's been around 40 years in the military, so he knows how to answer questions.[15]

All this hectoring of Mullen, and also of Ambassador Pickering, was too much for Democratic member Jackie Speier. At one point in the testimony she vented:

> You know, I am so outraged by the conduct of this committee today. There is 83 years worth of service to this country by these two men, and they are being treated shabbily, and I apologize to you for what I find to be just totally unnecessary.
>
> We are trying to get the facts. We are trying to prevent this from happening again, and badgering . . . does not achieve that goal.[16]

Hillary Clinton appeared at an October 22, 2015, hearing of the House Benghazi Select Committee chaired by Congressman Gowdy. Clinton expressed her extreme displeasure about Gowdy's questioning of Mullen's independence. "Mr. Chairman, I really don't care what you say about me. It doesn't bother me a bit. I do care about what you're implying about Admiral Mullen, and I will not sit here and hear that. . . . Admiral Mullen served this country with great distinction. He served the State Department with great distinction in being the co-chair of the Accountability Review Board . . . I'm sorry that the important work that was done by that board is held in such low regard by some members of this committee, and I deeply regret it."[17]

In January 2018, Trey Gowdy announced his retirement from Congress to enter the practice of law. His reason for retirement, he said, was that he wanted a job "where facts matter," adding that, "I don't see that in our current modern political environment" where, he suggested, it's "just about winning."[18]

Maybe, just maybe, Gowdy had the Benghazi hearings in mind.

I have attended a number of congressional hearings in my lengthy career, but Issa's hearing about the ARB report was the worst in terms of the treatment by members of Congress of prominent Americans who had served their country longer and far better than the harping boorish representatives who questioned them. After the hearing, Mike Mullen, Mike Levy, and I rode together in a car back to my law offices. Mullen said to me, "Jim, you asked me all the right questions in our practice sessions, but you really didn't prepare me for the level of vitriol that I experienced."

Mea culpa.

21

The Perils of Mock Trials

Litigators are familiar with mock trials or mini-trials used to test the strength of a client's position. At times these proceedings produce unexpected, embarrassing, or amusing results.

Mock trials begin when fifty or so "jurors" are assembled to hear an abbreviated version of a case. A lawyer representing the plaintiff or the government presents the affirmative case to the entire group of jurors. Next, a lawyer for the defense counters. The jurors are then split into several smaller groups to deliberate. The lawyers can see and hear the deliberations, but the jurors cannot see them. The jurors reach conclusions not only about the merits of the dispute but also about the quality of the lawyer's presentations.

In the 1990s I was involved in a mock trial in Charleston, West Virginia. Our client, a major accounting firm, was accused of audit shortcomings.

Before the arguments began, the mock-trial facilitator asked all the jurors, who were assembled in one large room, what person living or from history they admired the most. The purpose of this question was to obtain a feel for the people judging the case. The lawyers listened to the answers behind a one-way mirror that allowed us to look into the room while remaining hidden from the jurors.

Not surprisingly, being in West Virginia, a number people said the person they admired most was Senator Robert Byrd. (Several Charleston locales are named for him.) Several Black jurors named Jesse Jackson. I was struck by the scant mention of President Bill Clinton.

Finally, the question reached a middle-aged woman seated near the back of the room. She was very much a mountain woman; in accent and appearance she seemed to embody Appalachia.

"There are two people I admire most," she said. "One is Jesus Christ. The other," she said after a pause, "is Martha Stewart."

An unfortunate guffaw from the lawyer viewing space caused fifty heads in the large room to turn toward the one-way mirror.

I confess my indiscretion.

Several years later I participated in a mock trial in New York City. This time the case was one for customs fraud brought by the federal government. Our client was a subsidiary of a prominent Japanese trading company.

My then young partner, Mike Spafford, played the role of government attorney. I argued for the defense. Although I did my rhetorical best—striding up and down the aisle between the jurors while making my somewhat forced fervent argument—Spafford was more persuasive and won the day. (The client later settled the case, perhaps afraid that the government lawyer would be as good as Spafford.)

There comes a time in such proceedings when the jurors evaluate the lawyers. This can be a humbling experience.

One jury panel member was a formidable Black woman whose demeanor, language, and attire suggested that she had seen the rougher side of New York. She was forceful in expressing her opinions about the case.

She also had strong views about the lawyers who presented. When she got around to me, she said: "That lawyer Hamilton, he ain't bad. But he ain't no Johnny Cochran."

No dispute about that here.

22

"Dean of Vetting"

In 2008, Republican presidential candidate John McCain chose Alaska governor Sarah Palin as his running mate. That misguided choice is perhaps the best example of why rigorous vetting is mandatory before a candidate for high office is thrown onto the national stage.

In October 2016, when Hillary Clinton's transition team was gearing up for vetting potential candidates for her mistakenly expected administration, a *Politico* article referred to me as the "dean of vetting."[1] This chapter discusses my long involvement in vetting candidates for vice president, the cabinet, and the Supreme Court that prompted this accolade. I also lay out the procedures I think are required to ensure that qualified, ethical candidates are chosen. Along the way I describe some of my experiences, to the extent allowed by the demands of confidentiality.

I first became involved in the vetting process in 1992. Dick Moe, a prominent lawyer who later became head of the National Trust for Historic Preservation, had been asked to run the vetting process by Warren Christopher, who was heading Bill Clinton's vice-presidential search and later became his secretary of state. Dick asked me to assemble a team to vet first one, and then another, candidate. Because neither was chosen, I refrain from revealing their identities, although both were household names.

Christopher must have liked my detailed reports on these two candidates. After Bill Clinton won the election, he asked me to take charge of vetting candidates for Clinton's cabinet and senior White House staff.[2]

Early in Clinton's first term, Justice Byron White resigned. White House counsel Bernie Nussbaum then asked me to head the vetting for Clinton's potential Supreme Court nominees.

In 2000, when Al Gore was the apparent Democratic presidential candidate, Christopher was placed in charge of his vice-presidential search. He again requested that I head the vetting operation. The eventual nominee was Senator Joe Lieberman (D-CT).[3]

John Kerry's VP search in 2004 was conducted by Jim Johnson, a prominent Washingtonian who had been the CEO of Fannie Mae. (I later represented Jim in litigation and investigations relating to that company.) At Jim's behest, I led the VP vetting for Kerry. His eventual choice was Senator John Edwards (D-NC).

Jim also initially was in charge of the VP search process in 2008 for Barack Obama. Early in that year he asked me to run Obama's VP vetting process, but I declined because I was supporting Hillary Clinton, a longtime friend who already had requested my help on vetting. I told Jim that, if things didn't go Hillary's way, I would assist. When Jim asked me whom I would recommend to begin the project, I said Bill Taylor, a well-known DC white-collar lawyer who had worked with me before on various vetting projects.

When Hillary's campaign was folding, I contacted Jim to offer my services. Thereafter, Bill and I jointly ran the vetting effort with invaluable assistance from Bill's partner, Leslie Kiernan. Senator Joe Biden (D-DE) was chosen and became vice president when Obama was elected.[4]

When Obama won and John Podesta became chair of his Transition Committee, I advised John on the vetting process. I later vetted certain Obama candidates for cabinet, subcabinet, White House, and Supreme Court positions.

After Hillary entered the fray for the 2016 election, Podesta asked me to head VP vetting. This time my role was expanded: I also supervised the preparation of extensive prevetting memoranda on potential candidates. After extensive memo-writing and vetting, Senator Tim Kaine (D-NC) emerged as the choice. My law firm partner, Raechel Kummer, was of immense help on this project.

In the fall of 2016, I assisted the Clinton Transition Team in creating memo-writing and vetting teams to aid in staffing her cabinet. But that effort came to a sad screeching halt when Hillary lost the election to Donald Trump. By that time, I had was long aware that even the best vetting efforts are subject to election vagaries and may go wasted.

*   *   *

The VP vetting process, in my experience, begins when a presidential candidate and his closest advisers confer and develop a list of possible running mates. That list may be quite long. It is then whittled down to a manageable number of persons—usually no more than thirty—about whom detailed memoranda will be written.[5]

The VP prevetting memos are based on a comprehensive review of the *public* record. No interviews are conducted. Although formats may vary, the memos often begin with an overview of a potential candidate's life and professional career. The candidate's positions on important issues are examined. Areas of controversy, potential liabilities, or scandals are reviewed. The memos often conclude with an analysis of the pros and cons of choosing this particular candidate.

The vetting memos for VP (and cabinet, White House, and Supreme Court) candidates are prepared by lawyers from the nation's leading law firms. Preparing a proper vetting memo involves a substantial commitment of time, but all work is done on a volunteer basis.

The public record memos serve as the basis for the presidential candidate to decide which persons to subject to a comprehensive vet. Normally fewer than ten will be vetted for VP.

The vets are, again, done by lawyers from the nation's most prominent firms. Each candidate is assigned a team to them. The teams will have leaders or coleaders and from around ten to twenty members. Again, all this work is done on a volunteer basis. It cannot be counted as pro bono work because that would raise conflict and business issues within the lawyers' firms.

For the Hillary Clinton vets, some two hundred attorneys worked on memo-writing or on the vetting teams.[6] I never have had difficulty in recruiting lawyers for these projects. In fact, they flock to these tasks. They see the work as exciting and as a public service. Many of my vetters—whose names are generally confidential—have gone on to hold some of the highest positions in government.

Often the team leaders I choose are people I have known for years, who have my respect and trust and who have some personal loyalty to me. They are given considerable autonomy to conduct the vets in the ways they see fit. They involve other carefully chosen lawyers (whose selection I approve).

They often select young lawyers with the technical skills to find material on the internet. I have faith that the vetters will honor stringent confidentiality requirements.

Normally, the members of one vetting team do not know the other vetters involved. They normally do not know who else is being vetted besides the candidate they are examining. That said, for consistency's sake, I have chosen to use just one highly qualified doctor to review the medical records of all candidates vetted. And I have made available to all teams a single experienced tax lawyer to examine tax returns.

I have established four guiding principles for vets: thoroughness, confidentiality, expedition, and respect. Let me elaborate on those four principles.

Being thorough means knowing everything about a candidate's life that might have political consequences or be relevant to their ability to perform. We want to know about physical and mental health, business relationships, organizations joined, family matters—we may review the Facebook pages of a candidate's children—and marital and extramarital relations.[7] We want to see the last ten years of tax returns and other financial records. We want to read everything the candidate has ever written and transcripts or videos of their speeches.[8] We want to see health records and have permission to speak to doctors. We want to see press releases and any opposition research conducted on a candidate by the candidate's own staff. We want to read what has been written about the candidate—if a clip file is maintained, we want to see that. We want videotapes of political debates and copies of voting records. We want permission to speak with the candidate's accountant. Recognizing the tension between thoroughness and confidentiality, we may want to speak with family members, friends, employees, and business associates. We want to know the candidate's views on salient issues that may not be part of the public record. The list goes on.

The essential questions are contained in a questionnaire, which now has well over 120 questions. This questionnaire has been developed and added to over the years by both Democrats and Republicans, who likely now have their own version. The Democratic version is extremely invasive, probing every aspect of a person's life. Because of its extensive nature and its call for records, candidates often respond to it in writing.[9]

The ultimate goal of the questionnaire is to determine whether there is anything in the candidate's background that would be embarrassing if revealed. One of the final inquiries in the questionnaire goes directly to this issue. That said, a good vet also provides the decider with positive factors that may not be widely known.

Facing a vet is a daunting task. Some persons vetted have publicly commented on its extremely invasive nature.

Joe Lieberman, in his and his wife's book *An Amazing Adventure*, described the VP vetting process as "kind of like having a colonoscopy without anesthesia."[10]

Senator Sherrod Brown (D-OH) recounted his 2016 VP vetting experience in a July 24, 2017, *Washington Post* article:

> Yet for all his protestations, the Clinton team saw Brown as a definite possibility, who might help win over white working-class voters, especially men. So whether out of a sense of duty or secret ambition, Brown decided to go through the vetting process.
>
> "It was pretty uncomfortable," he said.
>
> "It was excruciating," [his wife Connie] Schultz said.
>
> Both Brown and Schultz spent nearly three hours locked in a room with lawyers, answering deeply invasive questions. They were asked about their acrimonious divorces from their first spouses. They were asked about decades worth of finances and every public statement they ever made. They were asked to share all their social media passwords. (That one, Schultz declined.)
>
> "Jesus, this is one hell of a process," Brown recalled telling one of the investigators during a bathroom break. "I've seen a lot worse than you," the lawyer replied.

I confess that I was the one who provided that comforting remark to Senator Brown.[11]

In an August 31, 2018, review of a book about Vice President Pence, Connie Schultz wrote: "My husband, Senator Sherrod Brown (D-Ohio), was vetted for vice president by Hillary Clinton's campaign, and I know it to be the most intrusive experience imaginable in the life of a marriage and a family."[12]

Despite such reactions, most people are willing to endure the process—although one well-known senator declined a VP vet when told what it entailed. The reason is that people want to be VP, or in the Cabinet or on the Supreme Court. They thus are willing to undergo the indignities of a vet and to answer questions truthfully.

For example, a number of affairs have been reported to me over the years. Some I have relayed up the chain; some that I thought irrelevant were put in my back pocket.

One concluding question usually asked is, "Why do you want to be Vice President?" Joe Biden's answer was described by him in an October 2020 article in the *Atlantic.*

"At the last meeting . . . there were all these high-powered lawyers in my Capitol office's so-called hideaway," Biden [said]. "And so they're all sitting there, eight, nine of these lawyers, and at the end, Jim Hamilton"—a Washington lawyer who assisted with the vetting of potential VPs—"Jim says, 'Well, just one last question, Mr. Chairman.' He said, 'Why do you want to be vice president?'"

"I don't," said Biden.

"And he looked at me—you can ask him—he looked at me and he said, 'No? Why?'"

"Guys," said Biden, "I'm not asking to be vice president, okay? If the president wants me to be vice president—our nominee wants me to be vice president, needs the help—obviously I'm not going to be able to say no. But if you're asking me why do I want to be—I don't want to be vice president."

"Is that really your final word, like, you know, your final answer?" Hamilton asked.

"Yeah, that's my final answer," said Biden.

"But I had decided by then, if [Obama] were to ask me, obviously I'd do it," Biden [said]. "If, in fact, they could show me that, (a) I could actually help him win in places like Pennsylvania and Ohio, etc., and if (b) in fact he really did want me to help him govern, what the hell do you say? But I never—swear to God—I never, ever, ever, ever thought that I'd be asked, and I never contemplated being vice president."[13]

On several occasions when I have seen Biden since his vetting, he brings up my question and his response. In September 2019, he did this again, adding that deciding to become Obama's running mate was "the best decision I ever made, at least for me, personally." I had the presence of mind to respond, "And for the country."

As noted, a vetter's chief role is to find embarrassing information about the potential candidate. That said, I have long viewed it as my role to go beyond that and to advise the decider about my views as what to do.

I traveled to Nashville, Tennessee, in August 2000 and met with Vice President Al Gore and his team in Gore's tenth floor suite in the Loews Vanderbilt Hotel on the night he chose his VP candidate. In the room were Warren Christopher, Bill Daley, Tom Nides, Frank Hunger (Gore's brother-in-law), Ron Klain, and a few others.[14]

As reported widely in the media, three candidates—Senators Joe Lieberman, John Kerry, and John Edwards (then a boyish looking legislator with just two years' service in the Senate)—were the finalists. Gore went around the room and asked us each to express our views as to who should be chosen. There was considerable sentiment, especially among the younger folks present, for John Edwards.

When my turn came, I said: "Mr. Vice President, I would not do that. He would have to debate a much older Dick Cheney. It would look like a boy against a man." Later, Christopher, a man of few words who obviously agreed with me and feared Edwards would be chosen, pulled me aside and quietly said, "Thank you."

Not finished, I continued: "As to Joe Lieberman, I think he helps you on the ethics issue, because he was the first to criticize Bill Clinton's conduct on the floor of the Senate. As to his being Jewish, I don't know ultimately how that will cut, but I do know this: Joe is orthodox, and religious people, whatever their stripe, often like other very religious people."

Gore thought a moment and then said, "I agree with you." Later that evening he chose Joe Lieberman.

The confidentiality requirement is crucial. Otherwise, a candidate will not provide the sensitive information being requested.

The confidentiality requirement is stressed to all vetters. They know that if they leak they will be immediately dismissed from the vetting team and never again asked to participate in any project I conduct. In the many vets I have run, which number over a hundred, I have never had a leak of sensitive confidential information obtained during the vet by any vetter. This book also does not reveal any such information not already public. I do offer, however, certain vetting stories to provide context and because stories shape history.

Warren Christopher had a particular penchant for secrecy. In my dealings with him, I thus decided never (or rarely) to ask him a question. He would tell me what he wanted me to know. Christopher appreciated my ability to keep a secret. An August 8, 2000, *New York Times* article on the VP selection process contained this line: "Mr. Christopher gives [Hamilton] perhaps his highest form of praise: 'He is very discreet.'"[15]

Several stories illustrate the stress put on secrecy.

Marna Tucker, a good friend, is a well-known DC family lawyer. She was a pioneer for women lawyers and was once president of the DC Bar. She was a vetter when I vetted Clinton's cabinet and White House staff.

During that time, Marna was featured in a flattering article in the *Washington Post*. Another old friend of hers, President Clinton, called Marna to congratulate her. In the conversation, Marna mentioned that she was coming to the White House that day to vet a potential member of the White House staff. When Clinton asked who, Marna said: "Mr. President, I can't tell you. Jim says all of this is secret."

Clinton replied, "Marna, I am the President. I will find out."

I am certain that, despite my instructions, he did.

In the summer of 2004, John Kerry was poised to choose his running mate. Jeff Liss—the vetting team leader for Senator John Edwards—Jim Johnson, and I proceeded to Kerry's office in the Russell Senate Office Building to report on the Edwards's vet. Kerry was not there, so the three of us waited in his private office.

A while later Kerry arrived followed by a gaggle of press. It was vice president picking time and the press was eager for news. When Kerry entered his office, the press encamped outside in the hall, not knowing that the three of us were inside.

For around an hour, Jeff—an accomplished, articulate lawyer—reported on the results of the Edwards vet. Kerry asked the questions on his mind. Then it was time to leave, but the press bevy was still in the hall.

Jeff and I probably could have walked out unnoticed. But Jim Johnson was recognizable, and his role in leading Kerry's vice-presidential selection team was well-known. He would have been besieged. We wanted our visit to remain confidential. So what to do?

Kerry's office was on the first floor of the Russell Building. But that actually is the second floor. Outside his office windows is a ledge twenty or thirty feet above the ground. Huge columns rest on this ledge, which is about five feet wide. There is no railing.

To make our escape, Jim, Jeff, and I crawled out one of Kerry's windows onto the ledge. We then, quite carefully, walked down the ledge around fifty-sixty feet to a window leading to Senator Ted Kennedy's office. The Kennedy staff was expecting us, and we crawled into his office through that now-opened window. Then, a bit rumpled and dusty, we walked out Kennedy's door, barely glancing at the oblivious press corps assembled down the hall. Houdini could not have done it better. Secrecy was preserved.

After Kerry chose Edwards—a pick he later regretted—but before his selection was announced, someone reported to the *New York Post* that the choice was Congressman Richard Gephardt (D-MO). The *Post* ran a banner headline: "KERRY'S CHOICE: Dem Picks Gephardt as VP Candidate," with a picture of Kerry and Gephardt apparently shaking hands.[16] I framed three copies of that front page. I gave one to Jim, another to Jeff. The third hangs in my office as an example of adherence to the demands of secrecy.

Vets must be expedited, but a thorough vet usually requires a minimum of two weeks. It takes time, for example, to obtain answers to the voluminous questionnaire, to read everything a candidate has written, and to examine carefully tax returns and medical records. However, at times exigencies demand a quicker turnaround, as was the case regarding the vet of Ruth Bader Ginsburg for the Supreme Court.

In June 1993, President Clinton was moving toward nominating Circuit Judge Stephen Breyer to the Supreme Court.[17] He had promised an announcement on Monday, June 14. But then a snag. As is now publicly known, the vetters discovered, and duly reported to the White House, that the Breyers had not paid Social Security taxes for a part-time housekeeper. After the Zoë Baird debacle, which is discussed below, this was the "crime du jour." President Clinton had not been informed about this discovery until late in the week before his planned announcement.

There was a meeting in the Oval Office on Friday evening, June 12, to decide what to do. Clinton felt blindsided and was agitated. He realized he might not be able to make a Monday announcement. He might have chosen New York governor Mario Cuomo, but Cuomo apparently was not interested (and thus had not been vetted).

There were fifteen to twenty people in the Oval Office, including George Stephanopoulos, Bernie Nussbaum (White House counsel), Vince Foster, and David Gergen. Clinton went around the room asking for opinions as how to proceed. When he got to me, his fury broke out. For five minutes—red faced, his finger wagging—he railed at me about being kept in the dark as to the results of the Breyer vet.

I calmly listened to this tirade because I knew—as David Gergen later said to me—that Clinton was not mad at me. I had done my job—discovered a problem and advised the White House. Somewhere in the White House there had been a failure of communication. At the end of the evening Clinton, realizing he had been a bit too harsh, gave me an awkward hug.

When Clinton's fulminating was over, I said, "Mr. President, I understand why you are upset. Let me vet Ruth Ginsburg over the weekend, so you can make an announcement on Monday." On Saturday afternoon, Stephanopoulos finally called and asked me to do so.

Fortunately, a good bit of background work on Ginsburg already had been done. All of her judicial opinions on the DC Circuit had been read. Her precourt legal career had been scrutinized. But the very personal questions contained in the vetting questionnaire had not been asked.

The vetting team, which included Vince Foster and Ron Klain, arrived at Ginsburg's Watergate apartment early Sunday morning. Ruth and her husband, Marty, met us at the door. Marty, a renowned cook and a delightful fellow, had prepared an excellent breakfast.

I began asking Ruth the relevant questions. Ruth was, as she has said publicly, "sober." She was also at times laconic, and her answers (all perfectly appropriate and benign) came carefully and slowly.

Clinton had never met Ginsburg, so a meeting between them was scheduled for late Sunday morning. By around 10:30 a.m. or 11:00 a.m. when she had to leave to drive to the White House, I had made little progress and was feeling frustrated.

An hour or so later she returned. I asked her how her meeting with the president had gone. The "sober" judge grabbed my arm and said, "Oh, he's so handsome."[18]

After her meeting with the President, which by her and Clinton's accounts went very well, her answers seemed to flow much more freely. We completed the vet that afternoon and reported to the White House that no issues had surfaced. The next day Clinton announced that he was nominating her to the Supreme Court. Justice Breyer was appointed the next year after Justice Harry Blackmun resigned.

The final guiding principle is respect. I have joked that a good vetter is a cross between a sadist and a voyeur. But that is only a joke, and perhaps a bad one. The people vetted for VP, cabinet, and the Supreme Court usually have risen to the pinnacle of US public life. They deserve respect and fair treatment, even when the most invasive questions are being asked. A respectful attitude also is the best approach to elicit candid answers.

I believe the goal of treating candidates with respect generally has been achieved. Candidates have cringed at questions asked, and perhaps occasionally become angry, but afterward many have expressed appreciation for how the vets have been handled.[19] Some lasting friendships have been cemented between skilled vetters and those vetted.

On August 2, 2016, after he was chosen to be Hillary Clinton's running mate, I received a note from Senator Tim Kaine, which read: "Thanks for your professionalism during my 08 and 16 vets. You know me pretty well by now."[20]

At the end of the process, reports on VP possibilities are made to the presidential candidate. Thus, on one day in the summer of 2016, a stream of vetting leaders entered Hillary Clinton's DC home to lay out what they had found. Their cogent presentations were well-received by an appreciative Clinton.

My practice is to allow the leaders of the individual vetting teams to take the lead in reporting. They have done the hard work; they know the facts best; they deserve the credit and face time with the person who may be our next president.

I instruct that these reports be made *orally,* not in writing. It is one thing to prepare written reports from the *public* record as foundations for the vets, even though these reports are treated as highly confidential and given limited circulation. It would be quite another matter to present written reports containing answers to all the sensitive, intrusive questions asked a candidate. I trust my vetters, but I want to minimize the possibility of a leak of a document that could prove harmful and unfair.[21]

At times, vets have disqualified candidates. In 1993, when Zoë Baird was to be attorney general, vetters discovered that she had hired undocumented immigrants and not paid her portion of their Social Security taxes. We duly reported these facts to Warren Christopher. Initially, Christopher, and apparently President Clinton, were not concerned about what they viewed as minor violations. But then a firestorm erupted over having an attorney general who had broken the law. Zoë was forced to withdraw.

The next candidate was respected district judge Kimba Wood. When asked to vet her, I promptly delegated the task to my law partner, Lester Hyman, because Kimba years before had been a close friend. The White House had asked Kimba if she had "a Zoë Baird problem," and Kimba truthfully (but perhaps with a lack of political astuteness) had said no. Zoë had hired undocumented immigrants and *had not* paid taxes. Kimba had hired an undocumented immigrant and *had* paid taxes. In fifteen minutes at lunch, Lester discovered this fact that the White House, in its interviews with Kimba, had missed by asking an imprecise question.

When we reported this to the White House, officials there were furious. They believed Kimba had misled them, and she was forced to withdraw. The White House then, spitefully and churlishly, leaked that, when she was at the London School of Economics in 1966, she had been for about five days in training as a Playboy Bunny.

I had been at the London School of Economics at the time and knew Kimba. When I heard she was in Bunny training, I (like others) told her that this was most unwise if she wanted to be a lawyer. I informed her that the octogenarians who had examined my fitness for the North Carolina Bar had worried about my membership in the Yale Law School World Community Association, fearing that this quite benign organization was a communist front. Bunny training, I said, could raise eyebrows down the road with some bar committee. Had I been prescient, I would have said, "Kimba this is really unwise because you want to be Attorney General someday." But I was not that farsighted.

In Supreme Court vets, health is a major factor. Any president wants his appointee to serve many years on the Court. Judge Richard Arnold of the Eighth Circuit Court of Appeals—a brilliant jurist and Arkansas native—was a favorite of President Clinton. As has been reported in the media, he was seriously vetted for the Supreme Court in 1993. The problem was that Judge Arnold had Lymphoma C. One can live years with this condition, but the predicted life expectancy then was around ten years. Clinton's intense interest in nominating Judge Arnold prompted him personally to call the National Institutes of Health to inquire about Arnold's survival prospects. In the end, Clinton went first with Ruth Bader Ginsburg, then with Steve Breyer. It has been reported that Clinton wept when he told Judge Arnold he would not appoint him to the Supreme Court. Richard Arnold died in 2004. Justice Breyer, thankfully, served with thoughtful, pragmatic distinction until his retirement in 2022.

Justice Ginsburg died in 2020 after twenty-seven honorable years on the High Court. She was the first woman to lie in state in the Capitol. The nation mourned.

23

A Concluding Word
for Young Lawyers

While writing this book, I also was giving my
oral history to the DC Circuit Court of Appeals Historical Society. This yet-
to-be released oral history covers many of the topics discussed in more depth
in this book. My interviewer was Bill Jeffress, one of DC's most respected
trial lawyers, who represented, among many prominent clients, Scooter
Libby, and who over the years has assisted me in VP vetting.

One question Bill asked was this: "You have spent much of your career in
large firms that have an eye on the bottom line. How were you able to participate in so many cases and political activities that were done pro bono or for
very little remuneration?" There are several answers to this salient question.

I was fortunate after Watergate, and after publishing a well-received book
on congressional investigations, to have a public presence that my law firms
thought valuable. My firms gave me freedom to take cases that enhanced
their reputations if not their pocketbooks. They also thought my leadership
in VP, cabinet, and Supreme Court vetting improved their public image.

I also was willing to take my lumps in the compensation process, which
invariably came, in order to shape the kind of law practice I wanted. Fortunately, I have been able to bring in a respectable number of good-paying
clients over the years and to achieve successes for them and other paying clients, all of which justified reasonable compensation. But if I had been, say,
a successful tax lawyer, my bank account would be much fatter. The freedom
to practice law my way was more valuable to me than a few extra dollars.

I have long said—and advised young lawyers and others starting out—that
there are four elements that comprise a successful career.

- You do need to make enough money to be comfortable. We must provide our families a home, educate our children, be able to travel, and, if one ever gets around to it, retire without undue concerns. Being in large law firms, such as those where I have been a partner, can be lucrative, but megafirms are not for everyone.
- You should work with people you enjoy and respect. On occasion, we all have had to deal with callous, distasteful, and dishonest folks who should be avoided. In Washington, this is sometimes hard to do. And on occasion the very nature of our work places us in unpleasant circumstances. However, having a compatible, ethical, and wise surrounding coterie should be a goal.

Young lawyers should be careful regarding the law firms they choose to join. Some firms rightly have the reputation of being difficult places to work, not only for the long hours demanded but also for the lack of respect and concern given to fellow attorneys and staff. Fortunately for me, the firm with which I have been most recently affiliated, Morgan, Lewis & Bockius—which is chaired by a woman, Jami McKeon—strives to govern humanely. Disrespect or mistreatment of firm employee is not tolerated.

- You should find work that interests you. Boredom is a curse. I learned that early on living in a small town, as charming and comfortable as at times it could be. I am fortunate in that I have found most legal controversies interesting either because of the facts, personalities, or legal issues involved, or the evil dragons to be slain.

Sadly, many lawyers do not find joy in the law. Young attorney may be stuck on drawn-out, tedious cases where document review is the principal activity. (I remember early in my career emerging from a dusty warehouse dirty and bloodied from moving around boxes of documents.) A caring mentor at a law firm may be essential in assisting a young lawyer to find meaningful work and avoid a dreary slog.

- At least part of the time, your accomplishments should be socially worthwhile. Frankly, not everything lawyers in large firms do meets that test. But both in law and politics, it is possible, if one makes an effort, to accomplish societal good. Many law firms offer young lawyers the chance to engage in significant pro bono endeavors. Those are the firms that young attorneys who want to contribute to their communities while earning a good wage should seek out.

Two final pieces of advice to lawyers young and old.

If you represent prominent clients and others whose reputations are under public attack, perhaps for the first time, realize your limitations. Clients may have critical needs most lawyers can't fulfill. Public attacks may create heretofore unknown anxiety, even depression. Clients with such issues may require a pastor, priest, rabbi, psychiatrist, or even a good friend to provide comfort and counsel. Steer them that way.

I learned this lesson the hard way in the Vince Foster tragedy. Since then, I have advised other clients under attack to seek the assistance they need from persons better equipped to provide it than I am. Regrettably, I was not wise enough to give that advice to Vince when I had the chance.

Last, some advice to attorneys dealing with the press. Be wary. Some lawyers become too infatuated with media attention and, in unguarded moments, say things not in their clients' best interests. Remember that your agenda and that of the media likely are not the same.

I was burned once during the Watergate investigation by a reporter I thought was friendly. After that, besides being careful about what I said, and often just refusing to comment, I have on many occasions adhered to the following approach: I will do an interview completely off the record, meaning that a reporter cannot publish what I say, even on background without attribution to me. Then, if the reporter wants to use a quote, I ask that it be sent to me in writing for my review so I can, if I agree it can be used, clarify what I meant or clean up my syntax or grammar before the quote is published. This practice has worked well for me as I have pursued my over fifty-year career on history's front lines.

Notes

1. The Path to Washington

1. Robert Tinkler, *James Hamilton of South Carolina* (Baton Rouge: Louisiana State University Press, 2004), 17.

2. My sister is also a prominent Washington painter.

3. Laski was a leading socialist politician, writer, and thinker in the mid-twentieth century. He was a professor at LSE from 1926 to 1950.

2. The Senate Watergate Committee: The White House Tapes Uncovered

1. Ervin and the other three Democrats, Herman Talmadge (Georgia), Dan Inouye (Hawaii), and Joe Montoya (New Mexico), were selected, in part, because none of them were going to run for president. The Republicans were Vice Chair Howard Baker (Tennessee), Ed Gurney (Florida), and Lowell Weicker (Connecticut).

2. Malek's withdrawal came after I testified about his involvement in the Responsiveness Program, which I had been coresponsible for investigating, before the Senate Governmental Affairs Committee, which was considering his nomination. Members of the committee, including my Yale Law School classmate Jack Danforth, were highly critical of Malek's Responsiveness Program conduct. Malek thus had reasons to dislike me, but he later showed he could rise above personal animus.

Joe Wright, Reagan's last director of the Office of Management and Budget, was a friend, client, and sometime tennis opponent. (Once or twice, we played on the White House tennis court.) Joe and Malek were close friends. When Joe married his wife, Ellen,—a sparkling woman—Malek hosted the engagement party in his mansion high above the Potomac River just off of Chain Bridge Road. Joe wanted me to come. I said, "Joe, you better speak to Fred about this. Might be a problem." Several days later, Joe called to say Malek would be delighted for me to attend. Before the evening was over, Malek and I, in a surreal moment, had a very friendly chat on a staircase landing underneath photographs of Nixon and his two principal aides, Bob Haldeman and John Ehrlichman.

3. The title I chose was a mistake. Many thought it sounded like a book on proctology.

4. Douglas E. Kneeland, "Inouye Says 'Thank You' to Senators—in Hawaiian," *New York Times*, August 3, 1973.

5. Herman E. Talmadge, *Talmadge: A Political Legacy, A Politician's Life* (Atlanta: Peachtree, 1987), 283-284. A few years later, Talmadge himself came under fire in a Senate Ethics Committee trial and a Department of Justice investigation about alleged financial improprieties. As discussed in chapter 3, I represented him in those matters.

6. Sam J. Ervin Jr., *The Whole Truth: The Watergate Conspiracy* (New York: Random House, 1980), 25 (emphasis added).

7. Fred D. Thompson, *At That Point in Time: The Inside Story of the Senate Watergate Committee* (New York: Quadrangle/New York Times Book Co., 1975), 83.

8. Carl Bernstein and Bob Woodward, *All the President's Men* (New York: Simon & Schuster, 1974), 330-331.

9. Thompson, *At That Point in Time*, 82n7.

10. John W. Dean, *Blind Ambition: The White House Years* (New York: Simon & Schuster, 1976), 332.

11. See generally James Hamilton, *The Power to Probe: A Study of Congressional Investigations* (New York: Random House, 1976), 85-91; James Hamilton, Robert F. Muse, and Kevin R. Amer, "Congressional Investigations: Politics and Process," *American Criminal Law Review* 44, no. 3 (Summer 2007): 1132-1133.

12. Samuel Dash, *Chief Counsel: Inside the Ervin Committee—The Untold Story of Watergate* (New York: Random House, 1976), 184.

13. *United States v. Nixon*, 418 U.S. 683 (1974).

14. *Senate Select Comm. on Presidential Campaign Activities v. Nixon*, 498 F.2d 725 (D.C. Cir. 1974).

15. *Comm. On Judiciary v. Miers*, 558 F.Supp. 2d 53 (D.D.C. 2008).

16. Pub.L. No. 95-521, §601(a), 92 Stat. 1824, 1867-1873 (1978).

17. As said at the beginning of this chapter, I was fortunate to participate in an event of the historical significance of Watergate. Recognizing the magnitude of the moment, I gave my all. A prized possession is a note to me from Senator Ervin, handwritten as committee operations wound down, expressing his appreciation for my "magnificent service" to the committee.

3. Senator Herman Talmadge: The Beneficent Overcoat

1. "Excerpts from Ehrlichman's Testimony before the Senate Watergate Committee," *New York Times*, July 26, 1973.

2. During the Watergate hearings people in airports would ask for Talmadge's auto-graph. At times, others would inquire whether he would run for president. He shrugged off that suggestion, being of the opinion after years in public life, "that in the mid-1970's it would be next to impossible for a politician from Georgia to be elected Pres-ident." Herman E. Talmadge, *Talmadge: A Political Legacy, A Politician's Life* (Atlanta: Peachtree, 1987), 265.

3. James Hamilton, *The Power to Probe: A Study of Congressional Investigations* (New York: Random House, 1976), back cover.

4. Senate Select Committee on Ethics, *Investigation of Senator Herman E. Talmadge–Open Session Hearings* (Washington, DC: US Government Printing Office, 1980), 313.

5. Ninety-Sixth Congress, *Senate Reports Vol. 10–Miscellaneous Reports* (Washington, DC: US Government Printing Office, 1979), 134.

6. Ninety-Sixth Congress, *Senate Reports Vol. 10*, 13.

7. Minchew was a personable native Georgian who had impressed Talmadge in his work as a lobbyist.

8. Bill Richards, "Talmadge Calls His Accuser a 'Proven Liar,'" *Washington Post*, May 1, 1979.

9. Richards, "Talmadge Calls His Accuser."

10. Senate Select Committee on Ethics, *Open Session Hearings*, vol. 2 (Washington, DC: US Government Printing Office, 1979), 1213.

11. Senate Select Committee on Ethics, *Investigation of Senator Herman E. Talmadge*, vol. 2, 6.

12. Nimetz was also a concert-level pianist and a Rhodes Scholar.

13. B. Drummond Ayres Jr., "Talmadge Lawyers Challenge Accuser," *New York Times*, June 12, 1979.

14. Senate Select Committee on Ethics, *Investigation of Senator Herman E. Talmadge–Open Session Hearings*, vol. 2, 981–982.

15. Senate Select Committee on Ethics, vol. 2, 1174.

16. Senate Select Committee on Ethics, vol. 2, 1175.

17. Senate Select Committee on Ethics, *Report of the Select Committee on Ethics to Accompany S. Res. 249 together with Additional Views*, vol. 1 (Washington, DC: US Gov-ernment Printing Office, 1980), 17.

18. Senate Select Committee on Ethics, *Report of the Select Committee on Ethics*, vol. 1, 18.

19. Senate Select Committee on Ethics, *Report of the Select Committee on Ethics*, vol. 1, 167.

20. "The Censure Case of Herman E. Talmadge of Georgia (1979)," US Senate, accessed August 9, 2021, https://www.senate.gov/about/powers-procedures/censure /139HermanTalmadge.htm.

21. "Senator Who Avoided Limelight," *New York Times*, October 12, 1979.

22. Timothy S. Robinson, "Talmadge Ex-Aide Minchew Sentenced to Four Months on Fake Voucher Count," *Washington Post*, October 11, 1979.

4. Senator Dave Durenberger: The Fallout of Bad Advice

1. Although I am a Democrat, I have represented many staunch Republicans, including former senator Phil Gramm and my good friend Joe Wright, President Reagan's last head of OMB. During Iran-Contra, I represented two prominent members of the Reagan administration whose conduct did not receive much public attention. For years I was outside general counsel for the American Bakers Association, which is mainly comprised of conservative Republican—and public-spirited—businessmen. My representation of conservative columnist Bob Novak is discussed in another chapter of this book.

2. Philip Shenon, "Washington Talk: Profile; Senator Durenberger Stirs New Concern with Outspokenness," *Washington Post*, April 8, 1987.

3. John M. Goshko and Bob Woodward, "Israeli Spy 'Recruited' by CIA," *Washington Post*, March 21, 1987.

4. Stephen Engelberg, "Senator Is Quoted as Saying U.S. Recruited Israeli Officer as a Spy," *New York Times*, March 21, 1987.

5. Robert L. Jackson and Ronald L. Ostrow, "Israeli Disclosure Raises Questions on U.S. Spying," *Los Angeles Times*, June 5, 1993.

6. William Safire, "Essay: Pollard Strikes Again," *New York Times*, March 30, 1987.

7. Former CIA director Casey, with whom Durenberger had on occasion clashed because of Casey's reticence to provide information to the Senate Intelligence Committee, previously had accused Durenberger of "repeated compromise of sensitive intelligence sources and methods." Philip Shenon, "Senator Durenberger Stirs New Concern with Outspokenness," *New York Times*, April 8, 1987.

8. Shenon, "Senator Durenberger Stirs New Concern with Outspokenness."

9. Goshko and Woodward, "Israeli Spy 'Recruited' by CIA."

10. Helen Dewar, "Ethics Panel Criticizes Durenberger's Remarks," *Washington Post*, April 30, 1988.

11. US Congress, *Journal of the Senate* (Washington, DC: US Government Printing Office, 1976), 16.

12. I had later encounters with Rudman, described in this book, that reinforced my view.

13. Irvin Molotsky, "Senate Ethics Panel Criticizes Durenberger on Talk," *New York Times*, April 30, 1988.

14. Molotsky, "Senate Ethics Panel Criticizes Durenberger on Talk."

15. Dewar, "Ethics Panel Criticizes Durenberger's Remarks."

16. Dewar, "Ethics Panel Criticizes Durenberger's Remarks."

17. US Senate Select Committee on Ethics, *Investigation of Senator David F. Durenberger–Exhibits*, vol. 4, part 7 (Washington, DC: US Government Printing Office, 1990), 10–13.

18. 2 U.S.C. § 31-1.

19. Senate Select Committee on Ethics, *Investigation of Senator David F. Durenberger–Exhibits*, vol. 4, part 2 (Washington, DC: Government Printing Office, 1990), 305.

20. Federal Election Commission, "First General Counsel's Report," January 29, 1991.

21. Federal Election Commission, "First General Counsel's Report."

22. Senate Select Committee on Ethics, *Investigation of Senator David F. Durenberger–Special Counsel Hearing Exhibits* (Washington, DC: US Government Printing Office, 1990), 387.

23. Senate Select Committee on Ethics, *Investigation of Senator David F. Durenberger–Special Counsel Hearing Exhibits*, 152.

24. Senate Select Committee on Ethics, *Investigation of Senator David F. Durenberger–Report* (Washington, DC: US Government Printing Office, 1990), 11.

25. Senate Select Committee on Ethics, *Investigation of Senator David F. Durenberger–Report*, 13.

26. Senate Select Committee on Ethics, 13.

27. Senate Select Committee on Ethics, 14.

5. The Keating Five: Senator DeConcini Fights Back

1. Helen Dewar, "'Keating Five' Hearings to Open Today," *Washington Post*, November 15, 1990.

2. John R. Cranford, "Public Could Affect 'Keating 5' Outcome," *Congressional Quarterly*, December 8, 1990.

3. Senate Select Committee on Ethics, *Preliminary Inquiry into Allegations Regarding Senators Cranston, DeConcini, Glenn, McCain, and Riegle, and Lincoln Savings and Loan—Part 2* (Washington, DC: US Government Printing Office, 1991), 122–123.

4. Senate Select Committee on Ethics, *Preliminary Inquiry into Allegations, Part 2*, 134.

5. Senate Select Committee on Ethics, *Part 2*, 141.

6. Senate Select Committee on Ethics, *Preliminary Inquiry into Allegations Regarding Senators Cranston, DeConcini, Glenn, McCain, and Riegle, and Lincoln Savings and Loan—Part 1* (Washington, DC: US Government Printing Office, 1991), 3–5.

7. Senate Select Committee on Ethics, *Part 1*, 175–177.

8. Senate Select Committee on Ethics, *Part 1*, 95.

9. Senate Select Committee on Ethics, *Part 1*, 95–96.

10. Senate Select Committee on Ethics, *Part 1*, 62–63.

11. Senate Select Committee on Ethics, *Part 1*, 33–35.

12. Senate Select Committee on Ethics, *Part 1*, 89–91.

13. Senate Select Committee on Ethics, *1*, 8–9.

14. U.S. Senate Select Committee on Ethics, *Preliminary Inquiry into Allegations Regarding Senators Cranston, DeConcini, Glenn, McCain, and Riegle, and Lincoln Savings and Loan—Part 8* (Washington, DC: US Government Printing Office, 1991), 105.

15. U.S. Senate Select Committee on Ethics, *Preliminary Inquiry into Allegations Regarding Senators Cranston, DeConcini, Glenn, McCain, and Riegle, and Lincoln Savings and Loan—Part 3* (Washington, DC: US Government Printing Office, 1991), 40.

16. U.S. Senate Select Committee on Ethics, *Part 3*, 11.

17. U.S. Senate Select Committee on Ethics, *Part 3*, 15.

18. U.S. Senate Select Committee on Ethics, *Part 3*, 16–19.

19. The televised hearings brought home to me that I was aging in another way. During Watergate, I received fan mail, sometimes suggestive, from young ladies. During the Keating Five hearings, almost twenty years later when I had begun to gray, my few pieces of fan mail came from retirement homes.

20. U.S. Senate Select Committee on Ethics, *Preliminary Inquiry into Allegations Regarding Senators Cranston, DeConcini, Glenn, McCain, and Riegle, and Lincoln Savings and Loan—Part 5* (Washington, DC: US Government Printing Office, 1991), 21–22.

21. U.S. Senate Select Committee on Ethics, *Part 8*, 94.

22. Before Dennis hired me, Kristina and I had dinner with him and his wife. Apparently he decided he wanted an attorney with a bit less bluster to represent him.

23. Senate Select Committee on Ethics, *Preliminary Inquiry into Allegations Regarding Senators Cranston, DeConcini, Glenn, McCain, and Riegle, and Lincoln Savings and Loan—Part 6* (Washington, DC: US Government Printing Office, 1991), 139.

24. U.S. Senate Select Committee on Ethics, *Part 8*, 136.

25. U.S. Senate Select Committee on Ethics, *Part 8*, 187.

26. Robert S. Bennett, *In the Ring: The Trials of a Washington Lawyer* (New York: Three Rivers Press, 2008), 148.

27. Senate Select Committee on Ethics, *Senate Ethics Manual* (Washington, DC: US Government Printing Office, 2000), 183.

28. "Cranston Reprimanded by Senate Ethics," *CQ Almanac* Online Edition, accessed August 11, 2021, https://alamedamgr.files.wordpress.com/2018/04/cq-almanac -online-edition-keating-five.pdf.

29. Senate Select Committee on Ethics, *Investigation of Senator Alan Cranston—Report* (Washington, DC: US Government Printing Office, 1991), 14.

30. Senate Select Committee on Ethics, *Investigation of Senator Alan Cranston—Report*, 15.

31. Senate Select Committee on Ethics, 15–16.

32. This comment related to Keating's not telling Dennis that he had entered into a consent decree with the Securities and Exchange Commission to resolve fraud charges before asking Dennis to assist him in his unsuccessful attempt to become US ambassador to the Bahamas.

33. Senate Select Committee on Ethics, 17.

34. Senate Select Committee on Ethics, 17.

35. Senate Select Committee on Ethics, 18.

36. Senate Select Committee on Ethics, 20.

37. Senate Select Committee on Ethics, 36.

38. At Yale Law School I was in a class with Alan. He was extremely sure of himself even then.

39. Martin Weil, "California Sen. Alan Cranston, 86, Dies," *Washington Post*, January 1, 2001.

40. Richard L. Berke, "Cranston Rebuked by Ethics Panel," *New York Times*, November 21, 1991.

6. Lawyers for Mississippi

1. Gesell became a good friend. For a while, I lived across the street from him in Georgetown, and on occasion I visited his home and his beloved farm in Leesburg, Virginia, where he spent most weekends.

As fate would have it, as a district judge Gesell was called upon to decide the Senate

Watergate Committee's case against Nixon for the White House tapes. He ruled against us on what I considered to be shaky grounds, which the Court of Appeals, although it affirmed, did not adopt.

In my book on congressional investigations, after praising Gesell's extraordinary gifts, I heavily criticized his opinion in a respectful tone. After the book came out, I sent him a copy. I then waited several weeks before I visited him in his chambers, as at times I did. When I walked in he said: "Read your book. Good book. You're wrong." That was the last we spoke of it. Our friendship continued.

2. *Sanders v. Russell*, 401 F.2d 241 (5th Cir. 1968).

3. "John C. Satterfield American Bar Association Collection," University of Mississippi, accessed August 11, 2021, https://egrove.olemiss.edu/satterfield/.

4. My Yale Law School classmate, the wonderful Marian Wright (now Marian Wright Edelman), who went on to found and lead the Children's Defense Fund, was on the brief with Coleman. Marian and I were the only South Carolinians in our law school class.

5. Brief for Petitioners, *Anderson v. Cox*, no. 25815 (5th Cir. 1968), 14.

6. *Sanders v. Russell*, 401 F.2d 241 (5th Cir. 1968).

7. *Sanders v. Russell*, 244.

8. *Sanders v. Russell*, 244–245.

9. *Sanders v. Russell*, 247.

7. "Otto the Terrible"

1. David D. Newsom, "An Outspoken Man," *Christian Science Monitor*, September 6, 1988.

2. "The Serendipitous Global Citizen Award—Remarks by Kul Chandra Gautam," National Peace Corps Association, accessed August 11, 2021, https://www.peacecorps connect.org/articles/the-serendipitous-global-citizen-award.

3. Newsom, "An Outspoken Man."

4. *Davis v. Passman*, 442 U.S. 228 (1979).

5. John MacDonald, "Congress Should Abide by the Laws It Imposes on Others," *Hartford Courant*, February 13, 1993.

6. *U.S. v. Passman*, 455 F.Supp. 794, 801 (D.D.C. 1978).

7. "Barrington D. Parker," *Washington Post*, June 5, 1993.

8. *Dusty v. United States*, 362 U.S. 402 (1960).

9. *U.S. v. Passman*, 455 F. Supp. 794, 795 (D.D.C. 1978).

10. *U.S. v. Passman*, 797.

11. *U.S. v. Passman*, 798.

12. *U.S. v. Passman*, 799.

13. *U.S. v. Passman*, 801.

14. William Safire, "Justice Finessed," *New York Times*, July 27, 1978.

8. Marina Oswald: "Nobody I Can Turn To"

1. Stokes was the first Black person elected to Congress from Ohio and served fifteen terms. He was chair of the House Intelligence Committee and a founding member and head of the Congressional Black Caucus.

2. A photograph of her appearing before the committee is found on page 136.

3. House of Representatives Select Committee on Assassinations, *Investigation of the Assassination of President John F. Kennedy–Volume II* (Washington, DC: US Government Printing Office, 1979), 308.

4. House of Representatives Select Committee on Assassinations, *Investigation of the Assassination of President John F. Kennedy–Volume II*, 232.

5. Select Committee on Assassinations, 249.

6. Select Committee on Assassinations, 257, 252.

7. Select Committee on Assassinations, 286, 300.

8. Select Committee on Assassinations, 262.

9. Select Committee on Assassinations, 312.

10. U.S. House of Representatives Select Committee on Assassinations, 278, 303, 312.

11. "JFK Assassination Records–Summary of Findings," National Archives, page last updated August 15, 2016, accessed August 11, 2021, https://www.archives.gov/research/jfk/select-committee-report/summary.html.

12. In December 1978, after the hearing concluded, I received a much-appreciated handwritten letter from Congressman Stokes, who before Congress had been a civil rights lawyer. The letter read in part:

Let me also take this opportunity to congratulate you for the dignity and professionalism which you brought to our hearings on each occasion when you represented clients before us. I happen to love the legal profession and think that there is no higher calling. Some lawyers who appeared here made me ashamed to be a member of the profession. . . .

Sincerely,

Lou

Stoke's letter referred to my representation of a witness in the investigation of Martin Luther King Jr.'s assassination, again at the DC Bar's request. For that witness's protection I had invoked a little-used House rule to bar television coverage of his testimony before the committee.

9. Danger in Distant Palau

1. Actually, I was told that he was only the acting Recklai because of a drinking problem.

2. William Chapman, "In Palau, Even God Is Said to Oppose Micronesian Unity," *Washington Post*, July 17, 1978.

3. United Nations Trusteeship Council, *Report of the United Nations Visiting Mission to Observe the Referendum in the Trust Territory of the Pacific Islands, 1978* (New York: United Nations, 1979), 52.

4. Philip Shenon, "Convictions Reversed in Island Slaying," *New York Times*, July 21, 1987.

5. United Nations Trusteeship Council, *Report of the United Nations Visiting Mission*, 53.

6. United Nations Trusteeship Council, 55.

7. United Nations Trusteeship Council, 62.

8. United Nations Trusteeship Council, 62.

10. Debategate

1. John Eby, "Reagan's 'Sparring Partner' Previews the Debate," *Dowagiac Daily News*, October 29, 1980.

2. House of Representatives Subcommittee on Human Resources, *Unauthorized Transfers of Nonpublic Information during the 1980 Presidential Election–Report*, part 1 (Washington, DC: US Government Printing Office, 1984), 110.

3. House of Representatives Subcommittee on Human Resources, *Unauthorized Transfers–Report*, part 1, 8–10.

4. House of Representatives Subcommittee on Human Resources, *Unauthorized Transfers of Nonpublic Information During the 1980 Presidential Election–Report*, part 2 (Washington, DC: Government Printing Office, 1984), 1087–1088.

5. Subcommittee on Human Resources, part 2, 122.

6. Subcommittee on Human Resources, part 2, 1236–1238.

7. Francis X. Clines, "Casey Says He 'Wouldn't Touch' Papers from the Carter Campaign," *New York Times*, July 6, 1983.

8. Subcommittee on Human Resources, part 2, 1105–1111.

9. Subcommittee on Human Resources, part 2, 1905.

10. Lou Cannon, "Casey Operated an 'Intelligence' System in 1980," *Washington Post*, July 1, 1983.

11. Martin Tolchin, "Panel Said to Find Casey Got Carter Papers," *New York Times*, May 23, 1984.

12. On Corbin, see generally Craig Shirley, *Rendezvous with Destiny: Ronald Reagan and the Campaign That Changed America* (Wilmington, DE: Intercollegiate Studies Institute, 2011), chapter 28.

13. Subcommittee on Human Resources, part 1, 123.

14. Shirley, *Rendezvous with Destiny*, 440.

15. Howard Kurtz, "Panel Cites Evidence of a Crime," *Washington Post*, May 24, 1984.

16. Subcommittee on Human Resources, part 1, 124.

17. Shirley, *Rendezvous with Destiny*, 438.

18. Shirley, 437.

19. Subcommittee on Human Resources, part 2, 1127–1128.

20. Subcommittee on Human Resources, part 2, 1107.

21. Subcommittee on Human Resources, part 2, 1090.

22. Isaac Chotiner, "George Will, Tea Party Tory," *New Republic*, February 11, 2014, https://newrepublic.com/article/116426/george-will-finds-his-wild-side.

23. Subcommittee on Human Resources, part 1, 23–24.

24. Subcommittee on Human Resources, part 2, 1860.

25. Subcommittee on Human Resources, part 2, 1905.

26. Subcommittee on Human Resources, part 2, 2145.

27. Subcommittee on Human Resources, part 2, 1133.

28. Subcommittee on Human Resources, part 2, 2146.

29. See, e.g., 18 U.S.C. 641 (theft of government property).

30. *Banzhaf v. Smith*, 588 F.Supp. 1498 (D.D.C.), vacated per curiam 737 F.2d 1167 (D.C. Cir. 1984).

31. *Unauthorized Transfers–Report*, part 2, 2151–2156.

32. *Banzhaf v. Smith*, 737 F.2d 1167, 1168 (D.C. Cir. 1984).

33. *Unauthorized Transfers–Report*, part 1, 124.

34. In September 2000, former congressman Tom Downey (D-NY) was assisting Vice President Al Gore in preparation for his debate with Governor George W. Bush. Gore received in the mail, from an unknown source, debate materials prepared for Bush.

Downey quickly sent the materials to the FBI and informed Bush's campaign manager what had happened. The Gore team did not use the Bush debate materials. The attentive learn history's lessons. Russell Berman, "'Uh-Oh, We Shouldn't Have This,'" *Atlantic*, June 14, 2019, https://www.theatlantic.com/politics/archive/2019/06/trump -fbi-foreign-election-interference-gore-downey/591748/.

11. *Impeachment Alaska Style*

1. State of Alaska Senate, *Report of the Grand Jury Concerning the Investigation Conducted Into the Fairbanks Consolidated State Office Lease with the Fifth Avenue Center* (Juneau, AK: Legislative Affairs Agency, 1985), 5.

2. State of Alaska Senate, *Report of the Grand Jury*, 6.

3. "Panel in Alaska Advises Ending Bid to Impeach," *New York Times*, August 4, 1985.

4. State of Alaska Senate, *Report of the Grand Jury*, 63–64.

5. State of Alaska Senate, *Report of the Grand Jury*, 68.

6. State of Alaska Senate, *Senate Journal* (Juneau, AK: Legislative Affairs Agency, 1985), 1490.

7. "Panel in Alaska Advises."

8. Alaska State Legislature, Senate Rules Committee, *Inquiry into the Report of the Grand Jury of the First Judicial District, Superior Court, State of Alaska Dated July 1, 1985,* Transcript, July 22, 1985, 79. http://archives2.legis.state.ak.us/PublicImageServer .cgi?lib/8502060Monday,%20July%2022,%201985.pdf

9. Alaska State Legislature, *Inquiry into the Report of the Grand Jury*, 122.

10. State of Alaska Senate, *Senate Journal*, 1493.

11. State of Alaska Senate, *Senate Journal*, 1491.

12. State of Alaska Senate, 1491.

13. State of Alaska Senate, 1491.

14. State of Alaska Senate, 1492.

15. State of Alaska Senate, 1492.

16. "Panel in Alaska Advises Ending Bid to Impeach," *New York Times*, August 4, 1985.

17. "Impeachment Inquiry Begins in Alaska," *New York Times*, July 23, 1985.

12. The Foster Notes

1. R. W. Apple Jr., "Note Left by White House Aide: Accusation, Anger and Despair," *New York Times*, August 11, 1993.

2. One staff member later was indicted for embezzlement but acquitted.

3. Attorney-client privilege protects information a client provides a lawyer for the purpose of obtaining legal advice.

4. Sometime after Vince's death, Bernie called to say that Hillary wanted me to take Vince's job as deputy White House counsel. I politely declined.

5. Materials prepared by an attorney in anticipation of litigation are protected by this doctrine.

6. The Whitewater affair involved the Clintons' financial matters.

7. Ruth Marcus, *Supreme Ambition: Brett Kavanaugh and the Conservative Takeover* (New York: Simon & Schuster, 2020), 129.

8. Brief for Petitioners, *Swidler & Berlin and James Hamilton v. United States*, no. 97-1192, 1998 WL 290366 at *3 (D.C. Cir., Apr. 29, 1998).

9. Appendix to Petition for Writ of Certiorari, *Swidler & Berlin and James Hamilton v. United States*, no. 97-1192 (December 31, 1997), 49.

10. Appendix to Petition for Writ of Certiorari, 50.

11. I next saw Judge Penn when I sat behind him at Harry Blackmun's funeral. He was clearly pleased with the Supreme Court's decision that sustained his views as to the notes.

12. *In re Sealed Case*, 124 F.3d 230, 231 (D.C. Cir. 1997).

13. *In re Sealed Case*, 235.

14. *In re Sealed Case*, 233.

15. Senate Committee on Banking, Housing, and Urban Affairs, *Hearings Related to Madison Guaranty S&L and the Whitewater Development Corporation–Washington, DC Phase, Vol. I* (Washington, DC: US Government Printing Office, 1994), 31.

16. Senate Committee on Banking, Housing, and Urban Affairs, *Investigation of Whitewater Development Corporation, Vol. III* (Washington, DC: US Government Printing Office, 1994), 434. The Pulitzer Prize–winning author James Stewart titled his book about Vince's death and other Clinton troubles *Blood Sport*.

17. *In re Sealed Case*, 124 F.3d 230, 236 (D.C. Cir. 1997).

18. *In re Sealed Case*, 236.

19. *In re Sealed Case*, 240 (emphasis in original).

20. *In re Sealed Case*, 239 (emphasis in original).

21. Appendix to Petition for Writ of Certiorari, *Swidler & Berlin and James Hamilton v. United States*, no. 97-1192 (December 31, 1997), 25.

22. *In re Sealed Case*, 124 F.3d 230, 236 (D.C. Cir. 1997).

23. *In re Sealed Case*, 129 F.3d 637, 638 (D.C. Cir. 1997).

24. *In re Sealed Case*, 638.

25. Official Transcript, *Swidler & Berlin and James Hamilton v. United States*, no. 97-1192, June 8, 1998, 21.

26. *Upjohn Co. v. U.S.*, 449 U.S. 383, 393 (1981).

27. *Northwest Airlines v. County of Kent, Michigan*, 510 U.S. 355, 364–365 (1994).

28. Official Transcript, *Swidler & Berlin and James Hamilton v. United States*, 37–38. See also "*Swidler & Berlin v. United States*," Oyez, accessed October 25, 2021, https://www.oyez.org/cases/1997/97-1192.

29. Official Transcript, at 48–49. See also "*Swidler & Berlin v. United States*," Oyez.

30. *Arizona v. Macumber*, 544 P.2d 1084 (Ariz. 1976). See also 582 P.2d 162 (Ariz. 1978).

31. *Brady v. Maryland*, 373 U.S. 83 (1963).

32. Official Transcript, *Swidler & Berlin and James Hamilton v. United States*, 25.

33. *Swidler & Berlin v. U.S.*, 524 U.S. 399, 408 (1998).

34. The Court thus was not required to reach the work-product issue.

35. *Swidler & Berlin v. U.S.*, 407.

36. *Swidler & Berlin v. U.S.*, 408.

37. *Moody v. IRS*, 654 F.2d 795, 800–801 (D.C. Cir. 1981).

38. "James Hamilton, Attorney for the Late Vince Foster—Holds News Conference on the Supreme Court Decision Regarding Attorney-Client Privilege When the Client Has Died," FDCH Political Transcripts, June 25, 1998.

39. The cartoon is reproduced on page 142.

13. The Foster Photographs

1. Petition for Writ of Certiorari, *Office of Independent Counsel v. Favish*, 2002 WL 32101044 (Ninth Cir., December 20, 2002), 5.

2. Petition for Writ of Certiorari, 1.

3. *Favish v. Office of Independent Counsel*, 217 F.3d 1168, 1174 (Ninth Cir. 2000).

4. *Favish v. Office of Independent Counsel*, 1172.

5. *Favish v. Office of Independent Counsel*, 2001 WL 770410 (C.D. Cal. Jan. 11, 2001), 1.

6. Joint Appendix, *Office of Independent Counsel v. Favish*, 2003 WL 21911171 (Sup. Ct. July 18, 2003), *93–95.

7. Joint Appendix, 91.

8. *Favish v. Office of Independent Counsel*, 217 F.3d 1168, 1174 (Ninth Cir. 2000).

9. *Favish v. Office of Independent Counsel*, 1172–1173.

10. *Favish v. Office of Independent Counsel*, 1168, 1174.

11. *Accuracy in Media, Inc. v. National Park Services*, 194 F.3d. 120 (D.C. Cir. 1999).

12. *Accuracy in Media, Inc. v. National Park Service*, 120, 121–123.

13. *Accuracy in Media, Inc. v. National Park Service*, 121, 124.

14. *New York Times Co. v. Nat'l Aeronautics & Space Admin.*, 782 F. Supp. 628, 631 (D.D.C. 1991).

15. *Katz v. Nat'l Archives & Records Admin.*, 862 F. Supp. 476, 485 (D.D.C. 1994) (emphasis in original).

16. Homer, *The Iliad*, trans. Richard Lattimore (Chicago: University of Chicago Press, 1951), Book 24. See also Brief for Respondents Sheila Foster Anthony and Lisa Foster Moody in *Support of Petitioner, Office of Independent Counsel v. Favish*, 2003 WL 21692827 (Sup. Ct. July 18, 2003), 27.

17. Support of Petitioner, *Office of Independent Counsel v. Favish*, 27. See also *Accuracy in Media, Inc. v. National Park Service*, 120, 123.

18. See, e.g., Brief on the Merits of Respondent Allan J. Favish, *Office of Independent Counsel v. Favish*, 2003 WL 21940001 (9th Cir. Aug. 6, 2003), 4–5, 50, 6–7.

19. Transcript of Proceedings, *Office of Independent Counsel v. Favish*, no. 02-954, December 3, 2003, 22. https://www.supremecourt.gov/oral_arguments/argument_tran scripts/2003/02-954.pdf

20. Transcript of Proceedings, 20.

21. Transcript of Proceedings, 21.

22. *National Archives and Records Admin. v. Favish*, 541 U.S. 157 (2004).

23. *National Archives and Records Admin. v. Favish*, 165.

24. *National Archives and Records Admin. v. Favish*, 167–168.

25. *National Archives and Records Admin. v. Favish*, 168.

26. *National Archives and Records Admin. v. Favish*, 170.

27. *National Archives and Records Admin. v. Favish*, 171–172.

28. *National Archives and Records Admin. v. Favish*, 175.

29. *Prison Legal News v. Exec. Office for U.S. Attorneys*, 628 F.3d 1243, 1248 (Tenth Cir. 2011); *Am. Civil Liberties Union v. U.S. Dep't of Homeland Sec.*, 738 F. Supp. 2d 93, 117 (D.D.C. 2010); *Catsouras v. Dep't of Ca. Highway Patrol*, 181 Cal. App. 4th 856, 864 (Ca. Ct. App. 2010); *Marsh v. Cty. Of San Diego*, 680 F.3d 1148, 1154–55 (Ninth Cir. 2012).

14. The Clinton Impeachment

1. Renaissance Weekends are diverse gatherings to discuss ideas of importance to society.

2. The picture on page 139 was taken that night.

3. Others testifying for Clinton included former attorney general Nicholas Katzenbach, former governor of Massachusetts William Weld, former members of Congress Robert Drinan (D-MA), Elizabeth Holtzman (D-NY), and Wayne Owens (D-UT), Yale Law School professor Bruce Ackerman, and former Watergate prosecutor Richard Ben-Veniste, who sat at the witness table with me.

4. "Madison Debates–September 8," transcript, Yale Law School Lillian Goldman Law Library, accessed August 16, 2021, https://avalon.law.yale.edu/18th_century/debates_908.asp.

5. House of Representatives Committee on the Judiciary, *Impeachment Inquiry: William Jefferson Clinton, President of the United States, Presentation on Behalf of the President* (Washington, DC: US Government Printing Office, 1998), 219.

6. House of Representatives Committee on the Judiciary, *Impeachment Inquiry*, 223.

7. House of Representatives Committee on the Judiciary, 224–225.

8. House of Representatives Committee on the Judiciary, 235.

9. House of Representatives Committee on the Judiciary, 259–260.

15. DNC Chair Don Fowler: A Friend in Need

1. Don's relationship with Harold—a tough, opinionated fellow—was tense. It is fair to say that Harold's relationships with a number of people were tense, given his forceful personality.

2. A conduit contribution is one made in the name of a person who does not provide the funds.

3. Use of that court was a special perk. One Saturday morning during the Clinton administration, my family and the family of Stan Smith, former Wimbledon and US Open champion, enjoyed some spirited social doubles on that court, made possible *not* by any campaign donations but by the kindness of then White House staffer Phil Lader.

4. The other board I have found particularly rewarding is the Board of the USO, to which President Barack Obama appointed me in 2011. Like PFIAB, the USO Board has had prominent members. The two chairs I have served under include Dick Myers, former chair of the Joint Chiefs of Staff, and General George Casey, former chief of

staff of the army. The USO is a national treasure that every day serves our troops and their families worldwide in innumerable ways.

5. Tom became a friend. My family and I later visited him in Tokyo when he was ambassador to Japan. Going to dinner with Tom at a Japanese restaurant was like traveling with the pope; the reverence this tall white-haired man received from the Japanese is memorable.

Tom also kindly entertained my wife and young twins for lunch at the ambassador's residence. The residence has an enormous formal room. At one end is a grand piano next to which Emperor Hirohito, in formal attire, and General Douglas MacArthur, in an open collar, were photographed after Japan surrendered in World War II.

6. See chapter 22.

7. I once introduced Bud at a DC Renaissance event. I said that the Lord, seeing the navy's great needs, placed the admiral at its helm, declaring, "This Bud's for you."

8. I did not take the ethical issue I was confronted with lightly. Over the years I have spent considerable time thinking about ethical concerns. In the late 1980s, I was chair of the DC Bar's Legal Ethics Committee. Shortly thereafter, when the bar's ethics rules underwent substantial revision, I was placed in charge of an ad hoc committee tasked with educating the many thousands of members of the DC Bar on the new rules. My committee won the bar's highest award for pro bono service. I also served for years on the board of the Ethics Research Center, which was a leader in promoting organizational ethics.

9. Steve was universally respected for his views on ethics in government, having held the position of head of OGE under both Presidents George H. W. Bush and Clinton. (I had strongly suggested to the Clinton White House that Steve be kept on after Clinton was elected.) Steve also was a world-class tennis player, having competed at both Wimbledon and the US Open. When he became older and tolerant of lesser players, we spent time together on the courts.

10. Senate Committee on Governmental Affairs, *Investigation of Illegal or Improper Activities in Connection with 1996 Federal Election Campaigns: Final Report of the Committee on Governmental Affairs*, Senate Rept. 105-167, vol. 2, "The Saga of Roger Tamraz," March 10, 1998, accessed August 16, 2021, https://fas.org/irp/congress/1998_rpt/sgo-sir/2-21.htm.

11. Edward Walsh, "Tamraz Defends Political Gifts for Clinton Access," *Washington Post*, September 19, 1997. See also: "The Saga of Roger Tamraz."

12. Walsh, "Tamraz Defends Political Gifts for Clinton Access."

13. Deposition of Donald Fowler, May 21, 1997, 242, as quoted in *Investigation of Illegal or Improper Activities in Connection with 1996 Federal Election Campaigns*.

14. "Ex-Chief of DNC Is Grilled on Donor; Republican Senators Put a Former Democratic Party Chairman on the Hot Seat," Associated Press, September 9, 1997.

15. "Ex-Chief of DNC Is Grilled on Donor."

16. Senate Committee on Governmental Affairs, *Investigation of Illegal or Improper Activities in Connection with the 1996 Federal Election Campaign*, part 6 (Washington, DC: US Government Printing Office, 1998), 378.

17. Senate Committee on Governmental Affairs, *Investigation of Illegal or Improper Activities*, part 6, 314–319.

16. A Disgruntled Prince Philip

1. See page 144 of this book.

2. Vanessa Thorpe, "Anti-Hunt Pack Hounds Philip," *Guardian*, March 9, 2002, https://www.theguardian.com/uk/2002/mar/10/hunting.immigrationpolicy.

17. James Lee Witt: "Chicken Feathers"

1. Bill McAllister, "FEMA Chief Given Cabinet Status," *Washington Post*, February 27, 1996.

2. "Short Takes, Quick Witt Helps," *Atlanta Journal-Constitution*, February 12, 1996.

18. Bob Novak and the Valerie Plame Saga

1. Robert D. Novak, *The Prince of Darkness: 50 Years Reporting in Washington* (New York: Three Rivers Press, 2007), 10.

2. Robert D. Novak, "Mission to Niger," *Washington Post*, July 14, 2003.

3. Novak, *The Prince of Darkness*, 602.

4. Novak, 608–609.

5. Robert Novak, "The CIA Leak," CNN, accessed August 17, 2021, https://www.cnn.com/2003/ALLPOLITICS/10/01/column.novak.opinion.leak/index.html.

6. Novak, *The Prince of Darkness*, 613.

7. That is what happened to *New York Times* reporter Judith Miller. Miller, who was represented by staunch First Amendment advocate Floyd Abrams, refused to answer

questions about her knowledge of the Plame affair and was sent to jail for many weeks by then District of Columbia chief judge Tom Hogan, who supervised Fitzgerald's grand jury. Miller was the wife of Jason Epstein, the prominent Random House editor who edited my first book.

8. "Statement of Robert D. Novak," from files of James Hamilton.

9. Novak, *The Prince of Darkness*, 616.

10. Novak, 616.

11. Letter from P. Fitzgerald to J. Hamilton, June 28, 2006, from the files of James Hamilton.

19. A Stain on Baseball

1. "The Mitchell Report," MLB.com, accessed August 17, 2021, http://mlb.mlb .com/mlb/news/mitchell/report.jsp?p=14.

2. "The Mitchell Report," MLB.com, accessed February 4, 2022, http://mlb.mlb .com/mlb/news/mitchell/report.jsp?p=369.

3. "The Mitchell Report," MLB.com, accessed February 4, 2022, http://mlb.mlb .com/mlb/news/mitchell/report.jsp?p=193.

20. The Disgraceful Interrogation of Admiral Mike Mullen

1. US Department of State Accountability Review Board (ARB) Unclassified Report, 4. https://2009-2017.state.gov/documents/organization/202446.pdf.

2. US Department of State ARB Unclassified Report, 30–303.

3. ARB Unclassified Report, 6.

4. ARB Unclassified Report, 6.

5. ARB Unclassified Report, 37.

6. ARB Unclassified Report, 7.

7. ARB Unclassified Report, 39.

8. House of Representatives Committee on Oversight and Government Reform, *Reviews of the Benghazi Attacks and Unanswered Questions* (Washington, DC: US Government Printing Office, 2013), 20.

9. House of Representatives Committee on Oversight and Government Reform, *Reviews of the Benghazi Attacks and Unanswered Questions*, 21.

10. Committee on Oversight and Government Reform, 24.

11. Committee on Oversight and Government Reform, 37–38.

12. Committee on Oversight and Government Reform, 46–48.

13. Committee on Oversight and Government Reform, 53.

14. Committee on Oversight and Government Reform, 76.

15. Committee on Oversight and Government Reform 76–77.

16. Committee on Oversight and Government Reform, 53.

17. House of Representatives Select Committee on the Events Surrounding the 2012 Terrorist Attack in Benghazi, *Hearing 4* (Washington, DC: US Government Publishing Office, 2016), 421.

18. Veronica Stracqualursi, "Gowdy on His Retirement from Congress: 'I Like Jobs Where Facts Matter,'" CNN, February, 2018, https://www.cnn.com/2018/02/14/poli tics/trey-gowdy-retirement-cnntv/index.html.

22. *"Dean of Vetting"*

1. Nancy Cook and Andrew Restuccia, "Clinton Transition Team Taps Lawyers to Help Vet Nominees," *Politico*, October 27, 2016, https://www.politico.com/story/2016 /10/hillary-clinton-transition-team-lawyers-vetting-230422.

2. Christopher later told Clinton that this vetting process was the best in history.

3. After the vet concluded, Christopher sent me a gracious handwritten note, which read in part:

Dear Jim,

. . .

Most of all, my gratitude goes to *you.* You managed the whole vetting process with consummate skill and the understated elegance that is your trademark.
You were a terrific partner to me and I hope there may be opportunities to reactivate our enterprise, which was so pleasurable and helpful to me.
As ever,
Chris

4. After I finished vetting work for Obama, I ran into a South Carolina friend who was having Sunday brunch with Rahm Emanuel, who was to become Obama's chief of staff and later mayor of Chicago. I mentioned that I had found Obama gracious, appreciative, and possessing a sense of humor, concluding with my view that he is a "nice

guy." Without cracking a smile, Emanuel, well-known for being acerbic, said: "Nice is overrated."

5. For cabinet and White House officials, far fewer memos are prepared for each position. Some people may be under consideration for more than one position.

6. In the 1993 vetting of Supreme Court nominees, some two hundred lawyers were also involved. Part of their job was to read some three thousand court opinions and other writings by individuals under consideration. The survey of opinions and writings was headed by Don Verrelli, who later became solicitor general in the Obama administration.

7. As he has stated publicly, Senator Kerry was asked questions about his conduct as a single man during his 2000 vet.

8. As the *New York Times* reported in an August 9, 2000, article, the vetting team examining Joe Lieberman in 2000 read every one of the more than eight hundred legal opinions Lieberman had issued from 1983 to 1989 as Connecticut's attorney general. I instruct vetters that, when reading everything a candidate has written, to review footnotes. Lani Guinier, whom I did not vet, was forced to withdraw as President Clinton's nominee for assistant attorney general for the Civil Rights Division in part because of a provocative footnote in one of her law review articles that arguably advocated for racial quotas in local legislatures. Her vetters had overlooked this footnote.

9. In cabinet and Supreme Court vets, the candidates also will be required to fill out an FBI questionnaire—Standard Form 86—and, if chosen, a questionnaire from the relevant Senate confirmation committee.

10. Joe Lieberman and Hadassah Lieberman, *An Amazing Adventure: Joe and Hadassah's Personal Notes on the 2000 Campaign* (New York: Simon & Schuster, 2003), 9.

11. Ben Terris, "Sherrod Brown Thinks He Could Have Helped Democrats Win in 2016. But What about 2020?" *Washington Post*, July 24, 2017.

12. Connie Schultz, "Is It God's Plan for Mike Pence to be President?" *Washington Post*, August 31, 2018.

13. Mark Bowden, "The Salesman," *Atlantic*, October 1, 2010.

14. A picture from that night is on page 141.

15. David Barstow and Katharine Q. Seelye, "In Selecting a No. 2, No Detail too Small," *New York Times*, August 9, 2000.

16. Years later, a knowledgeable friend told me who had provided that incorrect information to the *Post*. He was *not* a vetter in 2004 and was stricken from my list of vetters going forward.

17. We first interviewed Breyer in a hospital room in the Boston area, where he was recuperating from a bicycle accident.

18. While prepping Ginsburg for her confirmation hearing before the Senate Judiciary Committee, I tried to mimic the accent and manner of speech of Senator Strom Thurmond (R-SC), a member of the committee. Being from South Carolina myself, I thought my attempt was credible. The most I got from Ginsburg was a look somewhere between quizzical and bemused—but no real smile and certainly no laughter. She kindly did write me a note after she was confirmed thanking me for my "good counsel."

19. After the problems that beset the candidacies of Zoë Baird and Kimba Wood for attorney general in 1993, which are discussed below, Janet Reno, the next choice, was subjected to exceptionally intense scrutiny. This created no hostility, at least toward me. Several years later, after I wrote her about a health issue, she responded that my note "meant a lot to me for I respect and admire you so much. You are my example of what a Washington lawyer should be."

20. Kaine had been an Obama favorite in his 2008 search for a running mate. During the vetting team report on Kaine, Obama said. "I'm pulling for him"—an interesting statement for the decision-maker. It was clear to me that Obama advisers David Axelrod and David Ploufe wanted a more experienced candidate, such as Joe Biden, to pair with Obama, who then had been a senator for just two years.

21. Vetters are told to destroy or return any materials collected during the vetting process.

Index